Lincoln's Other
White House

Also by Elizabeth Smith Brownstein

If This House Could Talk:
Historic Homes, Extraordinary Americans

Lincoln's Other White House

The Untold Story of the Man and His Presidency

Elizabeth Smith Brownstein

WILEY

John Wiley & Sons, Inc.

This book is printed on acid-free paper. ∞

Copyright © 2005 by Elizabeth Smith Brownstein. All rights reserved

Published by John Wiley & Sons, Inc., Hoboken, New Jersey
Published simultaneously in Canada

Illustration credits: pages 9, 31, 35, 44, 86, and 192, the Library of Congress; pages 14, 77, 90, and 129, courtesy of the Lincoln Museum, Fort Wayne, Indiana; pages 22 and 97, the Albert H. Small Collection; page 25, copyright Applewood Books, Inc. Reproduced by permission of Applewood Books and harpersweekly.com; page 47, the Cooper-Hewitt National Design Museum, Smithsonian Institution; page 57, the Fort Ward Museum; page 62, the Missouri Historical Society, St. Louis; page 67, the Frank and Virginia Williams Collection of Lincolniana. Photograph by Virginia Williams; page 82, courtesy of LeRoy A. Fladseth, grandson of Sgt. Smith Stimmel, Union Light Guard; page 99, courtesy of the Illinois State Historical Library; page 115, reprinted by permission of the Friends of Jes W. Schlaikjer; page 121, the Gilder Lehrman Collection, on deposit at the New-York Historical Society (GLC 2572); page 133, the Smithsonian Institution Archives, record unit 95, box 28, folder 33, neg. no. 2003-19540; page 143, the Chicago Historical Society; page 155, the National Oceanic and Atmospheric Administration/Department of Commerce; pages 160, 186, and 200, courtesy of Picture History; page 166, the Foster Hall Collection, Center for American Music, University of Pittsburgh's Library System; page 170, Ronn Palm's Museum of Civil War Images, Gettysburg, Pennsylvania; page 210, Architect of the Capitol; page 227, the Alaska State Museum, Juneau (cat. no. II-B-833).

No part of this publication may be reproduced, stored in a retrieval system, or transmitted in any form or by any means, electronic, mechanical, photocopying, recording, scanning, or otherwise, except as permitted under Section 107 or 108 of the 1976 United States Copyright Act, without either the prior written permission of the Publisher, or authorization through payment of the appropriate per-copy fee to the Copyright Clearance Center, 222 Rosewood Drive, Danvers, MA 01923, (978) 750-8400, fax (978) 646-8600, or on the web at www.copyright.com. Requests to the Publisher for permission should be addressed to the Permissions Department, John Wiley & Sons, Inc., 111 River Street, Hoboken, NJ 07030, (201) 748-6011, fax (201) 748-6008, or online at http://www.wiley.com/go/permissions.

Limit of Liability/Disclaimer of Warranty: While the publisher and the author have used their best efforts in preparing this book, they make no representations or warranties with respect to the accuracy or completeness of the contents of this book and specifically disclaim any implied warranties of merchantability or fitness for a particular purpose. No warranty may be created or extended by sales representatives or written sales materials. The advice and strategies contained herein may not be suitable for your situation. You should consult with a professional where appropriate. Neither the publisher nor the author shall be liable for any loss of profit or any other commercial damages, including but not limited to special, incidental, consequential, or other damages.

For general information about our other products and services, please contact our Customer Care Department within the United States at (800) 762-2974, outside the United States at (317) 572-3993 or fax (317) 572-4002.

Wiley also publishes its books in a variety of electronic formats. Some content that appears in print may not be available in electronic books. For more information about Wiley products, visit our web site at www.wiley.com.

Library of Congress Cataloging-in-Publication Data:

Brownstein, Elizabeth Smith, date.
    Lincoln's other White House : the untold story of the man and his
presidency / Elizabeth Brownstein.
        p. cm.
    Includes bibliographical references and index.
    ISBN-13 978-0-471-48585-8 (cloth : alk. paper)
    ISBN-10 0-471-48585-3 (cloth : alk. paper)
    1. Lincoln, Abraham, 1809–1865—Homes and haunts—Washington (D.C.).
2. Cottages—Washington (D.C.)—History—19th century. 3. United States Soldiers'
Home—History—19th century. 4. Washington (D.C.)—History—Civil War, 1861–1865.
5. Washington (D.C.)—Buildings, structures, etc. 6. Lincoln, Abraham, 1809–1865—
Family. 7. Lincoln, Abraham, 1809–1865—Friends and associates. 8. United States—
Politics and government—1861–1865. 9. Presidents—United States—Biography. I. Title.

    E457.64.B76 2005
    973.7′092—dc22
                                                                2004029638
    ISBN 978-1-68162-005-3 (hc)
    ISBN 978-1-68162-000-8 (pbk)

To my great-grandfather, Patrick Edgar,
killed at the Battle of the Wilderness,
and to all the brave men and women who have
given their lives for our beloved country

CONTENTS

FOREWORD

As recently as 2000, Abraham Lincoln's "other White House" at the Soldiers' Home in Washington, D.C., was one of the city's—and the nation's—true hidden treasures, out of sight and largely forgotten by historians and the general public alike. In that year, efforts got under way to rescue the site from obscurity and return it to the spotlight it so richly deserves.

First, the National Trust for Historic Preservation included a cottage there on its 2000 list of America's Eleven Most Endangered Historic Places, noting that the Armed Forces Retirement Home, which owns the property, didn't have the funds to undertake a long-deferred and much-needed restoration. A short time later, President Clinton ensured that the site would be protected under federal law by officially designating it the President Lincoln and Soldiers' Home National Monument. Since then, an energetic and effective public/private partnership—involving the Armed Forces Retirement Home, the National Park Service, and an impressive array of preservationists, generous donors, public officials, and historians—has helped the National Trust develop an ambitious plan for converting this important piece of the nation's history into a publicly accessible historic site and premier learning center.

Why so much fuss over a relatively modest building on an out-of-the-way hilltop some distance removed from the capital's monumental core? The answer is simple: this is the most important "unknown" presidential site in the nation and, at least arguably, the site with the greatest potential to help us explore several aspects of Lincoln and his presidency that have been unknown, misunderstood, or underappreciated until now.

From 1862 to 1864, Lincoln and his family spent several months each year at the Soldiers' Home. In other words, the home was Lincoln's residence for almost a quarter of his presidency. It was here that he held important meetings and conferred privately (often late at night) with military leaders, members of Congress, and foreign diplomats—as well as with trusted advisors and friends. It was here that he spent hours brooding over the conduct of the war and agonizing over its impact on the nation. It was here that he refined his doctrine of emancipation.

But the Soldiers' Home was more than a busy workplace. It was also a breezy refuge from the din and heat and stench of downtown Washington, and it offered a welcome respite from the never ending stream of visitors and favor seekers who plagued Lincoln at the White House. It was a place where he could read, relax with his family, chat with the soldiers who guarded him, heal from the loss of his beloved Willie, restore his inner peace, and prepare himself for the rigors of another day as leader of a country at war.

This is what makes the Soldiers' Home unique—and uniquely important. Most of us are familiar with near iconic tales of Lincoln the gawky young lawyer known for his humor and homespun eloquence, the Illinois politician suddenly thrust onto the national stage, the martyred Father Abraham. But the Soldiers' Home offers new and enlightening perspectives on Lincoln the president and the man. Having admired Elizabeth Smith Brownstein's book *If This House Could Talk* very much, I know she was the perfect person to write this one, bringing together wonderfully, as she always does, the many stories gathered from newly revealed, original sources.

The very survival of the 160-year-old building now known as the Lincoln Cottage is a minor miracle, and its future promises to be as rich as its past. With the fresh information and insights she presents so engagingly in these pages and the help of our many partners and friends, the National Trust will ensure that the Lincolns' retreat is a place where everyone—students and teachers, scholars and tourists— can experience a new encounter with, and gain a new appreciation for, the rich heritage that is ours as Americans.

—Richard Moe
President of the National
Trust for Historic Preservation

PROLOGUE

The poet Walt Whitman attracted a glittering crowd of celebrities to the last of his famous lectures on the man he most loved—Abraham Lincoln. It was April 14, 1887, the twenty-second anniversary of the president's murder, and the poet himself had just a few more years to live. The steel magnate Andrew Carnegie was in the audience at the gorgeous little Madison Square Theater in midtown Manhattan. So were Mark Twain, the Civil War hero General William Tecumseh Sherman, the by then distinguished diplomat John Hay, the sculptor Augustus Saint-Gaudens, and many other cultural powerhouses of the day. "When Lilacs Last in the Dooryard Bloom'd," Whitman's powerful lament for Lincoln, "the sweetest, wisest soul of all my days and lands . . . the mighty Westerner," was well on its way to fame as the most moving elegy in the American anthology.

There were several ironies about Whitman's greatest poem. From the very first line, written only weeks after the assassination on April 14, 1865, Whitman returned again and again to the image of home. Yet, like Lincoln, Whitman would own only one home in his lifetime, and that one only as his own life drew to its end. Lincoln had detested the homes in which he'd lived more than half his life. Even sadder, as the poet and Lincoln biographer Carl Sandburg pointed out many years later, "There were thirty-one rooms in the White House and Lincoln was not at home in any of them. This was the house for which he had suffered so much."

But Whitman had spent over two years of the Civil War in and near Washington, moving from battlefront to camp, from hospital to hospital, caring tenderly, generously, in any way he could, for the war wounded and dying. He had come to understand, as had Louisa May Alcott and many other Civil War nurses, that the idea of home was a mighty refuge, both physical and emotional, an anchor that kept those soldiers clinging to life, and the folks back home moored

1

through four years of terrible civil war. It would take another war, in another century, for the patriotic concept of the "home front" to evolve, but at times during the Civil War, the longing for home was so acute that the nostalgic tune, "Home Sweet Home," was barred from Union camps. After one fierce battle, bands of both armies played the song together across the lines for the battered, homesick troops. Sentimental though Lincoln's taste in music was, perhaps understandably "Home Sweet Home" was never one of his favorites.

Abraham and Mary Todd Lincoln had hoped from the very beginning of his presidency that a cottage at the Soldiers' Home, then an asylum for disabled and homeless veterans three miles into the countryside north of the White House, established after years of political wrangling, would be just such a refuge for them. Lincoln's predecessor, James Buchanan, may have told them he slept better there during the summer. Two days after the inauguration on March 4, 1861, Mary Todd Lincoln went out to look it over. Lincoln hurried out before breakfast the very next day, probably alone, to see it for himself. Right away, the idea of the Soldiers' Home as a retreat pleased them both. "It was," Mary wrote an old friend in early July 1861, "a very beautiful place. . . . We will ride into the city every day & can be as secluded, as we please."

But that was not to be. Military and political crises in 1861 were so constant and calamitous, it would be another year—1862—before the Lincoln family could get away from Washington's dreaded, unhealthy "heated season," hoping to find at the Soldiers' Home the peace and quiet they craved after the loss of their adored second son, Willie, to typhoid fever that winter. But Mary was wiser after one year of living in a White House where the public roamed "the First Home" anywhere they pleased. She expected, even dreaded, that the Soldiers' Home might turn into an even "greater resort," and she was right. Perhaps wryly, she wrote, "Each day brings its visitors." A century and a half later, when the Soldiers' Home was dedicated as a national monument, another president, William Jefferson Clinton, would explain, "the Soldiers' Home gave the Lincolns refuge, but not escape."

In anticipation of at least some relief, Lincoln had ridden out to the Soldiers' Home days before the family moved out on June 13,

1862, and he was seen by a passerby "sitting upon the steps of that summer mansion . . . very sober, his head leaning upon his hand. The President had evidently gone out for a ride and stopped to refresh himself at the quiet retreat."

In the end, Lincoln would come to spend an astonishing quarter of his presidency—thirteen months—at the Soldiers' Home. The day before the assassination, he was seen heading toward it. So much of the site remains intact that it is remarkably easy to conjure up an immediate sense of Lincoln's presence there. Strange as it may seem, despite that immediacy, the Soldiers' Home is the least known significant presidential site in America. Even now, few know what happened to Lincoln there; few have even looked. Yet it is the only site in the country that encapsules Lincoln's life experience as father, husband, commander in chief, greatest and most beloved president. It is the only place left to offer fresh new insights into his startling physical appearance, his unusual temperament, the idiosyncratic character of his leadership, and the intensity and breadth of his political and personal relationships. It would be the last home the Lincolns would share together. It is the missing link in the study of his presidency. This is that untold story.

PART ONE

Lincoln's Long Journey to the Soldiers' Home

CHAPTER 1

―――――――――――∞∞∞―――――――――――

Beginnings

THE PICTURESQUE COUNTRY COTTAGE where tradition holds that the Lincolns stayed at the Soldiers' Home for the three seasons was surely the most comfortable, even fashionable, home Lincoln ever knew. With two floors of spacious, airy rooms and more on the third, the cottage was worlds apart from the cramped log cabins of Lincoln's miserable earlier years. As if those crude shelters weren't bad enough for a young man with Lincoln's drive and genius, after hacking their way in 1816 through thick forests to Little Pigeon Creek, Indiana, seven-year-old Lincoln, his father, Thomas, mother, Nancy, and older sister, Sarah, even lived for a time in what was called a "pole shelter" or "half-faced camp." William O. Stoddard, Lincoln's dashing third secretary in the White House, later offered a journalist's vivid, if imaginative, description: "It was a shed, log-walled on three sides, open on the south and roofed with riven slabs. It was about fourteen feet square with the 'fire-place' out on the ground on the open side. Its floor was the earth and it had neither window, door, nor chimney. It was the poorest home to which Nancy (Hanks) Lincoln's husband had brought her." Years later historian George Dangerfield embellished that description: "The sides and roof were covered with poles, branches, brush, dried grass, mud; chinks were stuffed where the wind or rain were trying to come through."

Thomas Lincoln managed to build a log cabin in time. A succession of these cabins has been re-created—and revered—all the way from Kentucky through Indiana to Illinois. A massive temple now covers the tiny cabin at Sinking Springs Farm near Hodgenville, Kentucky, where Lincoln was born on February 12, 1809. Each of the fifty-six steps leading up to it is meant to represent a year in his life. It wasn't until he'd lived more than half those years that he escaped the humiliation widely associated in those days with such crude places.

Even though the Harrison-Tyler presidential campaign of 1840 had made log cabins somewhat respectable, however hypocritically (Harrison had been raised in a mansion), and though Lincoln had been railroaded at the 1860 nominating convention by some well-meaning supporters into endorsing what became a smashingly successful railsplitter image, the presidential hopeful dismissed his log-cabin years with a single line from Thomas Gray's elegy, "the short and simple annals of the poor." Paradoxically, the cabins move millions of people today as indispensable symbols of our faith in democratic government. They shore up our conviction—indestructible up to now, at least—that anyone in America can aspire to be anything one wishes, no matter how humble one's beginnings. Lincoln later explained this basic American ideal to some Union soldiers. "The purpose of the war," he told them, was that "each of you may have through this free government which we have enjoyed, an open field and fair chance for your industry, enterprise and intelligence." As for himself, Lincoln was confident enough in his ability and destiny to have taken to heart two other lines from Gray's elegy: he was determined not to become another "flower born to blush unseen and waste its sweetness on the desert air."

In some ways the Little Pigeon Creek cabin must have been an improvement on the half-faced camp where they had first lived, but the 1820 census of Spencer County, Indiana, gave some hint of how miserable the family's living conditions still must have been. The census recorded a total of eight people, including the future president, his father, his new stepmother, Sarah Bush Johnston (Nancy Hanks had died in 1818), and her children, all living in one three-hundred-sixty-square-foot room, just a few square feet larger than the squalid three-room tenements of New York's Lower East Side.

ABRAHAM LINCOLN,

Sixteenth President of the United States.

Born February 12, 1809.   Died April 15, 1865.

Lincoln had lived only in log cabins before he moved to Springfield, Illinois, in April 1837 at the age of twenty-eight. The house at Eighth and Jackson was the only home he ever owned.

These would be put up for maximum profit and minimum comfort during the Civil War to house the hordes of immigrants flooding into the city who were to make up about a quarter of Lincoln's Union Army.

Materially and emotionally, Sarah brought much to the cabin, and Lincoln loved her for all of it: her affection and understanding, her Bible, decent clothes rather than buckskins, beds, glazed windows, a door that really shut. Even in the White House, journalist Noah Brooks reported that Lincoln could still remember "how he lay in bed of a bitter, cold morning, listening for [Sarah's] footsteps rattling the slabs of the rough oaken floor as she came to arouse him from his pretended sleep."

That harsh existence changed radically once Lincoln got to Springfield, Illinois, where he arrived in April 1837, with two saddlebags to his name, a self-taught lawyer ready to start a practice. By the time he left Springfield for Washington as President-elect on a bleak February day in 1861, Lincoln and Mary Todd, his wife of nineteen years, and their three surviving children—Robert, Willie, and Tad—were living in one of the most respectable houses in town.

Lincoln had once said to a friend that "it isn't the best thing for a man ... to build a house so much better than his neighbors." But by 1860 he had. We know now from the stunning discoveries of the Lincoln Legal Papers Project that he could well afford it. Lincoln may have started out as a poor country lawyer, but by 1860 he was one of the most prominent attorneys on the frontier, and even had been admitted to practice before the Illinois and United States supreme courts. His legal practice had provided most of the one thousand dollars he needed to buy a one-and-a-half-story Greek Revival cottage on the edge of the prairie in 1844, two years after he and Mary Todd married. A back-breaking load of cases, five thousand in all—from petty thefts to murder to corporate liability—tried in anything from crude log courtrooms to ornate federal court chambers, had enabled him and Mary to keep on enlarging the house until it had two full stories and five bedrooms. Fees as high as five thousand dollars for one case, but usually around fifty dollars, laid the financial base for their political and material ambitions.

For all that, their marriage paid a price. Lincoln's law practice took him away as much as twenty weeks each year. It was his only source of income, because he had chosen not to add to it by land or real estate speculation, as had many of his associates, or by farming, which he loathed. He told a friend, Joseph Gillespie, that he "had no capacity whatever for speculation and never attempted it."

After Lincoln's nomination on May 18, 1860, as the new Republican Party's candidate and the country's first presidential nominee born west of the Appalachians, politicians and the press swarmed to the house at Eighth and Jackson. The none-too-friendly *New York Herald* gave the house, and the Lincolns, good reviews:

> It is like the residence of an American gentleman in easy circumstances, and it is furnished in like manner...there is no aristocracy about it; but it is a comfortable, cozy home, in which it would seem that a man could enjoy life, surrounded by his family...the internal appointments of his house are plain but tasteful, and clearly show the impress of Mrs. Lincoln's hand, who is really an amiable and accomplished lady.

The *New York Evening Post* found Mr. Lincoln

> living in a handsome but not pretentious, double story house, with parlors on both sides neatly but not ostentatiously furnished. It was just such a dwelling as a majority of the well-to-do of those fine western towns occupy. Everything about it had a look of comfort and independence. The library, I remarked on passing, particularly, that I was pleased to see long rows of books, which told of scholarly tastes and culture of the family.

The *Utica Morning Herald* correspondent confessed that he had "an instinctive aversion to dogging the footsteps of distinguished men," and "nothing seemed more impossible than that I should ever...join the great mob of those who should pay [Lincoln] their respects." But he did, and was pleasantly surprised both by the house and the Lincolns.

> After you have been five minutes in his company you cease to think that he is either homely or awkward. You recognize in him a high-toned, unassuming, chivalrous-minded gentleman, fully posted

in all the essential amenities of social life, and sustained by the infallible monitor of common sense.

As for Mary,

You would have known instantly that she who presided over that modest household was a true type of American lady. There were flowers upon the table; there were pictures upon the walls. The adornments were few, but chastely appropriate; everything was in its place, and ministered to the general effect. The hand of the domestic artist was everywhere visible. The thought that involuntarily blossomed into speech was, "What a pleasant home Abe Lincoln has."

These were valuable clues to what she would later try to do to make the Soldiers' Home just as pleasant for the family's summer stays. Mary had other motives in mind when she turned the White House from a dirty, tattered place that looked like a down-at-the-heels, third-rate hotel into a shining and elegant place that impressed even her many savage critics.

CHAPTER 2

The Riggs Villa

THE COTTAGE MARY DEARLY LOVED at the Soldiers' Home had been built in 1842 in the "Rural Gothic" style for a prominent, wealthy young Washingtonian, George W. Riggs. One look at it shows how carefully Riggs and the builder, William H. Degges, followed the recommendations of the predominant tastemaker of the 1830s and 1840s, Andrew Jackson Downing. Downing's views on what was architecturally suitable for country residences for rich and poor alike had begun to percolate nationally in the 1830s, when he was in his midtwenties. His 1841 *Treatise on the Theory and Practice of Landscape Gardening* was a best-seller despite its high price ($3.50), and would become one of the most influential books on the subject published in the nineteenth century. His *Cottage Residences* of 1842 put the final seal of approval on the Gothic Revival style.

It was clear that Riggs, as "a retired gentleman of fortune," should build a "beautiful and picturesque villa" in the Rural Gothic style, Downing wrote, "the lines of which point upwards in the pyramidal gables, tall clusters of chimneys, finials and the several other portions of its varied outline, harmoniz[ing] easily with the tall trees, and tapering masses of foliage, or the surrounding hills." Even if the villa did not have its unique connection with Abraham Lincoln, the cottage would stand by itself as a rare survivor of early Gothic Revival architecture in the nation's capital.

In this "perfect gem of a country residence," Riggs intended to introduce his growing family to the charms and benefits of the rural

Mary Todd Lincoln included this picture of the Soldiers' Home cottage she loved so much in the Lincoln family album.

life that he'd enjoyed as a child on his family's Maryland plantations, where slavery had made life easier. He'd already made what would amount to millions today in the banking business with his older partner, William Corcoran, known as "the American Rothschild" and a connoisseur and collector of art. But Riggs was more conservative, and growing tired of the risks and worries Corcoran thrived on. He was uncomfortable with the bank's heavy investments in loans to the federal government for the war in Mexico, in railroads, and in land speculation. "I think it wrong," he wrote, "for persons who do a banking or collecting business to operate in stocks unless possessed of money to carry on such operations without taking from the regular business. Our situation here induces many people to put confidence in us such as would not be placed if it were known that we speculated largely."

So finally, in January 1849 (he'd already tried to convince his father to "keep out of Wall Street a little"), Riggs explained to a friend,

> I am engaged in winding up my affairs with Corcoran & Riggs, in which I had an interest. After that is over I shall have my whole

time to devote to my family and my little farm. I have not the
large fortune that the public give me but I have enough to live on
if I live moderately and I want to try to do so [George Riggs was
being modest here about his fortune, for a young man of thirty-
five, his net worth already must have exceeded two hundred thousand dollars—a very large figure for his day] . . . I am confident I
have adopted the prudent and wise course in withdrawing. I am a
happier, if poorer man. Contentment is, after all, riches, not possession of money.

A year later, he wrote the friend again:

I am living quietly in the country, out of business entirely, except-
ing the charge of the books of the old firm of Corcoran & Riggs.

But a year and a half later, to the same, probably astonished
friend, Riggs announced that:

this last winter, I sold my country place to the Government for a
site for a military asylum. I did it at the earnest request and advice
of my father & brother . . . both of whom are desirous to have me
remove to New York or the vicinity.

The death at the farm of their youngest daughter may have
haunted the Riggses away, just as Willie's death would make the Lincolns eager to escape the White House. In any event, the $58,111.75
Riggs received from the government for the house, out-buildings,
and 256 acres was not a bad price for the time. Riggs was soon back
in business—in Washington again—with a bank of his own.

Lincoln had deposited his first paycheck at George Riggs's bank
on April 5, 1861 (for the month of March he earned $2,083.33), but
that was nothing new for the Riggs Bank. President John Tyler
before him had banked with Corcoran & Riggs, and most of Lincoln's cabinet already had accounts at Riggs. But Lincoln and
George Riggs never met. According to the vehement testimony of
Riggs's two granddaughters, Riggs was a "Lincoln hater" and made
it clear to his many friends in the Washington establishment that
Lincoln would not be welcome in his house. It didn't help that
Riggs was treasurer of the national committee of the Southern wing
of the Democratic Party that in 1860 had nominated John C. Breck-
inridge, who had been defeated by Lincoln.

Among the many other ironies of Lincoln's attachment to the Soldiers' Home was that one of the prime movers in Congress to establish the Soldiers' Home institution was log cabin–born Senator Jefferson Davis of Mississippi, later president of the Confederacy. And as far back as 1840, Major Robert Anderson, who would be in command at Fort Sumter in April 1861, was pleading for its creation. "Let the soldier know that a home is prepared for him, where he will be kindly welcomed and well taken care of, and he will be more active and zealous in the discharge of his duties, more willing to incur fatigue and danger, than can now be the case, when he knows that the greater the suffering he endures, the sooner is his constitution destroyed, and he, by discharge, deprived of the means of obtaining his daily bread." (General Winfield Scott, Lincoln's first military adviser, was the third cofounder.)

The Riggs cottage would be enlarged before the Lincolns came to use it, in order to serve temporarily as the "inmates'" living quarters, and from the records of their meetings, it's clear the governors of the institution didn't care to spend their limited funds on amenities. Major Thomas Alexander, a very nice, considerate man who ran the institution during the time the Lincolns used it, and who visited them often, pleaded for a modest sum to furnish his quarters. In six years, he said, he'd received nothing and was having a hard time getting along with what was there. His own property had been destroyed in a fire at his previous post. (Much of the Lincolns' Springfield furniture had been sold when they left for Washington and was also destroyed in the great Chicago fire of 1871.) That history of parsimony surely explains why it took a long train of wagons to transport the Lincolns' belongings from the White House when they moved out for the summer and explains the long list of embellishments (gilt paper and borders, lace curtains, mirrors, and more) Mary ordered to refurbish the cottage for what would turn out to be their final summer of residence, 1864.

Mary was not unaccustomed to luxury when she'd married Lincoln, and she had done her best with their modest home in Springfield. She would struggle to turn the White House into a glittering symbol of national pride. For Mary had been raised in great comfort in Lexington, Kentucky, the daughter of a wealthy aristocrat, Robert Todd. She'd been accustomed to life with slaves and politically influential family friends, including Henry Clay, and was given a superior education. Marrying Lincoln had changed all that. She had to learn to cook, sew, and keep house, with the help of a servant or two, none of whom stayed long. Life with Lincoln was made no easier, she also knew, by their "opposite natures."

So their house at Eighth and Jackson in Springfield is a monument to the many things that kept the two devoted to each other to the end, as eyewitnesses to their days at the Soldiers' Home would later confirm. What bound them was their ambition and fascination with politics, their love of children and friends, shared memories of their "desolate" childhoods, their passion for poetry, theater, books . . . and each other.

It is likely the Lincolns had separate bedrooms at the Soldiers' Home, just as they had at the house in Springfield and in the White House, an arrangement expected of couples in their respectable position in those days. Perhaps, too, at the Soldiers' Home Lincoln continued his practice of occasionally receiving visitors in his bedroom as he did at the White House, where he was sometimes so exhausted he had to meet with colleagues while in bed. Given his nightmares and Mary's migraines, such an arrangement was even more practical. In Springfield, it may also have been a means of spacing the births of their four children.

We know that there were, at the very least, seventy visitors to the Soldiers' Home during their stays: old friends, generals, politicians, members of the cabinet, the brazen, and the curious. If the Lincolns entertained at all, it was not remotely on the scale of their efforts in Springfield, where five hundred people were invited to one party ("owing to an unlucky rain, three hundred only favored us by their presence," Mary wrote to her sister, Emily Todd Helm). Anguish over Willie's death in the White House in February 1862 was too constant, and massive public receptions there more than took care of their social and political obligations. These White House events were usually open to all, as the soldiers of Lincoln's guard reported in their letters home and in their memoirs. Sergeant

Smith Stimmel, a member of the Union Light Guard of Ohio, Lincoln's cavalry escort to and from the Soldiers' Home in 1863, wrote:

> When not on duty, it was our privilege to attend his public receptions if we wished to do so. . . . One evening three or four of us boys concluded to slick up and take in the President's reception . . . we stood in the anteroom for some time, watching the dignitaries pass in, before we could make up our minds to venture into the presence of the President. Cabinet Ministers, the Judges of the Supreme Court, Senators and Congressmen, Foreign Ambassadors in their dazzling uniforms, accompanied by their wives, army and navy officers of high rank, and the aristocracy of the city, all in full evening dress, were there. Naturally we boys in the garb of the common soldier, felt a little timid in the presence of such an assemblage . . . the door-keeper said 'Go on in, boys, he would rather see you boys than all the rest of these people.' So we plucked up courage and went in. The President gave us a cordial shake of the hand. We bowed to Mrs. Lincoln and the others and passed on into the large East room with the rest of the guests. At first it was a little like taking a cold bath when the water is a little extra chilly, but the first douse took off the chill, and after that we felt quite at home.

Private Willard Cutter decided not to go to the New Year's reception in 1863, "for fear I would jerk old Abe off his legs . . . [the guests] shook old Abe most to pieces. I guess he was glad when they shut the House up."

Cutter was only partly right. No one really could shut the White House up. Walt Whitman had seen firsthand what Lincoln would face there as he began his presidency on March 4, 1861. The only peace Lincoln could hope to get was when he left it.

A few tantalizing clues now suggest that the Lincolns may also have at times occupied another house on the Soldiers' Home grounds during their residency there. The National Trust is still pursuing these leads as it continues its extensive restoration of the Riggs villa.

CHAPTER 3

Washington and the White House

Eighteen Sixty-One

Arm'd year—year of the struggle,

No dainty rhymes or sentimental love verses for you
    terrible year,

Not you as some pale poetling seated at a desk lisping
    cadenzas piano,

But as a strong man erect, clothed in blue clothes,
    advancing, carrying a rifle on your shoulder,

With well-gristled body and sunburnt face and hands,
    with a knife in the belt at your side,

As I hear you shouting loud, your sonorous voice ringing
    across the continent

Your masculine voice O year, as rising amid the great
    cities,

Amid the men of Manhattan I saw you as one of the
    workmen, the dwellers in Manhattan,

Or with large steps crossing the prairies out of
    Illinois and Indiana,

Rapidly crossing the West with springy gait and
    descending the Alleghanies,

Or down from the great lakes or in Pennsylvania, or on
    deck along the Ohio river,

> Or southward along the Tennessee or Cumberland rivers,
>   or at Chattanooga on the mountain top,
> Saw I your gait and saw I your sinewy limbs clothed in
>   blue, bearing weapons, robust year,
> Heard your determin'd voice launch'd forth again and
>   again,
> Year that suddenly sang by the mouths of the round-
>   lipp'd cannon,
> I repeat you, hurrying, crashing, sad, distracted year.

Walt Whitman wrote his poem "Eighteen Sixty-One" after that "terrible year" was over, but President-elect Lincoln arrived in the nation's capital as "the hurrying, crashing, sad, distracted year" was just beginning. Lincoln had not exaggerated when he told his friends at the railroad station in Springfield that he was leaving them "with a task before me greater than that which rested upon Washington." But it would take just one day after his inauguration on March 4, 1861, for him to realize that he had, in fact, totally underestimated what he would face in the next four years. Any hopes of finding peace for the Lincolns at the Soldiers' Home that summer must have begun to fade right there.

Six southern states had already fallen like dominoes after South Carolina voted in a special convention just a few days before Christmas 1860 to dissolve "the union now subsisting between South Carolina and the other states." Like a "prairie fire," Louisiana senator Judah P. Benjamin described it, even a "revolution," Mississippi followed on January 9, 1861, Florida on January 10, Alabama on the eleventh, Georgia on the nineteenth, Louisiana on the twenty-sixth, and Texas on February 1. So before Lincoln had even left Springfield for Washington on February the eleventh, the entire Lower South— seven out of thirty-four states, fifteen of them slave-holding—was now in rebellion, although that, of course, is not how they looked at it. In less that six weeks, just eighty-five years after the first Declaration of Independence, the seven states had now declared their own: the Confederate States of America.

Naively, Lincoln refused for a time to believe, despite all the contrary evidence—the continual failure of efforts to compromise, the gory rhetoric, the secessionists' seizure of federal property (mints,

forts, arsenals, and customs houses in the seven states)—that somehow they could be coaxed back into the Union. To Lincoln, secession was "the essence of anarchy," tragic evidence that disproved
the notion he cherished above all, that government by the people—
the Union—"is not an absurdity."

On March 5, his very first full day in office, an urgent message
was already waiting for him from Major Robert Anderson, the commander of Fort Sumter, the Union's new installation at the entrance
to Charleston's harbor: there were just six weeks left between his
small garrison and starvation. The fort was of little military value to
the Union, but now its symbolic importance to both North and South
was magnified. Was it worth fighting for? Or should Anderson just
surrender? Would that keep the peace? Or was war inevitable? Lincoln himself had said, "The tug has to come, & better now than at
any time hereafter." And while Lincoln was on his way to Washington, the new Confederacy's president, Jefferson Davis, warned, "the
South is determined to maintain her position and make all who
oppose her smell Southern powder and feel Southern steel."

Lincoln had barely finished putting together his cabinet of seven
advisers before the inauguration. He needed time to get that small
but critically important group of men, so disparate in ambition, temperament, and political persuasion, to work together effectively. He
needed time to convince them—and the country—and even himself
that he was up to the job. He knew that he "was entirely ignorant
not only of the duties but of the manner of doing business." He'd
even confessed to his new secretaries of state and the navy that he
didn't know a thing about foreign affairs, or ships. And how was he
to keep the eight other slave states in the Upper South from join-
ing the seven who'd left? Would the new Confederacy give heart
to those who believed the Union might just as well break up into
several more confederacies? And what did he have to fight with, if
it came to that? Anderson had warned that it would take twenty
thousand men to keep the fort in Union hands. But there weren't
even that many in the entire regular United States Army, and troops
were scattered all over the country. The navy was in no better
shape. Both services were already being severely depleted as Southern loyalists, who were their backbone, left to join the Confederacy.

The White House (center) was the hub of Lincoln's presidency. Key departments were just steps away through dark and unguarded woods.

The hundreds of political appointees from the outgoing Democratic administration would have to be replaced, as was the custom in the days before civil service reform. Many who remained were hardly Union supporters. Washington was "thick with treason," suspected Lincoln's secretary of the navy, Gideon Welles. The strains on Lincoln were so intense as he grappled with all this, Mary Lincoln reported he "keeled over" and had to be put to bed.

The war some feared and others on both sides welcomed had finally come at 4:30 A.M. on April 12, when Confederate guns opened up on Fort Sumter before the supplies that Lincoln had finally decided, after weeks of agonizing, seesawing debate, could be delivered. The bloodiest war of the nineteenth century had begun, and in a few more weeks the Confederacy grew larger: four more states, Virginia, Tennessee, Arkansas, and North Carolina, left the Union by the end of May. Arguably, Virginia was the worst loss, strategically. With her went the huge and vital Navy Yard at Norfolk, the armory and arsenal at Harper's Ferry, the Tredegar Iron Works in Richmond—and Colonel Robert E. Lee. What made it even worse was

Virginia's taunting location. Lincoln could see Confederate flags flying just across the Potomac from his office window. When the Confederacy moved its capital up to Richmond from Montgomery, Alabama, the two capitals were only a frustrating hundred miles apart. It would take four years and thousands upon thousands of casualties for the Union army to capture Richmond, after coming time and time again within a few miles.

The loss of the Norfolk Navy Yard was particularly devastating for Secretary of the Navy Gideon Welles. A disciplined diarist, of those first traumatic months Welles wrote: "Few know or can appreciate the actual condition of things and state of feeling of the members of the Administration in those days. Nearly sixty years of peace had unfitted us for any war, but the most terrible of all wars, a civil one, was upon us and it had to be met. Congress had adjourned without making any provisions for the storm, though aware it was at hand and soon to burst upon the country. . . . A new Administration scarcely acquainted with each other, and differing essentially in the past, was compelled to act, promptly and decisively." Some, including Lincoln's private secretaries, John Nicolay and John Hay, would differ with Welles on that last point, although Welles himself quickly did wonders to assemble a motley fleet. Years later, they wrote, "No one believed yet that Lincoln was the better man. So administration policy was necessarily passive, expectant, cautious, tentative." Young Henry Adams agreed. He and his father, Charles Francis Adams, of the formidable Quincy, Massachusetts, political dynasty, had not yet left for England, where Henry would serve as his father's secretary at the United States Mission to the Court of St. James's. Henry Adams was not impressed by Lincoln, or by anybody, for that matter, except elegant, cosmopolitan Charles Sumner, the vehemently abolitionist senator from Massachusetts. "Any private secretary in the least fit for his business," Adams wrote later in his autobiography, *The Education of Henry Adams*, "would have thought, as Adams did, that no man living needed so much education as the new President, but that all the education he could get would not be enough." What was worse, Adams wrote astutely, in what was for him an unusually empathetic vein, "No one in Washington was fitted for his duties, or rather, no duties in March were fitted for the duties in April."

But Lincoln did act, insecure and inexperienced though he certainly was. Whether he actually maneuvered the South into war is still debated, but the most plausible explanation for Lincoln's final decision to resupply Fort Sumter, according to the Civil War historian James McPherson, is that "Lincoln would have been happy to preserve the peace, but probably expected the Confederacy to open fire; either way he won. . . . His new concept of the resupply undertaking was a stroke of genius."

On April 15, Lincoln issued the first of many calls in the next four years—for seventy-five thousand volunteers. Eventually as many as two and a half million would ultimately serve in the Union Army. There was no formal declaration of war. Congress was not in session, so Lincoln could use his powers as commander in chief again and again to get the Union ready to fight.

At times, not only in those first dangerous spring months of 1861 but also throughout his four years in the White House, as the war raged up and down Virginia and into Pennsylvania, threatening the capital itself more than once, Lincoln must have wondered about the wisdom of the Founding Fathers' choice of a swampy site on the east bank of the Potomac River as the place to build a new national capital from scratch. As a young Illinois legislator, Lincoln had been deeply involved in the 1837 campaign to move the state capital from Vandalia, a small town in the southern part of the state, to Springfield, by then Lincoln's home base and a more central, rapidly developing town. Some opponents of the move from Vandalia accused the backers of Springfield—including Lincoln—with logrolling, even corruption, trading votes to support relocation for all kinds of improvements—from canals to turnpikes to railroads—that would benefit the losing towns.

Lincoln would have appreciated the high political and economic stakes involved in the deal regarding the location of the national capital that James Madison made with Alexander Hamilton at Thomas Jefferson's dinner table (at least that was Jefferson's version of how the Potomac Compromise of 1790 was finally made). The capital would be where Madison, George Washington, and other Virginians wanted it, and believed it to be the most useful to a growing nation—on the Potomac River.

The nation's still raw, young capital was in a precarious military position throughout the Civil War, with the Confederate capital just a hundred miles away. (Illustration copyright Applewood Books, Inc.)

In exchange, they would support Hamilton's conviction that the federal government must assume the states' Revolutionary War debts, and be allowed to strengthen its ability to deal with its own domestic and foreign debt, if the new country were ever to be considered a viable world power. Such a compromise was vital at that early stage in the new government's existence. In fact, Jefferson believed that "without some kind of breakthrough, the entire experiment with republican government at the national level would burst and vanish and the states separate to take care of everyone of itself."

As many as fifty localities over time had seen themselves as ideally situated to be the nation's permanent capital. Far more was involved in the selection than the hope for riches to be won when land prices ballooned around the final choice. George Washington was hardly the only land speculator in the new nation. He did own twenty thousand acres of land near the Potomac, and even prudent Madison had a stake as comparatively small as he was himself (five hundred acres) in an eventually failed site on the river near Great

Falls. Both men were also investors in the Potomac Company, which planned to open the river as far as possible to the West. But their interests were greater than that: they believed, however unrealistically, in the "grand Virginia illusion" that the Potomac River provided the best access to the lands that lay open for development farther west. Furthermore, the Potomac site was neither too far north nor too far south, they argued, to raise fears of dominance by one section of the infant republic over the rights and interests of the others, and its natural setting, they continued, was ideal for both defense and western expansion. Its selection would be a fitting, unifying conclusion to the American Revolution.

But the Washington/Madison victory in the Potomac Compromise of 1790 had exposed fundamental differences that would come to haunt Lincoln in 1861. Where did power and allegiance really lie—in the states or in the Union? It began to look as if that decision would have to be made by civil war.

The losers in 1790 were skeptical. In Philadelphia, a chief competitor for the honor, there were complaints that it was "abhorrent to common sense to suppose they are to have a place dug out of the rocky wilderness, for the use of Congress only four months in the year and all the rest of the time to be inhabited by wild beasts." In 1800, Abigail Adams rendered one of her acerbic opinions, "[It] is the very dirtiest hole I ever saw for a place of any trade or respectability of inhabitants." Washington himself knew it would take time for the city to "stand upon much higher ground than [it does] at present." The victors' vision indeed had grave shortcomings, and the Lincolns soon began to realize them.

In 1861 they came to a city that was still, seventy-one years after the Potomac Compromise, "the City of Magnificent Distances." James Fenimore Cooper, the novelist, said kindly in 1838, "Washington has certainly an air of more magnificence than any other American town. It is mean in detail, but the outline has a certain grandeur about it." A few years later, Charles Dickens called it the city of "Magnificent Intentions . . . spacious avenues that begin in nothing, and lead nowhere; streets, mile-long, that only want houses, roads, and inhabitants; public buildings that need but a public to be complete." Henry Adams had the longest perspective. His great-grandparents John and Abigail had come in 1800, and he had seen the capital in 1850. "Ten years had passed since his last visit," he wrote, "but very little had changed. As in 1800 and 1850, the same rude colony was camped in the same forest, with the same unfinished Greek temples for work rooms and sloughs for roads . . . right or wrong, secession was likely to be easy where there was so little to secede from." For that matter, Lincoln could see that little had changed since he'd left Congress in 1849.

What was even worse, the burning of the White House in 1814 by the British had certainly destroyed any vestige of the Founders' claims to the capital's defensibility. This Lincoln realized as he looked anxiously from his window after Fort Sumter fell for Union troops to arrive from the North, asking, "Why don't they come? Why don't they come?" When the Sixth Massachusetts militia regiment finally did arrive in Washington on April 19, Lincoln told the commanding colonel, "If you had not arrived tonight, we should have been in the hands of the rebels before morning."

Lincoln looked back on those first days a year later, on May 16, 1862:

> All the roads and avenues to this city were obstructed, and the capital was put into the condition of a siege. The mails in every direction were stopped and the lines of telegraph cut off by the insurgents, and military and naval forces which had been called out by the government for the defense of Washington were prevented from reaching the city by organized and combined treasonable resistance in the State of Maryland. . . . It became necessary for me to choose whether, using only the existing means . . . I should let the government fall at once into ruin or whether, availing myself of the broader powers conferred by the Constitution in cases of insurrection, I would make an effort to save it with all its blessing for the present age and for posterity.

It seems strange to us now, when Lincoln has consistently ranked first in every scholarly assessment of presidential leadership for the past sixty years, that his capacity to save the Union remained in doubt for his entire presidency. Was he up to it? Were his generals and admirals? His cabinet? One of the country's most colorful politicians concluded Lincoln was up to it. He was the brilliant, audacious

German American Carl Schurz. Schurz was just twenty-three when he arrived in the United States as a political refugee nine years before the Civil War began, already famous for his part in the 1848 revolutionary movement in Germany. He had escaped imprisonment or worse through a sewer, then rescued one of the leading figures of the movement in a daring raid on Spandau Prison. Immediately on arriving in America, Schurz threw himself into Republican politics, then into diplomacy, then into the war—and at Lincoln—with a vengeance. His visit to the Soldiers' Home in August 1864 was one of the many, usually impassioned, meetings on political and military strategies with the president, which perhaps led to Lincoln's wry correction of another general's pronunciation of Carl Schurz's name: "It's not Shurs, General Couch, but Shoorts." And it was now General Schurz to boot.

A prolific polemicist, Schurz, in an 1865 memorial essay on Lincoln, described as "appalling" the wider situation the new president faced in the spring of 1861, adding to Secretary of the Navy Gideon Welles's litany of the obstacles Lincoln faced with "an empty treasury, departments honeycombed with disloyalty, cries for peace at any price . . . and a Europe hoping to see the United States fall apart."

But Schurz believed he knew why Lincoln had been able to save the government.

> He instinctively understood . . . that this war would have to be carried on, not by means of a ready-made machinery, ruled by an undisputed, absolute will, but by means to be furnished by the voluntary action of the people . . . he would have to take into account all the influences strongly affecting the current of popular thought and feeling, and direct while appearing to obey. . . . For this leadership, Abraham Lincoln was admirably fitted. He understood the plain people, with all their loves and hates, their prejudices and their noble impulses, their weaknesses and their strength, as he understood himself, and his sympathetic nature was apt to draw their sympathy to him. . . . In fifty years, perhaps much sooner, Lincoln's name will stand written upon the honor roll of the American Republic next to that of Washington, and there it will remain for all time.

The philosopher-poet Ralph Waldo Emerson's explanation echoed Carl Schurz's. "[Lincoln was] the true representative of this continent, an entirely public man, father of his country, the pulse of twenty million throbbing in his heart, the thought of their mind articulated by his tongue." There was simply no other way to explain Lincoln's unprecedented willingness to welcome into his office the throngs of people who began lining up in and around the White House at dawn to see him. Lincoln had various names for this phenomenon: "the Beggar's Opera"—his "public opinion baths." They were his simple version of today's public opinion polls. Mary's cousin, Elizabeth Todd Grimsley, saw citizens swarming throughout the mansion during her six months at the White House in the Lincolns' first days there. "The halls, corridors, offices and even private apartments were invaded, and this throng continued increasing for weeks, intercepting the President on his way to his meals, and . . . almost every tenth man claimed the honor of having raised Mr. Lincoln to the Presidency."

One of the first supplicants had written the president-elect even before he left Springfield. An opera singer, Mrs. Amalia M. Valtellina, "Italian married Lady with two American sons," had fallen on rough times after her concert tour in Mexico. She had not been able to sell her house in Rahway, New Jersey, evidently one of many unsuccessful commercial speculations. Nor had she had any luck imploring his Grace, the "Duck of Cornwall"[sic], or Lincoln's predecessor, James Buchanan, so she and her children were about to be put out on the street. "Save me and my children, Do Sir! Take up the mortgage!" An equally desperate old woman showed up at the White House wanting Lincoln's help in getting a boarder to pay his overdue bill of seventy dollars. Lincoln patiently told her that he was "not here to collect small debts."

Despite the fact that many requests were "frivolous," Lincoln held his "promiscuous receptions" twice a week up to a few weeks before his assassination. "I feel—though the tax on my time is heavy—no hours of my day are better employed than those which thus bring me again within the direct contact and atmosphere of the average of our whole people. Men moving only in an official circle are apt to become merely official—not to say arbitrary—in their ideas; and are apter and apter, with each passing day, to forget that they only hold power in a representative capacity. Now this is all wrong. . . . They don't want much. They don't get but little, and I must see them."

What did bother Lincoln much more were the office seekers. He grew to dread, even detest them. As the war drew to an end, he told Schurz, a determined advocate of civil service reform in later years, "The rebellion is hard enough to overcome, but there you see something which in the course of time will become a greater danger to the Republic than the rebellion itself." "There" were the hundreds, even thousands, of men and women who flocked to Washington from all over the country, hoping to be given a political appointment: to a local post office, a city customs house, anything the new political party now had the power to dispense. Hundreds more prospects opened up with the war: young men wanted commissions in the regular army, older men wanted to raise *and* command regiments or battalions, independent of what the states were doing to recruit. Others wanted to supply the army with goods; inventors came full of ideas.

The line in the White House was never-ending. But political patronage was an accepted adhesive for nineteenth-century political parties. In fact, Lincoln, according to historian Mark Neely, "had initiated the most sweeping removal of federal office holders in the country's history up to that time. Of 1,520 presidential office holders, 1,195 were removed, and since most Southern offices were left unfilled, that was almost a complete overturn. He appointed Republicans to almost all of the jobs. His administration, the President explained frankly in 1862, 'distributed to its party friends as nearly all of the civil patronage as any administration ever did.'"

The hordes of office seekers were so obtrusive throughout the war, they became grist for the humorists of the day. One character—the creation of journalist Robert Henry Newell—even got his name, "Orpheus C. Kerr," from the phenomenon. The traveling showman Artemus Ward, an invention of Charles Farrar Browne, wrote of his "visit" to Lincoln at his home in Springfield. "The house, dooryard, barngs, woodshed was now full, and when *another* crowd cum I told 'em not to go away for want of room as the hog-pen was still empty. 'Good God!' cried Old Abe. 'They cum upon me from the skize—down the chimneys, and from the bowels of the yerth!" Artemus

Every day for four years, Lincoln was besieged by men, women, and even children wanting his help. But office seekers like these were the bane of Lincoln's existence.

Ward tried to help Lincoln deal with the infestation. "I wish there was furrin missions to be filled on varis lonely Islands where eprydemics rage incessantly, and if I was in Old Abe's place I'd send every mother's son of you to them." Lincoln had another idea: once when he came down with varioloid, a milder but contagious version of smallpox, he said now he'd willingly let the office seekers come, for at last he had something to give them all!

The office seekers did serve a useful immediate purpose. As they waited to see the president, Tad Lincoln, the Lincolns' enterprising youngest son, collected five cents from each one, for the support of civilian efforts to do something about the pitiful medical conditions in the army. But the toll on Lincoln was severe. "When I get through with such a day's work there is only one word which can express my condition, and that is—flabbiness." A congressional critic observed, "There were moments when his face was the picture of an indescribable weariness and despair." What seemed to distress Lincoln most was his conclusion that "seven-eighths of them were trying to find out how to live at the expense of the other eighth," and that for each position he filled from perhaps twenty applicants, "of these I must make nineteen enemies." By 1864, he'd had enough, and he was no longer so dependent on party loyalty. "I think now I will not remove a single man except for delinquency." Carl Schurz came to believe that Lincoln had begun to realize the danger to the republic of using public office as party spoils, and that he perhaps would have become a pioneer in civil service reform had he lived.

Several members of his new cabinet thought this presidential open house was an unwise use of Lincoln's time. Secretary of State William Seward let him know—in one of the most tactless, brazen messages any president ever received from his immediate circle. But Lincoln displayed his power at once, squelching Seward's pompous proposal that he in essence run the country since it looked as if Lincoln wasn't going to do it, he was so occupied with minutiae.

Secretary of War Edwin M. Stanton had no such ambitions. He allotted just one hour each morning to receiving seekers after one favor or another from his department. A disgusted Benjamin Brown French, the exuberant commissioner of public buildings, called those who approached him "office Beggars," although he had been quite persistent himself in seeking his own post from Lincoln, and regretted that his predecessor had shelled out most of the patronage jobs, leaving him with "the mere gleanings."

Navy Secretary Gideon Welles was a close observer of Lincoln for those four arduous years, one of only two cabinet members we know to have visited the Soldiers' Home. He was perhaps the first in the cabinet to appreciate the qualities for which Lincoln is now revered. Very early in the war, Welles wrote that Lincoln had "learned he must not give implicit trust to anyone . . . in a gentle manner he gradually let it be understood that Abraham Lincoln was the chief." But Welles was also a constant critic (at least to his diary) of Lincoln's management style. His never-ending gripe was that Lincoln did not consult the entire cabinet on critical issues, and often the cabinet met only to be told there was "no business." As the war came to an end, Welles wrote that it would hardly surprise him if Lincoln "were to undertake to arrange terms of peace without consulting anyone." When complaints from the cabinet and the Senate reached a crisis in December 1862, Lincoln explained that they were all too busy to meet more frequently, that it would take too much time for each member to be briefed sufficiently for him to make a valid contribution, and that dissension would be costly and unproductive. When the cabinet did meet, the atmosphere appeared quite casual, at least to William O. Stoddard, Lincoln's third secretary. "I have seen one stretched on the sofa with a cigar in his mouth, another with his heels on the table, another nursing his knee abstractly, the President with his leg over the arm of his chair, and not a man of them all in any wise sitting." Lincoln cultivated this harmonious atmosphere deliberately. But Welles insisted (to his diary) throughout the war that it would have been better for Lincoln to get a broader view before coming to a decision, wise though that might be, and it would certainly have been helpful, at least to Welles, to have heard others' opinions on important naval matters. As it was, he had to make crucial decisions on his own. Fortunately, he was usually right.

Welles was particularly put out by Lincoln's intimacy with Secretary of State William Seward, who could "watch and wait on the President daily because he has few active duties." Welles distrusted and blamed Seward for some of Lincoln's mistakes. The two men would go off into a corner with Seward whispering in Lincoln's ear, leaving the rest of the cabinet at loose ends. Secretary of War Edwin Stanton did the same, and Welles didn't think much of him either, calling him insincere, overbearing, and rude. Lincoln was very inquisitive, Welles observed, and had a weakness for political gossip, an appetite that Seward fed. "It is an infirmity of the President that he permits the little newsmongers to come around him and be intimate, encouraged by Seward." (Welles had a low opinion of the press, too, despite his own journalistic past.) And "Lincoln was constantly imposed on by sharpers and adventurers, peddling one scheme or another." As late as March 23, 1865, just a few days before Lincoln's murder, Welles wrote, "Lincoln makes the office much more laborious than he should. He does not generalize and takes upon himself questions that properly belong to the departments, often causing derangement and irregularities. The more he yields, the greater the pressure on him. It has now become such that he is compelled to flee." But when Lincoln did flee to the Soldiers' Home, much of the pressure followed him there. Welles felt strongly that "when he relies on his own right intentions and good common sense, he is strongest. . . . [he is] a much more shrewd and accurate observer of the characteristics of men, [and he] better and more correctly informed an estimation of their power and capabilities than most others." He is "a singular man and not fully understood." The two men respected each other very much.

Few praised Lincoln's day-to-day management of "the shop," either. "He was extremely unmethodical," reminisced exhausted, overburdened John Hay. "It was a four year's struggle on Nicolay's part and mine to get him to adopt some systematic rules. He would break through every regulation as fast as it was made." George Boutwell, Lincoln's commissioner of internal revenue, recollected that "Mr. Lincoln was indifferent to those matters of government that were relatively unimportant, but he devoted himself with conscientious diligence to the graver questions and topics of official duty, and in the first months of his administration, at a moment of supreme peril, by his pre-eminent wisdom, of which there remains indubitable proof, he saved the country from a foreign war." "He was an unconscious driver [of his small staff] and was unintentionally, though unrelentingly, exacting," wrote William Stoddard. "No person employed in connection with Mr. Lincoln's work would willingly have been out of call when wanted, but when the President did call for a man, and couldn't find him, he would at once send for another. He managed his generals and sea captains somewhat on the same principles, except that now and then he dropped one of them and did not afterwards make any effort to find him."

The *Times of London* correspondent, William Russell, felt sorry for Lincoln in the early days of the war. "This poor President! He is to be pitied . . . trying with all his might to understand strategy, naval warfare, big guns, the movements of troops, military maps, reconnaissances, occupations, internal and exterior lines, and all the technical details of the art of slaying. He runs from one house to another, armed with plans, mss, reports, recommendations, sometimes good-humored, never angry, occasionally dejected and always a little fussy."

It was unusual for Lincoln to just sit in a chair. His legs were so long, Frederick Douglass said, that when Lincoln arose, "he slowly drew his feet in from various parts of the room."

Hell seemed more on Lincoln's mind than heaven as he faced the calamities that kept coming at him year after year. "Hell has no terror for me," he said after the Union troops' ignominious retreat from its first test at Bull Run in July 1861. "If there was any worse Hell than he had been in for two days, he would like to know it," Lincoln told a friend after the hideous slaughter at Fredericksburg in December 1862. And to another friend, "If to be the head of Hell is as hard as what I have to undergo here, I could find it in my heart to pity Satan himself."

Yet two years later things had improved. "The tycoon is in fine whack," wrote John Hay in August 1863. "I have rarely seen him more serene and busy. He is managing this war, the draft, foreign relations, and planning a reconstruction of the Union, all at once. I never knew with what tyrannous authority he rules the Cabinet until now. There is no man in the country so wise, so gentle, and so firm. I believe the hand of God placed him where he is." Lincoln had by then issued the Emancipation Proclamation on his own terms, he had faced down Senate radicals who wanted changes in his cabinet and his own behavior, and he had kept the country out of war with Great Britain over the seizure of two ardent Confederate agents on their way to London hoping to get British recognition of the Confederacy. In what Gideon Welles pointed to later as a perfect example of Lincoln's courageous leadership, he had taken the risk of reappointing the discredited warrior, George B. McClellan, to command the Army of the Potomac after another demoralizing defeat at Second Bull Run in August 1862.

Mary Todd Lincoln worried constantly about her husband's health, and she was under enormous strain herself. "The White House has been quite a *Mecca* of late," she wrote to her old friend Mercy Levering Conkling. "I consider myself fortunate if at eleven o'clock, I find myself, in my pleasant room & very especially, if my tired & weary Husband, is *there*, resting in the lounge to receive me—to chat over the occurrences of the day."

At least the couple did not have to go very far to find one another. By then, "in the new republic, only the White House functioned both as an officeholder's residence and as a center of political activity, combining functions that had traditionally been united in the palaces of kings." The place had become an anachronism. Lincoln may have received some comfort from the White House's symbolic value as the Union's "First Home"; he insisted that the Capitol be finished despite the war, as proof of the Union's strength and permanence. And by the 1870s, President Grant dismissed the idea of presidents living anywhere else. The White House was now too historic for that. Ironically, Lincoln had made it so.

The Lincolns had very different views of how palatial the "President's House" should be. Lincoln did not seem to notice—or care—that their entire house in Springfield could have fit into the East Room, or that the White House was then the largest house in the country. To him, it was simply "this damned old house . . . furnished better than any one we ever lived in." "I have but a dull sense of the beautiful," he once said as he watched people enjoying a Marine Band concert on the White House's south lawn on a lovely day. "As a student in a rugged school, I have through life been obliged to strip ideas of their ornaments and make them facts before I conquered them.... What began in a narrow necessity remains a habit. I may have gained in precision, concentration, or that hard power of arrangement we draw from mathematics, at the cost, maybe, of the silent pleasure an eye educated to beauty can always drink in at a glance."

As in so many other traits, Mary was his opposite. When she got through with it, the White House was going to be not only a shining symbol of the Union, inside and out, but also a testimony to her taste and sophistication. When they moved in, cousin Elizabeth Todd Grimsley shared her opinion that the executive mansion was seedy and dilapidated, and they weren't the only ones to notice. "Miserable ... gloomy ... like an old and unsuccessful hotel ... an ill-kept and dirty rickety concern" were other reactions from friends and staff. By the time all the work was completed, Mary had overrun her entire four-year budget of twenty thousand dollars, the customary congressional appropriation for White House repairs, by close to seven thousand dollars. It had taken months to get everything done, including Mary's several well-publicized (and exaggerated) shopping trips to New York and Philadelphia. John Hay was still complaining in the fall of 1861 about the smell of paint and workmen everywhere. But the refurbished mansion was now in splendid shape. Even the hard-boiled William Russell praised "the stamp of [Mary's] exquisite taste ... on the furnishing of the President's Mansion that never looked so well as now." One of the country boys assigned to guard the president at the Soldiers' Home and the White House beginning in September 1862 was also impressed and wrote to his mother: "I wish you could see the inside of the [front] room it would make your eyes glitter ... there is Chandeleers [*sic*] in the front room and there is more than one waggon load of glass in them and looking glasses 8 feet long ... there is lights all a round the house ... you can see to pick up a pin it is so light at all the places where we guard."

It is not too difficult to understand some of the brutal criticisms Mary Todd Lincoln did suffer. Her husband was furious at her overspending. He realized that "it would stink in the land to have it said that an appropriation of twenty thousand dollars for furnishing the house had been overrun by the President when the poor freezing soldiers could not have blankets." The government was faced with the frightening challenge of financing a war that would cost six billion dollars before it was over. Congress had had to appropriate twenty thousand dollars apiece just to enlarge the Navy and War Department buildings, both more critical to the war effort than Mary's new carpets and drapes. If she had had a keener sense of public relations, she would perhaps not have become so vilified over the White House redecoration, or any of the other generous and courageous things she did as first lady. Her loyal aide, "Stod," believed a few White House teas with cake for the press after one of her frequent hospital visits would have done wonders. Mary could have learned something about the value of good PR from Julia Gardiner Tyler, the handsome young second wife of the tenth president, John Tyler. Julia had always had a flair for publicity, and hired a press agent to burnish her image as first lady. A supporter of slavery despite her New York origins, she got away with behaving like a queen, receiving guests while seated on a raised platform, with a tiaralike arrangement of feathers in her hair, and wearing a gown with a regal train.

What refurbishing the independently wealthy Julia Tyler did in her one-year reign at the White House she could and did pay for herself. Mary had to work with an appropriation that had not been increased in years. Thirty years before, President Andrew Jackson had even gotten away with spending thirty thousand dollars, but his successor, the eighth president, Martin Van Buren, was subjected to a three-day tirade from a Pennsylvania congressman for his "palace as splendid as that of the Caesars, and as richly adorned as the proudest Asiatic mansion."

Nor was Mary alone in going to New York and Philadelphia for major purchases for the White House. Even the beloved Dolley Madison had offended Mrs. Sweeney, a local upholsterer, "at my leaving her but little to do in the house." The ruthless scrutiny of Southern sympathizers who had ruled Washington society until the war and felt that Mary was a traitor to her Southern background, as well as the scorn of Northerners who were suspicious of it, made it almost inevitable that Mary would be blamed for extravagance and everything else she did. She was given "the cold shoulder," her loyal friend, Elizabeth Blair Lee, regretted in one of her long letters to her husband, an admiral in the United States Navy.

Despite their fatigue and worry and growing sadness, the Lincolns tried valiantly to keep up appearances throughout the war, carrying on the tradition of greeting personally the thousands of people who crammed into the White House on New Year's Day and on other occasions. It was Benjamin French's official duty as commissioner of public buildings to introduce the visitors to Mrs. Lincoln "every Saturday from 1 to 3 pm & every Tuesday from $\frac{1}{2}$ past 8 to $\frac{1}{2}$ past 10. . . . It is a terrible bore, but as a duty I *must* do it, and it leads to an acquaintance with very many celebrities of whom I should otherwise have no personal knowledge." Oftentimes, friends noticed that the president seemed to be miles away as he held out his enormous kid-gloved hand. His arm became so stiff and sore from shaking hands at the New Year's reception on January 1, 1863, he was concerned about signing the Emancipation Proclamation later that day. If his signature were shaky, he wondered, would the people think he had doubts about it?

In his journal, French consistently gave the Lincolns' receptions high marks:

> January 8, 1862: I have never seen so elegant a reception, or one that went off better. [Mrs. Lincoln] was 'got up' in excellent taste and *looked* the Queen.

> Just before Christmas in 1863: a reception

> [for visiting Russian naval officers] . . . was the most brilliant I ever attended because it was the only one where the mud-stained people did not mingle with the court.

> January 3, 1864: at $\frac{1}{2}$ past 11 am Mrs. L. appeared and did her part of the reception with her usual ease and urbanity.

> February 22, 1864: attended the President's and Mrs. Lincoln's reception . . . it was a very crowded and brilliant one. The President and Mrs. L. affable and pleasant as they always are on such occasions.

March 3, 1864: In the evening a reception at the President's . . . I think I never saw such a crowd in the White House in my life, and it was a steady stream of humanity for 2 ½ hours of all sorts and kinds of people. Ladies in magnificent toilets and in the plainest garb imaginable. The Major General in his dress coat, and the common soldier in his patched great coat, and boots covered with mud halfway up the leg . . . citizens in all sorts of dress, from the finished & perfumed dandy down to the shabbiest of the shabby.

As the war drew to a close, on January 22, 1865, French attended another

large and brilliant reception at the White House . . . the President appeared well and in excellent spirits, and Mrs. Lincoln never appeared better. She was dressed in admirable taste . . . I never was much at describing ladies' dresses, but I know that her *toute ensemble* never had a more favorable impression upon me . . . and she greeted every guest with such cheerful good will and kindness as to do infinite credit to her position and her heart.

Incredibly, at their last reception, after Lincoln's second inauguration, French noted in his diary on March 5, 1865:

the largest I ever saw . . . from 8 til ¼ past 11 pm, the President shook hands steadily at the rate of 100 every 4 minutes, with about 5000 persons, and when they came the thickest he was not over 3 minutes, never over 5. It was a grand oration of the people to their President, whom they dearly love. Mrs. Lincoln was present throughout the reception and avowed her intention to remain till morning, rather than have the doors closed on a single visitor. She appeared very gracious and well. She certainly is a woman of endurance, having been all the morning at the Capitol.

John Fleming, a "Bucktail" in Company K of the 150th Pennsylvania Regiment, the president's guard for three years, wrote to his parents that he had gone to one of the receptions because he wasn't on duty. The job of those who were on duty was to keep the crowd under control, or at least try. "I went in and took of [*sic*] my hat to mrs. lincoln and then went on and shook with old abe and then passed in the east room there is where the prommading [*sic*] was done it almost scared me to see so many richly dressed ladies and gentlemen but I waded around among them for an hour and then scrabeled out the crowd did not get all through till twelve o'clock."

There was a downside to all this republican hospitality. It almost left much of the White House in tatters. Mary's elegant and costly efforts were so badly vandalized by visitors wanting souvenirs, the journalist Noah Brooks couldn't believe his eyes. By late November 1864, carpets, upholstery, drapes, and even the wallpaper and fixtures in the public rooms had been cut up, ripped off, wrenched out, and carted away. By 1865, Commissioner French reported to congress that "no private gentleman would suffer his house and grounds to remain in such dilapidated condition." French went on to say that he had repeatedly informed them of the "depredations upon the fixtures and furniture of the house, which can be avoided in no other way that I can devise but by hiring a day watchman to accompany all visitors through the public rooms." This perhaps explains why Mary Todd Lincoln at least wanted their retreat at the Soldiers' Home spruced up for the summer of 1864.

The Lincolns had more control over who came to the private entertainments they arranged in the White House from time to time. One of Mary's major purchases in 1861 from the Philadelphia firm of William H. Carryl, which certainly did not help her budget, was an elaborately carved rosewood grand piano, on which Willie and Tad Lincoln undoubtedly suffered lessons from Professor Alexander Wolowski. More appropriately, in 1863, the nine-year-old prodigy, temperamental Teresa Careno, was invited to play. She didn't think too much of the piano but was prevailed upon to play some popular sentimental tunes, driving her father to despair for not playing Bach. But the president was pleased, she remembered later. "He patted me on the cheek and asked me if I could play 'The Mocking Bird.'" She did, and "then went off in a series of impromptu variations that threatened to go on forever. When I stopped, it was from sheer exhaustion."

A young Washington opera singer, Meda Blanchard, gave a performance for Mary Todd Lincoln and her friends, which tempted the president down from his office as she was about to finish. Accompanying herself on the piano, she sang an aria from Bellini's *Norma*.

Lincoln then asked her to sing "The Marseillaise," which was banned in France at the time. A young Native American singer, Larooqua, also pleased the Lincolns with "wood notes wild." So did Commodore G. W. Morrison Nutt, in a performance of songs for Lincoln and the cabinet. Nutt was "a most polite and refined gentleman" just twenty-nine inches tall, a member of P. T. Barnum's troupe. The impresario's stars, Mr. and Mrs. Tom Thumb, were given a reception at the White House (Robert Todd Lincoln disapproved of such levity, and would not attend). Lincoln invited the Shakespearean actor James H. Hackett to the White House during his run as Falstaff at Ford's Theater, and Commissioner French noted in his journal that on Sunday, November 4, 1861, he and his family had gone to the White House to "witness the performance of Monsieur Hermann . . . the Great Prestidigitator." About a hundred people were there: four cabinet secretaries, several generals, "& many officers of lower rank whom I did not know and some I did know. There was quite a number of ladies, some handsome, some homely . . . the performance did not commence until toward eleven, when Hermann astonished his audience by some of the best slight [sic] of hand performances I ever saw, and I have seen a great many."

Since the Soldiers' Home was suitable as a retreat only in warmer weather, the Lincolns were compelled to look within the city itself for other relaxation. They were steady patrons at the two major theaters in town: Ford's and Grover's. The young managers, John Ford and Leonard Grover, were rivals for Lincoln's patronage, and tried to outdo each other. After a huge fire, Ford erected a "magnificent new Thespian temple." So then Grover enlarged his theater to twenty-five hundred seats, and boasted that Lincoln had attended performances there at least a hundred times. Mary Lincoln particularly loved the opera, which she attended with her favorite escort, Senator Charles Sumner, if Lincoln was too busy. Although Lincoln loved Shakespeare's tragedies above all, the local press reported that Lincoln went to the opera at least twice in one week in April 1863, and, unlikely as it seems, that he heard three operas in two days in March 1865. The Canterbury Music Hall, "a sink of corruption," was surely off-limits to the Lincolns, with its "barelegged dancing girls," but young John Hay did attend, and admitted that one of the shows was "filthy and not funny."

There was even a theater at Campbell Hospital on Seventh Street, Lincoln's usual route to the Soldiers' Home. Campbell was one of many military hospitals in Washington. Together they cared for sometimes as many as twenty thousand casualties at one time. (Estimates of the number of hospitals operating in Washington during the war vary from twenty-one to seventy. Many were temporary, set up in churches, schools, and even private homes.) An enlightened surgeon at Campbell, and the hospital chaplain, believed that it was as important to heal the soldiers' minds as their bodies, so Campbell had its own five-hundred-seat theater. The patients had their own drama company, and professional actors playing in town came out to entertain. Lincoln was among the invitees, of course, and John Wilkes Booth knew that. Before his intention became deadly, Booth had planned to kidnap Lincoln there, then spirit him off to the Confederacy as a hostage.

The Lincolns' visits to all the hospitals around the city were hardly joyful, but they persisted in going throughout the war, sometimes together, sometimes alone. Lincoln's mere appearance was enough to boost morale, but he did more than that; he would go from bed to bed with a personal word for each soldier. As for Mary Todd Lincoln, "among the ladies who visit the hospitals none is more indefatigable," said at least one favorable reviewer. She wrote letters home for the soldiers, raised money for badly needed fruit and vegetables when scurvy became a problem for the poorly fed patients, brought flowers she loved from the White House gardens, and even served Christmas dinner to the wounded in 1862.

Captain Aldace Walker, stationed with a Vermont regiment for eighteen months in the defenses around Washington, was one of the few who was favorably impressed at least with the three Washington hospitals he visited (Mount Pleasant, Carver, and Columbia College). "They all seemed neat and well kept. The rooms are cleanly—all that I saw. The iron cots are comfortable, with springy slats, white cover lids, and mattresses, etc. They are not so crowded as I supposed, and they say other hospitals in the city are in better condition than these . . . the wounds are everywhere. Some are shockingly mangled. I did not go about much, for I do not like such scenes." Benjamin French concluded otherwise. On November 7, 1862, his diary noted that his wife and a friend had been to two hospitals in

No matter where he went in Washington, Lincoln passed hospitals for the wounded. Comparatively "neat and clean" 3,000-bed Harewood was on his route to the Soldiers' Home.

Washington "distributing food & clothing to the sick. They gave an account of Emory Hospital that makes one shudder, and ought to disgrace those who have the control of it. The Buildings are mere rough board shanties, not a fire or the means of having a fire in them, and the poor sick soldiers lying on beds covered with snow."

Louisa May Alcott shared that view. A self-styled "red hot abolitionist" not yet famous for her novel *Little Women*, she came down from Massachusetts in early 1863 to work as an army nurse. Alcott arrived in the capital after dark, which was just as well. All she could think of to say was "splendid," because she couldn't see what she was supposed to be admiring. Reality set in later; the city was "a camp of hospitals" and in her brief experience at one of them, "the Hurly Burly Hotel" she called it in her *Hospital Sketches*, "disorder, discomfort, bad management, and no visible head, reduced things to a condition which I despair of describing." Alcott got typhoid fever from the unsanitary conditions at the hospital, became so ill she had to go home after just one month, and never fully recovered. She did not get to meet Lincoln, "that much abused gentleman," but she did visit the Senate chamber, and wrote at length about one of Washington's more surprising sights: the pigs that roamed Washington's streets, "enjoy[ing] a greater liberty than many of its human citizens."

Jane Swisshelm, also an ardent abolitionist and feminist, came to Washington in 1863 to help out, and spent most of her time at Campbell Hospital. Many other respectable women volunteered as nurses during the war, for there was not a single trained nurse, as we would recognize her, in the entire country. Most army nurses, in fact, were male, some still convalescing from their own wounds, and of little use. The redoubtable reformer Dorothea Dix, a longtime crusader for better treatment of the mentally ill and for better prison conditions, had volunteered her services. She was quickly made superintendent of female nurses in June 1861, to select and supervise the most suitable applicants. To her that meant, for starters, past thirty years old, healthy, "plain almost to repulsion in dress, and devoid of personal attractions." The salary was forty cents a day and one ration. With her own formidable personality and notoriety, Swisshelm was effective in the few months she served, even facing down Dix herself when Swisshelm felt she should go into the field at Fredericksburg to deal with the even worse conditions for the wounded there.

Most of the three thousand women who served as army nurses, with or without Dix's imprimatur, were like Alcott and Swisshelm, using their common sense, humor, courage, and kindness to combat the prejudices against working women, as well as the senseless bureaucracy, incompetence, and indifference. Jane Swisshelm was proud of her ability to nurse amputees back to health. She had seen a demonstration on how to make amputees' stumps more comfortable and clean by observing a doctor demonstrate on a watermelon!

Veterans of Korean War MASH units would have been appalled at the care of wounded in Civil War field hospitals, although perhaps anything would have been better than being left, as many were, to lie out on the battlefield for three or more days without food or water, and covered with maggots. Clara Barton, "the Angel of the Battlefield," made prodigious efforts to deal with those conditions. She "followed the cannon" and arrived ahead of almost everyone with wagons of food and supplies that she proceeded to dispense, sometimes up to her ankles in blood and mud. Her most memorable experience during the war, she said, was crossing a creek on a bridge made of the left knees of soldiers, who knelt on their right knees in the water to help her cross, like latter-day Sir Walter Raleighs. With a letter of support from President Lincoln, whom she never managed to meet directly, Barton remained in Washington after the war trying to locate sixty-two thousand men missing in action. She found twenty-two thousand.

As wars went in the nineteenth century, the Civil War was a comparatively healthy one. Dysentery, cholera, scurvy, and "fevers" had killed over 70 percent of the twenty-five thousand men in the first expeditionary force to the Crimea. After Florence Nightingale exposed that debacle, reforms in Europe did make an impression on Civil War sanitary practice, and although the public health movement in the United States lagged behind Europe's, it grew strong enough to support the creation of the United States Sanitary Commission in 1861, a group of professionals who were determined to provide efficient and decent care to the wounded. Still, the record is abysmal. The Union Army lost close to two hundred and twenty-five thousand men to disease, one hundred and ten thousand to battle. The Confederate Army lost one hundred and sixty-four thousand men to disease, ninety-four thousand to battle.

Conditions in the capital itself were not propitious for the health of civilians, either, as the Lincolns would discover tragically in 1862. On the Lincolns' daily afternoon carriage rides together around the city, some ingenuity must have been required of their coachman to avoid the scavenging and dying animals in the streets, including Alcott's pigs. But these were not the only problem. Washingtonians complained bitterly about the mud in winter and the dust in summer. "It is the mudyest place I ever thought of seeing for the capital of the U.S. or any other big city you can hardly get a cross from one side of the street to the other," wrote Private Willard Cutter of Company K. Captain Aldace Walker was more precise. "The mud here is good on one account—it is very thin—of no more constituency [*sic*] than so much water . . . & though I was covered from head to foot, it was not very hard for the horse." Commissioner French noted that one of General Daniel Sickles's men told him that his horse "absolutely swam" through the mud on one of the main streets.

Then there was the dust! Walt Whitman dreaded it—"I don't mind the mud." A local newspaper carried a notice of a meeting

Winslow Homer's intimate, powerful sketches of Civil War battlefields for Harper's Weekly *made him famous.*

before Lincoln's first inauguration on how to deal with "Dust! Dust! Dust!" on Pennsylvania Avenue. Commissioner French noted that the main thoroughfare was "one cloud of dust from end to end and it was nearly as much as one's life was worth to pass up or down 7th St., the wind being N. W. seemed to whirl all through that street in eddies, whirling the dust in thick clouds in every direction."

The city's population was exploding all around the Lincolns. In 1860 there were seventy-five thousand inhabitants, by the end of 1863 perhaps as many as three hundred and fifty thousand. (The population decreased in the 1870 census, which counted one hundred thirty-one thousand seven hundred residents.) Among them, Walt Whitman wrote, were "a huge mess of traitors, loafers, axe-grinders, incompetencies and officials." The Lincoln boys' tutor, a mild-mannered Scot, Alexander Williamson, saw the city

swarming not only with troops, but with vagabonds, vampires, and harpies of every description . . . low women were continually caught selling whiskey to the soldiers in bottles suspended from the hoops of their crinolines ... whole streets were occupied by prostitutes ... then such a roar as there continually was in the city, day and night. Droves of mules from Kentucky, brought in for drawing the quartermaster's stores; horses by the thousands, for cavalry and other service ... herds of cattle, for feeding the army, bellowing and stampeding through the streets. Then there were the dying and the dead, arriving in ship-loads at our wharves.

Frederick Law Olmsted, the formidable first executive director of the United States Sanitary Commission, weighed in with a perspective based on his three intensive prewar journeys through the South, studying slavery and the social and economic conditions there. He saw Washington as a "reflection of frontier indifference and the laziness of a slave society." He was equally critical of Lincoln at first but soon decided that "his frankness and courageous directness overcame all critical disposition." "Oh, how I wish this war were over," wrote French. "If for nothing else, that this city may once more be a civil city, instead of a city of Camps, corrals and soldiers . . . a goodly number of whom are continually drunk."

As usual, Walt Whitman saw the city with a poet's eye.

My first impressions, architectural, etc., were not favorable; but upon the whole, the city, the spaces, buildings, etc., make no unfit emblem of our country, so far, so broadly planned, everything in plenty, money and materials staggering with plenty, but the fruit of the plans, the knit, the combination yet wanting—Determined to express ourselves greatly in a Capitol but no fit Capitol yet here (time, associations, wanting, I suppose) many a hiatus yet—many a thing to be taken down and done over again yet—perhaps an entire change of base—maybe a succession of changes.

Whitman observed and loved President Lincoln.

He has a face like a Hoosier Michelangelo, so awful ugly it becomes beautiful, with its strange mouth, its deep cut, criss-cross lines, and its doughnut complexion ... I do not dwell on the supposed failures of his government; he has shown, I sometimes think an almost supernatural tact in keeping the ship afloat at all ... I say never yet captain, never ruler, had such a perplexing dangerous task as his, the past two years. I more and more rely upon his idiomatic western genius, careless of court dress or court decorum.

Whitman was right in his assessment of Lincoln's leadership—and about the city's "staggering plenty." There were toy shops, jewelry stores, book stores, photo studios, good restaurants and oyster houses, stationery shops, millinery and fancy good stores, dressmakers, confectioners, markets, hotels, saloons, and of course the theaters enjoyed by the Lincolns. "Life was anything but monotonous ... in the little, great city," wrote Lt. Col. Thomas Chamberlin in his history of the 150th Regiment. "The town was full of life, full of business and social enterprise, with a feverish desire on the part of its permanent and transient population to be amused. In spite of the 'horrors of war' and in the face of depressing reverses to our armies, people ate, drank and were merry." The special correspondent of the *Chicago Evening Journal* sensed the same vitality (June 16, 1864). "Pennsylvania Avenue is a museum without a Barnum. Every calling has its representative man": organ grinders, coffin makers, bootblacks, umbrella repairmen, ice cream vendors, advertisers for embalmers, theater performances, and second-hand furniture sellers. ... [It is] "a thoroughfare where at almost every step Yesterday seems looking over the Shoulder of Today, and Tomorrow peers smilingly between."

For the Lincolns, neither yesterday nor tomorrow smiled. After Mary had left Washington as a widow, she wrote, "All the sorrows of my life occurred there & that Whited Sepulcure broke my heart." And sensitive young Tad, after Lincoln's assassination, said: "I am glad he has gone [to heaven], for he never was happy here. This was not a good place for him."

It remained, then, for the Soldiers' Home to provide the ill-fated couple with whatever real happiness in Washington was to be theirs.

PART TWO

Lincoln at the
Soldiers' Home

CHAPTER 4

⟨❧⟩

Embattled Retreat

IF THE WHITE HOUSE WAS in the worst possible location in the nation's capital, then the Soldiers' Home was surely in one of the very best. The contrast was more than sad—it was frightening. "There is a soap factory south east of the President's Mansion," complained Lincoln's commissioner of public buildings, Benjamin French, to the Board of Health, "the stench from which, when the wind direction is South East, is almost unindurable [*sic*] at the mansion, at the Treasury Department, and at all other places in that vicinity. Mrs. Lincoln has especially complained concerning it." French went even further with a warning to the United States Senate: "The Washington Canal [that flowed into the Potomac not far from the White House to the south] is the grand receptacle of all the filth of the city . . . the waste from all the public buildings, the hotels, and very many private residences is drained into it . . . unless something is done to clean away this immense mass of fetid and corrupt matter, the good citizens of Washington must, during some hot season, find themselves visited by a pestilence . . . the health of the entire population and the lives of thousands depend on it." John Hay added his two cents' worth: "The ghosts of twenty thousand drowned cats come in nights through the South Windows."

French's warning came too late for Willie Lincoln. The pestilence he feared had already struck the White House. That "vast septic tank," the Potomac, which supplied the White House with water for washing, was most probably the cause of the eleven-year-old boy's death of typhoid fever in February 1862. Tad Lincoln had almost died. Now two of the four Lincoln boys (Eddie had died in 1850) were gone. So whatever military or political crises had kept the Lincolns from their eagerly anticipated retreat at the Soldiers' Home that first summer of 1861, there was no way Mary would risk another summer in "the City of Stink." And from the fall of 1861 to the spring of 1862, the Union Army had performed well, with a succession of significant victories throughout the Confederate states. New Orleans was in Union hands; McClellan was within a few miles of the Confederate capital, Richmond.

So the Lincolns moved out to the country in early June 1862 and didn't return to the city until the middle of November. The pattern was much the same in 1863 and 1864. Their prolonged reliance on the Soldiers' Home was such an obvious retreat from the miseries and dangers of living in the White House that in 1866, just one year after the three surviving Lincolns were gone from it, a site adjacent to the Soldiers' Home grounds was proposed as the ideal place for a new presidential mansion to be built. Mary had not exaggerated when she wrote to Hannah Shearer, a Springfield neighbor, that the Soldiers' Home was "a very beautiful place." Banker George Riggs had chosen well the site for his new home. The land had once been part of a large plantation known as "Pleasant Hills." He bought part of that very desirable real estate at auction in June 1842, impressed by the description: "[It] lies on a commanding height overlooking the city of Washington . . . it is distinguished by its beauty of site [and] has been enriched by high cultivation and contains thriving orchards of well selected fruit." Even today, with the city closing in on the few hundred acres that remain of the original property, and with more buildings on the grounds to house over a thousand veterans, the hilltop still can be a welcome ten degrees cooler than downtown in the summer.

Just before the family moved out to the Soldiers' Home for the summer of 1862, Mary had written another Springfield neighbor, Julia Ann Sprigg, "When we are in sorrow, quiet is very necessary to us." Both parents had had such high hopes for Willie, their poised, considerate, highly intelligent third son, the one most like Lincoln himself, people said. But unlike Thomas Jefferson's retreat,

Poplar Forest, ninety miles from Monticello, where he could find "the solitude of a hermit," the Soldiers' Home was just a few miles north of the chaos of the capital city. The times were so turbulent, the fighting so close by, and Lincoln's responsibilities so overwhelming, for the family to find the peace they longed for at the Soldiers' Home was next to impossible. The ride out to the Soldiers' Home was disturbing enough, with its rumbling ambulances, military hospitals, and contraband camps along the way. Everyday sounds of the immense mobilization of men and materiel needed to fight a war being waged on a continental scale surrounded them. A young soldier camped on the grounds wrote his brother in September 1862, "There was fifty thousand troops passed up 7th St. on Saturday." This was Lincoln's usual route into the Soldiers' Home grounds from the White House, and a major commercial route from the city's docks to the north. A year later, the same soldier wrote: "There is 1800 mules not far from here that keeps muleing all night and make a devilish noise." Not only that, he reported, "two of the old soldiers at the home had a big fight one was stone blind and both big fat stout men the blind man kicked bully for him."

Then there was the hundred-man Company K, the president's guard, which had arrived at the Soldiers' Home in early September 1862 to provide Lincoln at last with the protection he detested ("an almost morbid dislike," said his journalist friend, Noah Brooks) and eluded as often as he could. Their camp was within sight of the Lincoln cottage; the drills, the drums, the rifle practice, even the music of its two bands must have added to the din. At least once, Mary Lincoln had to ask them to stop playing. Add to that the clankings of the cavalry escort that accompanied Lincoln from the Soldiers' Home into town, which made so much noise on the way that he and Mary could hardly hear themselves talk. On top of that was the constant traffic at the military cemetery just down the hill from the Soldiers' Home as new war dead were brought in to be buried, and old dead exhumed to be taken home for permanent burial. The clattering telegraph installed at the Soldiers' Home by July 1863 was sure to have Lincoln hovering over it, for he communicated with his field commanders at all hours of the day and night.

On October 1, 1862, Mary Lincoln mentioned far more ominous sounds to a favorite in her most intimate circle, General Daniel Sickles. "When we are within hearing, as we on this elevation have been, for the last two or three days, of the roaring cannon, we can but pause and think." That was not the first or the last time sounds of battle reached the Soldiers' Home, and in July 1864, the war came within just a few miles as the Union Army fought off Jubal Early's invasion of the capital itself in a two-day battle at Fort Stevens. Perhaps inured by then to war, the Lincolns didn't flee from it; instead, they headed out to the fort to see the action for themselves.

So those who call the Soldiers' Home Lincoln's "embattled retreat" would be closer to reality. Even so, it's unlikely the Lincolns would have agreed with Company K's Private Willard Cutter when he confessed to his brother back home in Meadville, Pennsylvania, that he was glad when the troops moved back to the city in late October 1863. "There is more going on in the city than at the Soldiers' Home." For at the very least, the Lincolns' house at the Soldiers' Home was all theirs. There were no offices or secretaries, no office seekers crowding the halls and stairways, no curious citizens to make off with slices of carpet, drapes, or curtains (once an entire lace curtain disappeared for lack of a day watchman, Commissioner French complained), and no young soldiers coming in to sit down and write letters (it was the people's house, wasn't it?). And on a sunny day, summer or winter, the Riggs cottage then, as it is today, was bright, airy, high-ceilinged, and spacious. The fourteen-inch-thick brick exterior walls helped keep the house cool in the "heated season." Architects have discovered that if the entrance door on the north side and the jib windows on the south side facing the city are kept open, fresh, clean air circulates throughout the house. (The National Trust may continue to rely largely on this natural ventilation in the preserved cottage.) Seven marble-manteled fireplaces still in place today would have provided some warmth in the colder months, and the cottage kitchen was "nice and warm—a good coal fire is burning all night," Private Cutter was pleased to find.

Lincoln was noticeably impatient to escape the White House for the Soldiers' Home by four or five o'clock every afternoon, but it seems he was too courteous, perhaps too curious, and even hopeful for a rare bit of good news, to send anyone away who followed him

In July 1864 Lincoln was exposed to enemy fire at Fort Stevens, not far from the Soldiers' Home, where Union troops held back a Confederate raid on the panicked capital.

out there, no matter what the hour. And plenty did. Some callers arrived so late at night that the servant who opened the door saw fit to comment on their intrusion. Ironically, it is thanks to that very intrusiveness that we have some of the most dramatic and poignant images of the president that exist. Some visitors were so desperate, some so angry, others so embarrassed by their thoughtlessness once they got a look at Lincoln, they paid little attention to the house itself. So it is not surprising that all we have are a few references to "a dark parlor," a "dimly lighted hall," and just a few hints of "a scantily furnished sort of parlor," "a plainly furnished room" with a marble table in the center, "a neatly furnished drawing room," "a haircloth-covered sofa," a chandelier.

But of Lincoln himself, the impressions were vivid. As late as August 1864, Lincoln appeared to one group of late-nighttime callers "holding a candle high above his head" to light his way downstairs, "clad in decidedly scant attire," most likely his night-shirt, for we know from other accounts that he was delightfully unaware of how he looked in it when he had something else on his mind. ("He seemed to dislike clothing and in private wore as little of it as he could," wrote the humorist David Ross Locke, creator of a favorite Lincoln character, Petroleum V. Nasby). He sometimes even "perambulate[d] through the [White] House" in his night-shirt, perhaps to share an amusing story with John Hay and John Nicolay, who slept there, or to dance a jig with the naval officer and general who brought good news to him in the middle of the night. When Lincoln realized there were women with these particular nighttime visitors, however, one of them recorded that he "beat a retreat and soon reappeared in more suitable apparel" to listen to their story.

Colonel Silas W. Burt's nighttime visit to the Soldiers' Home in 1863 was so excruciating that he refused for years to talk about it publicly. "It was very evident," Burt finally wrote many years later, "that [Lincoln] had just got up from his bed, or had been very nearly into it when we were announced." Burt was appalled by Lincoln's appearance that evening. "It was the face that in every line told the story of anxiety and weariness. [It] was so pitiful that I could almost have fallen on my knees and begged pardon for my part in the cruel presumption and impudence that had thus invaded his repose." The president tried to keep awake during his visit, which began well after nine o'clock. "But the gaunt figure of the President had gradually slid lower on that slippery sofa, and his long legs were stretched out in front, the loose slippers half fallen from his feet, while the drowsy eyelids had almost closed over his eyes, and his jaded features had taken on the suggestion of relaxation in sleep." It was June 26, 1863. Colonel Burt and his party did not know that the president had just made the agonizing decision to remove General Joseph Hooker, whom he liked very much, from command of the Army of the Potomac after his defeat at Chancellorsville, and to replace him with General George Meade just a few days before the critical battle of Gettysburg. It was Lincoln's third change in the command of the hapless Army of the Potomac in one year.

As if their timing weren't bad enough, after Burt's group had delivered its message of support from a formidable Democratic opponent, the governor of New York, Horatio Seymour, which Lincoln did not appear to regard as particularly significant, one of Burt's companions that night, a major, who Burt noticed too late on the way out, had had too much whiskey, proceeded to slap the exhausted Lincoln on the knee and say, "Mr. President, tell us one of your good stories. . . . If the floor had opened and dropped me out of sight," Burt recalled, "I should have been happy." Lincoln contained himself, but turned his back on the major, and then explained in words Burt wrote down that same night:

> I believe I have the popular reputation of being a story-teller, but I do not deserve the name in its general sense; for it is not the story itself, but its purpose, or its effect, that interests me. I often avoid a long and useless discussion by others or a laborious explanation on my part by a short story that illustrates my point of view. So, too, the sharpness of a refusal or the edge of a rebuke may be blunted by an appropriate story, so as to save wounded feeling and yet serve the purpose. No, I am not simply a story-teller, but storytelling as an emollient saves me much friction and distress.

More tersely and poignantly, Lincoln once put it another way: "I laugh because I must not weep. That's all, that's all."

Fortunately, some would-be visitors lost their way in "the intricacies of this labyrinth," as Lincoln's old friend, attorney Leonard Swett, described the route to the Soldiers' Home, wooded and pitch black at night. Even in the daytime, it took sixteen-year-old drummer boy Harry Kieffer from noon to nightfall to find his way there from the city. When he finally arrived, a certain casualness was evident in the reception he got from the soldiers who had guarded Lincoln briefly before their unit went into battle. "Halt! Who goes there? A friend. Advance, friend, and give the countersign. Hello, Elias! said I, peering through the bushes, is that you? That isn't the countersign, friend. You'd better give the countersign, or you're a dead man." This banter went on for some time until Kieffer, who had been in the hospital with heat exhaustion, was marched off to bed with instructions to "beat reveille at daybreak."

As soon as the Lincolns moved out of the White House for their first season at the Soldiers' Home, they learned that enough of the essential, even the extraneous, visitors could find their way there day or night. Jay Cooke, the "financier of the Civil War" and key adviser to Lincoln's secretary of the treasury, Salmon P. Chase, was one of the first to describe the warlike atmosphere at the Soldiers' Home. One night in the fall of 1862, he arrived to find Lincoln "surrounded by a small army of officers and civilians coming and going." Lincoln asked Cooke to wait until ten that evening, when the others would be gone. Cooke had already been phenomenally successful at raising millions of dollars for the war effort, and would continue to be so throughout the war and afterward. But he was convinced that General George Brinton McClellan, the "young Napoleon," had to go. By then, Cooke had become totally disenchanted, as was Lincoln, by McClellan's whining, procrastinating, even paranoid performance as head of the Army of the Potomac. (Some called him "Oliver Twist II" because he was always asking for more: troops, horses, anything, it seemed, to avoid action.) To Cooke, McClellan's notorious "slows," as Lincoln put it, were impeding his ability to raise the millions more needed to keep the war going. People were losing confidence, he argued, because they saw that McClellan "was entirely unfitted for the position of vast responsibility so unfortunately given him." One week after Cooke's Soldiers' Home meeting, McClellan was indeed gone, despite pressure from his avid supporters to keep him. Cooke was relieved that "the sale of bonds increased and public confidence was restored."

Two years later, in the summer of 1864, arguably his worst both politically and militarily, Lincoln was still trudging down the stairs to receive visitors, in one case at midnight, to see the feisty Baltimore lawyer, Charles Gwynn. He was not even a political supporter, and, even more surprisingly, he was on business Lincoln had already taken care of, sparing the lives of several men sentenced to die the next morning as spies. Lincoln would have had every reason to excuse himself from meeting Gwynn at all, much less in the middle of the night. But he did not, and Gwynn was grateful: "Although you had decided to extend mercy to the prisoners without reference to any interview with me, I nevertheless acknowledge the promptness and genuine kindness, with which you exerted yourself to make that purpose effectual."

That same summer of 1864, an English lawyer, George Borrett, visited Washington, and as evidence of his earlier astute observation, at least as it applied to Lincoln, that "public life in America has no private side at all," found himself late one night at the Soldiers' Home, thanks to the daughter of a Treasury official. Borrett wrote,

> She was emphatically one of those strong-minded young ladies (and what American girl is not?) who can take care of themselves without *chaperones*, and very well too. It was dark when we reached the

President's residence, so that we could see little of what it was like beyond the fact that it stood in a sort of park and was guarded by a regiment of troops encamped picturesquely about the grounds. . . . We were waited upon by a buttonless "buttons," apparently the sole domestic on the premises, to whom we told our wish. He suggested that it was rather late for an interview with Mr. and Mrs. Lincoln and as it was then considerably past eight, I thought the hint very reasonable. Not so the Secretary's daughter. With ready wit and admirable *aplomb*, she bade the officious page to go in and tell his master that there were three gentlemen there, who had come three thousand miles for the express purpose of seeing him and his lady, and did not intend to go away until they had done so.

"I must confess," continued Borrett, "I was very much ashamed of myself for disturbing a quiet couple in this unceremonious way, but it seemed to be all *en règle* . . . we had sat there but a few minutes, when there entered through the folding doors [a] long, lanky, lath-like figure with hair ruffled, and eyes very sleepy and . . . feet enveloped in carpet slippers." Borrett's initial reaction to seeing Lincoln in the city from afar earlier that day had been patronizing and harsh: Lincoln was "very ugly, and awkward and ungainly." But as the conversation in the parlor went on and on, "briskly kept up by the President," and covering everything from the United States Constitution, comparative legal systems, and problems of land acquisition in the two countries, to his early life and English poetry, Borrett, like so many others, became a convert: "Sit and talk with him for an hour, and note the instinctive kindliness of his every thought and word, and say if you have ever known a warmer-hearted noble spirit . . . one of the great historical characters of this century." Mrs. Lincoln, less inclined than her husband to be imposed upon, did not appear that evening.

On at least one spectacular occasion, Lincoln was not so hospitable to those who interrupted his evening peace. "It was late Saturday afternoon," wrote John R. French, a former journalist, and now a Treasury employee. "Mr. Lincoln had left [the White House] wearier even than was his wont, for his retreat at the Soldiers' Home; and in the hope of an undisturbed evening, and a quiet Sabbath, that he might gather some strength for the coming week, expected to be one of stirring events." (The Battle of Second Bull Run was

An amateur French artist, Pierre Morand, made a number of sketches of Lincoln, this one probably at the Soldiers' Home. He never got Lincoln's long legs quite right.

about to begin in late August, 1862, hopefully giving Lincoln the military victory he had been advised to claim before announcing his preliminary Emancipation Proclamation.) French arrived with a Colonel Scott, who wanted Lincoln's permission, over Secretary of War Stanton's refusal, to enter the war zone in Virginia to retrieve the body of his wife, who had drowned after successfully nursing him back to health. "It was in the deepening twilight," French remembered. "The House was still and dark. . . . In the gloaming, entirely alone, sat Mr. Lincoln. In his escape, as he had supposed, from all visitors, and weary with the care and heat of the day, he had thrown off coat and shoes, and with a large palm-leaf fan in his hand, as he reposed in a broad chair, one leg hanging over its arm, he seemed to be in deep thought, perhaps studying the chances of the impending battle." After hearing the colonel's story, "Lincoln rose to his feet, and in a voice of mingled vexation and sadness, asked: 'Am

I to have no rest? Is there no hour or spot when or where I may escape this constant call? Why do you follow me out here with such business as this? . . . Go to the War Department. Your business belongs there. If they cannot help you, then bear your burden, as we all must, until this war is over. Everything must yield to the paramount duty of finishing the war.'" The colonel and his companion were stunned by this "totally unexpected rebuff" and left in despair. But the next morning, Sunday, that longed-for quiet day now ruined for the president, the colonel was astonished to find Lincoln at his hotel room door, apologizing: "I was a brute last night!" Lincoln had already made all the necessary arrangements for the colonel to get to his wife's body. "I have my carriage here and will go with you to the wharf . . . notwithstanding my apparent indifference last night, I honor you from the bottom of my heart for your manly love for your wife and devotion to her memory."

Lincoln's extraordinary memory saved another larger entourage from a similar rebuff. The group had arrived late one night that same summer, awakening Lincoln to plead for the lives of three alleged Confederate spies who were to hang the next morning. It did not take Lincoln long to recollect that a couple in the group, a Mr. and Mrs. Gittings, had helped save Mary Lincoln and their three sons from a potentially violent attack by an angry mob as they passed through Baltimore on their way to his inauguration three years before. Lincoln said, "Madam, I owe you a debt. . . . You took my family into your home in the midst of a hostile mob. . . . You gave my family succor and helped them on their way. That debt has never been paid, and I am glad of the opportunity to do so now, for I shall save the lives of these men." When Mrs. Gittings showed up once again, however, Lincoln ignored her plea for the life of another condemned Confederate officer. He felt that he already had liquidated his debt.

After-hours or early-morning interruptions by members of his cabinet, political supporters, and even influential opponents were at least more understandable. "I go there, unattended, at all hours, by daylight and moonlight, by starlight and without any light," said Secretary of State William Seward, rather poetically, if somewhat vainly. Both he and first-term vice president Hannibal Hamlin met with Lincoln at the Soldiers' Home until midnight more than once. For one summer, at least, Secretary of War Edwin Stanton occupied another house on the Soldiers' Home grounds, which surely meant many meetings between the two men there. Senator Orville Hickman Browning was a long-time friend and confidant of the new president until the two men's views on the advisability of an Emancipation Proclamation divided them. He visited the Soldiers' Home four times, usually at night, in the summer of 1862. (He appeared at the White House almost every day.) Browning seemed inclined to bring others along with him to the Soldiers' Home. One politician he brought had been so obviously hoping for advancement that Lincoln hurried Browning out to the steps of the house to talk about something else, ending their conversation by reciting a few verses from a popular poem, "Fanny," which satirized a nouveau riche father and daughter whose social pretensions caused their ultimate ruin. Browning could not understand why Lincoln found the "ludicrous conclusion" so amusing. Surrounded as he was by so many climbers and poseurs, it is not so surprising that Lincoln laughed.

Perhaps the most important and interesting visitor Browning brought with him—for breakfast on June 18, 1862—was "the great New York Merchant," philanthropist, and contractor for supplies to the Union Army and Navy, Alexander T. Stewart, an Irish immigrant, a brilliant businessman, and a staunch Republican with strong views on how the army was being led. He had no confidence in McClellan by that time, either. Stewart's enormous "marble emporium" on Broadway, carrying the latest fashions and setting new and clever standards for service, provided him by that time with an average annual income of two million dollars. Mary Todd Lincoln had bought several thousand dollars' worth of rugs and curtains there in one day the year before for her White House renovation, and Stewart had given her a dinner party. He also presented her with an expensive shawl, and as has always been the case with first ladies, it was difficult for Mary to distinguish between a gift, a bribe, and an expected purchase. She, of course, preferred to consider it a gift, but Stewart sent her a bill four months later. Henry James was certainly correct when he described Stewart's store as "fatal to feminine nerves." Mary couldn't stay away, and ended up heavily in debt to

Stewart after Lincoln's assassination. He threatened to sue, but there is no evidence that he ever did.

Washington was not considered a prestigious post for foreign diplomats in those days, but from Lincoln's perspective, keeping Britain and France from recognizing the Confederacy was vital. Relations with Britain were particularly volatile throughout the war, beginning as early as December 1861. Fortunately for Lincoln, her majesty's representative in Washington was the seasoned, wily, albeit humorless Lord Lyons, Richard Bickerton Pemmell Lyons. He found the summer heat of the capital "abominable . . . overwhelming" and was undoubtedly grateful for the opportunity to feel the cool breezes at the Soldiers' Home.

Secretary of State William Seward had arranged for Lyons to visit Lincoln there at eight-thirty one Sunday evening in June 1863. It perhaps still rankled the president that, in order to avoid fighting a second war in December 1861, he had had to surrender two Confederate envoys whom an overly zealous United States Navy captain, Charles Wilkes, had taken from a British mail steamer, the *Trent*. Lyons had worked brilliantly to defuse that dangerous crisis. Confederate actions launched against the Union from the British possession, Canada, were a constant and dangerous irritant, and it didn't help at all that British shipyards were building blockade runners and commerce raiders for the Confederate Navy, with devastating consequences for Union shipping. But Lincoln was in a good mood that Sunday, John Hay noted. In the morning, he'd even written an atrocious bit of doggerel about Lee's retreat from Pennsylvania. And by then, Lincoln and Lord Lyons had arrived at a relationship Lyons described as "affectionate." Commissioner French noted that Lord Lyons "was received with peculiar distinction & seemed to be particularly pleased to be present."

Lyons kept himself extremely well informed through a powerful intelligence network that extended from Canada to Mexico to Cuba, softening up members of Congress with the best champagne (he'd come with a hundred bottles), which of course would not have worked with teetotaling Lincoln. But Lincoln must have recognized and appreciated that Lyons, too, was working himself to exhaustion to keep the two countries from colliding. "I have no time to think whether I am amused or not," Lyons wrote the British foreign minister, Lord Russell. In just one year, his tiny legation had sent over eight thousand dispatches and letters, and had received six and a half thousand, most if not all of which Lyons had read and signed.

Lincoln was not above teasing diplomats, and Lyons, a bachelor, came in for his share. When he announced formally to Lincoln that Queen Victoria's daughter was now married, Lincoln responded, "Go thou and do likewise." This was not to be. Despite the urgings of Queen Victoria herself, Lyons had long ago taken his position. "I am afraid marriage is better never than late. The American women are undoubtedly very pretty, but my heart is too old and too callous to be wounded by their charms."

Another victim of Lincoln's teasing, said to be an unnamed foreign minister, had been assured by Lincoln that the fruit of the persimmon tree they were passing by (which Lincoln explained was "our golden yellow wrong-side-out, a very delicious plum imported from Patagonia") was "far superior to pears. In order to get the exquisite ripeness you must eat very rapidly." When the diplomat bit into the bitter fruit and realized he'd been tricked, Lincoln roared with delight, undiplomatically as that might have appeared to some.

By mid-August 1864, it was obvious that Lincoln was half dead with war weariness and worry. "Careworn," the adjective used most often to describe his appearance, was no longer adequate. There was good reason: Lincoln believed his defeat for reelection that November was a distinct possibility, and if he did lose, the victors would then agree to "the dismemberment of the Union." Three years of death and destruction would have been in vain. Richmond had not yet fallen, and the hundred thousand casualties in the Army of the Potomac over the past three years had accomplished next to nothing. Criticism of his handling of the war was more intense than ever. Even his old friend Browning wrote, "I fear he is a failure." After his victory in November, Lincoln told his dear old friend, Joshua Speed, "I am a little alarmed about myself; just feel my hand." It was "cold and clammy," Speed said, and Lincoln then put his stockinged feet so close to the fire they steamed. Would it have been less tragic for the nation had Lincoln not lived through his second term? Mary certainly thought that was a possibility.

Mary Lincoln and many others thought Lincoln might not live through his second term because he was so worn out. This photograph of Lincoln from March 6, 1865, shows why they worried. It may be the last image of Lincoln taken while he was alive.

"Poor Mr. Lincoln is looking so broken-hearted, so completely worn out, I fear he will not get through the next four years."

So the Soldiers' Home did not turn out to be quite the tranquil haven he and Mary had hoped for. Others who visited could see that: "Says Gov [Alexander] Randall," wrote Judge Joseph Mills in his diary after the two Wisconsin politicians visited the Soldiers' Home in mid-August 1864, "why cant you Mr. P seek some place of retirement for a few weeks. you would be reinvigorated. Aye said the President, 3 weeks would do me no good—my thoughts my solicitude for this great country follow me where ever I go." And Willie was never far from his thoughts, either. Nor from Mary's, who wrote to her friend Mrs. Charles Eames, a prominent Washington social leader, from the Soldiers' Home in July 1862, "In the loss of our idolized boy, we naturally have suffered such intense grief that a removal from the scene of our misery was found very necessary. Yet, in this sweet spot, that his bright nature, would have so well loved, *he is not with us,* and the anguish of the thought, oftentimes, for days overcomes me." Laura Redden, a deaf journalist who wrote under the name Howard Glyndon, saw Mary at the Soldiers' Home months after Willie's death, and found that "her affliction seemed as fresh as ever."

But Mary at least could leave town altogether, and hope that her own grief over Willie's death and her worries about the war and her husband's survival would stay behind. Every summer she and the boys escaped, leaving Lincoln alone at the Soldiers' Home for weeks, sometimes months, at a time. This was quite the reverse of their experience in Springfield, where Lincoln's law practice took him away for as much as a third of the year. Resentful though she had been back then, unconscious retaliation for those absences was surely not Mary's motivation. She was terrified that the dreaded "miasma" permeating Washington in the summertime, and feared by everyone, would kill the two boys she had left. Robert was out of danger at college in Boston or visiting friends for much of the time, but Tad, their "troublesome little sunshine," was frail, often ill, and affected by the death and tension all around him.

Still, there was much all the Lincolns loved about the Soldiers' Home—"that sweet spot"—that would keep them coming back to it.

In her 1862 letter to Mrs. Eames, Mary added that "We are truly delighted with this retreat, the drives and walks around here are delightful." Visits from Elizabeth Blair Lee, her gossipy "in the know" friend, must have been a pleasure. From Chicago in August 1865, Mary would write her, "How dearly I loved the Soldiers Home & I little supposed, one year since, that I should be so *far removed* from it, broken hearted, and praying for death, to remove me, from a life so full of agony." Mary kept a photograph of the cottage in the Lincoln family album, the strongest evidence for the Lincolns' occupancy.

Mary had asked Commissioner French for three thousand dollars in May 1864 to fix it up. This is somewhat puzzling, because Lincoln's chances of reelection that fall were so uncertain. It may have been Mary's way of keeping her mind off her own troubles, which included serious debt her husband knew nothing about, but which would have been revealed had he been defeated. Her beautification attack on the Riggs cottage was as ambitious as her renovation of the shabby White House had been. It's more than likely that the cottage had served a utilitarian function for the Soldiers' Home institution itself in the wintertime, and at the very least, needed a thorough cleaning before Mary would move her family in. Commissioner French's invoices to John Alexander, a local home furnishings merchant, listed "washing floors, windows and paint—$81.01, 4 large buckets $8.00, 3 large scrub brushes $3.60, 3 mops $6.50, cleaning chair covers $27.00." Mirrors and paintings were rehung, chair covers repaired and cleaned. Then Mary went full tilt at the decoration. If their Springfield home was any indication, the wallpaper she ordered from Alexander was the latest fashion, colorful, with lots of glitter. Years later, during her self-imposed exile in Europe, she would write to her daughter-in-law, Mary Harlan Lincoln, "papering is a great improvement—makes a house look homelike—use it all the different patterns . . . you never see a place in E[urope] which is not papered." Mary ordered enough rolls to paper eight of the cottage's many rooms! Yards and yards of expensive cocoa matting were also ordered, to be laid over the pine floors. Lincoln may have worn those loose carpet slippers that visitors commented on to keep from damaging the matting, or scratching his feet, which in any event, always gave him great discomfort. (He was overjoyed to find a foot doctor who was so effective that Lincoln wanted to send him into the field to minister to foot-weary troops.) The Alexander invoices mention carpeting for the halls and staircases. All the handsome marble mantelpieces in the cottage remained. So did the shellacked pine paneling in the library.

Some hints do exist of the private, more social, even relaxed times at the Soldiers' Home, perhaps evenings of whist, chess, singing, or checkers, assisted by a small staff (just a cook, a manservant, and a housekeeper). On September 30, 1862, Mary invited her controversial but "kind-hearted" friend, General Daniel Sickles, to come out to the Soldiers' Home for a really good chat, because "we always have so many evening callers, that our conversations, necessarily are general." Mary was restrained, she told Sickles, "because Mr. L. has so much to excite his mind, with fears for the Army, that I am quite considerate in expressing my doubts and fears to him concerning passing events." (There is considerable evidence quite to the contrary in the Lincolns' relationship; Lincoln knew very well Mary's opinion of General Grant—"a butcher," that Secretary of State Seward was not to be trusted, and that the cabinet was full of her husband's enemies.)

Mary encouraged other friends to visit the Lincolns at the Soldiers' Home. To Brigadier General George Ramsay, Chief of Ordnance, in July 1864 Mary wrote, "It is such a pleasure, *especially*, at such a charming place as *this*, to receive one's friends. I trust that Mrs. Ramsey [sic] Miss R. & yourself will favor me by frequently driving out these delightful evenings." Secretary of War Edwin Stanton didn't like Ramsay, and Mary didn't like Stanton, so there was more to this invitation than meets the eye. Affable, courteous, courageous Ramsay, whom the president also admired and trusted, had risked his career in the second year of the war by disobeying Stanton's order, just before the battle of Antietam, to ship all the weapons stored in his arsenal out of Washington to New York. Thanks to Ramsay's not following the order, the arms were available for McClellan at that crucial battle, and Lincoln was able at last to issue the preliminary Emancipation Proclamation on the strength of it. But Stanton, in retaliation, then placed Ramsay in an untenable position as Chief of Ordnance, and soon after Mary's invitation he got rid of him altogether.

Several visitors actually did think it appropriate to use the word "entertainment" at the Soldiers' Home, and the Lincolns were charming, experienced hosts. Lincoln liked to serve dinner guests himself. With the "elasticity of spirits" Judge Mills noted in his diary, Lincoln was able to turn quickly from their intense discussion that night of the disastrous consequences for the country if he were to be defeated for reelection, to pleasure. He "entertained us with reminiscences of the past . . . it is such social tete a tetes among his friends that enables Mr. Lincoln to endure mental toils & application that would crush any other man. The President now in full flow of spirits, scattered his repartee in all directions." Stalwart family nurse Rebecca Pomroy saw the same quality: "The strong will of the man combined with his wonderful facility in extracting comfort out of the pleasant trivialities of everyday life."

Together with the theater—Shakespeare's plays of civil war and succession quite understandably Lincoln's preference by far—storytelling, even storytelling contests, were his favorite form of entertainment. Hugh McCulloch, who would become Lincoln's third secretary of the treasury in 1865, visited the Soldiers' Home one autumn evening in 1864. The postmaster general and a few of Lincoln's personal friends were there. "For two hours there was a constant run of story-telling—Lincoln leading and [the postmaster] following—a contest between them as to which should tell the best story and provoke the heartiest laughter. The stories were not such as would be listened to with pleasure by very refined ears, but they were exceedingly funny. The verdict of the listeners was that, while the stories were equally good, Mr. Lincoln had displayed the most humor and skill."

Journalist Noah Brooks described several of those casual evenings: "A little party from the city was being entertained at Mr. Lincoln's summer White House . . . the President, standing with his back to the fire and his legs spread apart, recited from memory" a story of the popular Civil War humorist Orpheus C. Kerr [Robert Henry Newell] that satirized Secretary of the Navy Gideon Welles, who, Kerr claimed, was very busy examining a model of Noah's Ark with a view of introducing it into the United States Navy. Then Lincoln asked his guests not to tell Welles about the story because it might hurt his feelings, explaining later to a somewhat offended

Brooks that one of the guests that evening was "a leaky vessel" and this was Lincoln's subtle way of warning the man against repeating what he might hear at the Soldiers' Home. On another evening at the Soldiers' Home, Brooks wrote, Lincoln stood again before the fireplace and recited from memory one of his favorite "Petroleum V. Nasby" [David Ross Locke] letters, another character whose influence on public opinion of the day was significant. Lincoln lulled an overworked John Hay to sleep one evening there, reading "the end of *Henry VI*, and the beginning of *Richard III*, until my heavy eyelids caught his considerate notice & he sent me to bed."

Most listeners were sensitive enough to appreciate that storytelling in particular was Lincoln's safety valve, as he had explained to Colonel Silas Burt, a nineteenth-century version of antidepressant medication, if you will. Pompous, hostile General McClellan, of course, thought Lincoln's stories were "ever unworthy of one holding his high position, at least on public occasions." Curiously enough, Frederick Douglass never saw that side of Lincoln. "I could as well dance at a funeral as to jest in the presence of such a man."

It would not be correct to assume that when men came out to the Soldiers' Home with their wives, conversations were any less freighted. Mary Todd Lincoln was not the only Civil War wife with political savvy who was intensely watchful of her husband's reputation. Mrs. Margaret Heintzelman went to see Lincoln at the Soldiers' Home on August 8, 1862, at her husband's request. At the time, General Samuel Heintzelman was commanding McClellan's Third Corps during the ill-fated Peninsula Campaign. Margaret and her husband had been in constant communication in the weeks before her appointment with Lincoln, sometimes with daily letters discussing his frustrations and concerns.

Heintzelman was distraught over the prospect of withdrawal of Union troops from the Peninsula. "If it is done the country is ruined," he wrote in his journal. "All we want is reinforcements that are within reach and we will advance.... It is sad to see the imbecility in Washington.... Reinforce us and we will take Richmond." But he had not been able to get leave to argue his own case, and so Mrs. Heintzelman went instead, and the day after her visit, she sent Lincoln a long abstract outlining her husband's views, which she had discussed with Lincoln in surely more politic but still strong terms the previous evening. But the Army of the Potomac was withdrawn, and Heintzelman was furious. As the troops retreated, he ordered the regimental musicians to "Play! Play! It is all you're good for. Play, damn it! Play some marching tune. Play Yankee Doodle, or any doodle you can think of, only play something!" The general's only visit to the Soldiers' Home the following summer was purely for pleasure, not to see Lincoln. Even during the war, the beautiful grounds were a favorite destination for sweltering city dwellers. But even that excursion backfired. "Warm! Warm! Clear 91 degrees. It was too dusty to be pleasant." Heintzelman gets little attention in broad Civil War histories, but some of his colleagues felt his achievements throughout the war, including his defense of the capital, had been greatly underestimated. They wrote to Lincoln that he was "rust[ing] out" unfairly in one of his later backwater assignments. Mary Lincoln may have wanted to make some amends for all that by telling the general at the White House in April 1863 that his son Charles would indeed be going to West Point. In response to one of Lincoln's classic equivocations about the appointment to Heintzelman earlier that year, the general wrote in his journal, "Was ever such an endorsement made?"

Several officers in command at the Soldiers' Home installation became friendly with the Lincolns over their three seasons, and they must have provided company for Lincoln when Mary and the boys were away. Deputy Governor Thomas L. Alexander had run the Home since 1858, and he was apparently a gem: a kind, modest man who put the soldiers' welfare before his own. Shortly after Alexander resigned in 1864, having lost out on a promotion to the governorship of the institution, Lincoln wrote General-in-Chief Henry Halleck the next best thing to a recommendation: "The relations between Colonel Alexander and myself at the Soldiers' Home have been very agreeable, and I feel a great kindness for him and his family." It is difficult today, looking at the Home's large, well-stocked library, for example, to appreciate how hard Alexander had to fight to get any amenities at all for the veterans, including basic reading material. He knew how dissatisfied they had been with their treatment. The year he arrived, for example, about a quarter of the men had complained to a United States senator that the funds they provided to the home were being misused, and that they felt imprisoned there. In 1862, there was even more to grouse about. The Board of Commissioners of the Home voted to discontinue the veterans' tobacco allowance, and made other economy moves so unpopular they had to be rescinded the next month. Alexander tried to put in a bowling alley, a smoking room (no smoking was allowed in the men's quarters), a laundry room, and a bathhouse. Only the latter two survived the board's consideration. Alexander also wanted a decent library for the men, and was able to add historical works and novels to the Bibles and few newspapers already authorized. If there was any truth to the accusations that Alexander was actually a rebel sympathizer and "his wife an avid secessionist," Lincoln didn't seem to notice, although the first deputy governor of the Home and the first secretary-treasurer had indeed resigned to serve in the Confederate army. Elizabeth Blair Lee, Mary's good friend, wrote her husband that she'd had to assure Mary that [the Alexanders] "were the best & most *loyal hearted* people in the world," and that Sallie Alexander had insisted, "If we were secesh I would be vastly more afraid of her, but as I am not I anticipate her residence there with great pleasure."

Mary was more than disappointed when the Alexanders left, but not so with the Home's surgeon, Dr. Benjamin King, who was not the kind of man to hide whatever light he had under a barrel. King, who had been at the Soldiers' Home in one capacity or another since its founding in 1851, was cantankerous, demanding, self-satisfied, and as opinionated as he was quarrelsome. He'd resigned in a huff more than once, declaring in his 1859 effort that "four-fifths of the inmates [or "members" as they were called by the time the Lincolns lived there] are good and excellent men while others are so bad as to put to shame a penitentiary convict." But Lincoln took his chances with them. He sometimes ate with the veterans, and one of them said that Lincoln was very kind and familiar with them all. At any one time, between ninety-nine and a hundred and forty-two members resided at the Soldiers' Home over the five Civil War years.

*   *   *

Journalist Brooks observed that "no family that ever lived in the Executive Mansion was so irregular in its method of living as were the Lincolns." As Tad's pet goat was able to find its way unhindered up the stairs to rest on the boy's bed at the Soldiers' Home cottage, life there was probably even more so. Mary and Tad were away at the time "Nanny" went exploring in the house, having eaten so many of the flowers in the garden she was ultimately exiled to the White House, but the tone of Lincoln's letter describing the animal's behavior is so playful, it's clear he expected Mary to be just as amused as he was. (She never received the letter. Somehow it came into the hands of a soldier, who turned it over to a postmaster in upstate New York, who returned it to Lincoln the following spring.)

Evidently a sizable menagerie (ponies, goats, cats, and once, perhaps, Jack the turkey) made the annual move from the White House to the Soldiers' Home. Tad refused to leave the city until all were accounted for. Lincoln himself once went looking for Tad's cat before the long wagon caravan of family, furniture, and pets could set off. Lincoln didn't mind at all when the kittens Secretary Seward's family had given his boys climbed all over him even as he worked. After all, as far back as 1848, while Lincoln was in Congress, Mary Todd Lincoln wrote to her "dear boy" from her father's house in Lexington, Kentucky, "Boby [sic: Robert Todd Lincoln] came across in a yard, a kitten, *your hobby*." When Mary's stepmother found he'd brought it into the house, she ordered that it be thrown out, much to the boy's and Mary's distress. One account of Lincoln's inaugural journey to Washington describes his stopping the train when he saw a terrapin beside the tracks. He had it brought into the train for Tad to play with. The two of them would play for hours with the pet goats on the White House lawn, which Lincoln insisted to Mary's dressmaker, Elizabeth Keckley, would come when he called. Their antics provided him with some diversion. "'See, Madam Elizabeth— my pets recognize me . . . there they go again; what jolly fun! And he laughed outright as the goats bounded swiftly to the other side of the yard.'" Lincoln's thought then turned, according to Madam Keckley, to the real bounders, the bounty hunters and their agents, the men who "plunder the national treasure in the name of patriotism."

As for meals, when Mrs. Lincoln was away, "I generally browse around," Lincoln told some visitors. His general disinterest in what he ate suggests a certain casualness about mealtimes, and perhaps explains Tad's frequent appearances at Company K's mess at dinnertime.

The Lincolns were extraordinarily permissive parents by Victorian standards. Even their eldest son, the somewhat stuffy, publicity-shy Robert ("all Todd"), could get annoyed at Tad's constant and clever pranks. But Lincoln insisted, "It is my pleasure that my children are free—happy and unrestrained by parental tyranny. Love is the chain whereby to lock a child to its parents." Neither he nor Mary had had a particularly happy childhood. (Mary's was "desolate," she said.) Lincoln's was no better.

Only seven years old when the Lincolns arrived in Washington, Tad was the focus of attention for the better part of the Lincolns' life in the capital. Robert was studying at Harvard most of the time. For those who did not think Tad was a spoiled brat, he provided what we might call today comic relief—finding the mechanism that would set all the executive mansion's bells ringing, driving his cart and goat through the public rooms during receptions, bringing street urchins in for dinner, waving the Confederate flag from the White House window. He could swear like a trooper, and even managed to appear several times as an extra on stage at the National Theater, much to his father's amusement. Tad may not have been able to read or write well, but Noah Brooks saw that he "comprehended many practical realities that are far beyond the grasp of most boys . . . he knew much about the costs of things, the details of trade, the principles of mechanics, and the habits of animals, all of which showed the activity of his mind and the odd turn of his thoughts." Tad was a fearless rider, a shrewd judge of character, imaginative, compassionate, and utterly devoted to both his father and mother. He and Lincoln were inseparable after Willie's death, appearing together even in some situations others thought inappropriate. Lincoln believed Tad "will be what the women all dote on—a good provider."

The boy did later provide his mother with faithful companionship in Chicago and then Europe, staying with her loyally during her years of wandering, and turning with dogged effort into a handsome,

Tad Lincoln was a clever, mischievous boy. In a typical prank, he marked up his photo in the family album. He's wearing a miniature Zouave uniform.

quite literate young man. But eventually Tad became so homesick and "wild to come home" to see Robert, his wife, and their new baby girl, that mother and son set sail for the United States from Liverpool in May 1871. Tad caught a cold during the passage, which turned into "pleurisy, probably tubercular in origin," and died on July 15, 1871. He was just eighteen.

After his death Mary's reliance on spiritualism—the great quasi-religious phenomenon of its day—was still alive. Despite her increasingly pitiful physical condition, she tried to establish contact with Tad, as she'd done with Willie—sometimes without the help of a medium—after his death in 1862. During the war, she'd joined millions of other Americans fascinated and given solace by the claims of spiritualists to communicate with the dead. Elizabeth Keckley, Mary's closest confidant for years, reached her only son, who'd been killed in an early battle. Secretary of the Navy Gideon Welles and his wife, Mary Jane, hoped to communicate with their six dead children, Harriet Beecher Stowe with her son who had drowned, and Horace Greeley with his. Mary's faith in spiritualism had been bolstered when she learned that Queen Victoria and Empress Eugenie were believers. So was Commodore Vanderbilt, although he apparently felt this was a way he might get new business ideas, and perhaps exorcise the spirits of those killed while riding in his various conveyances. Even Frederick Douglass was said to be interested in the phenomenon.

A few years before the war began, there were more spiritualists in Boston than there were abolitionists, and an estimated forty thousand spiritualists were operating in that city alone during the war. Lincoln, of course, was among the skeptics, but he attended a few séances with Mary, who was convinced that a well-known medium in Georgetown had indeed "made wonderful revelations to her about her little son Willy," the adored child who had been so promising, so like Lincoln himself. On a drive out to the Soldiers' Home on New Year's Day 1863, Mary revealed to Orville Hickman Browning that the Georgetown medium, Mrs. Laurie, had revealed to her that Lincoln's cabinet was full of his enemies "working for themselves." That was not altogether far-fetched, for Lincoln's cabinet was indeed riven with rivalries, jealousies, and fundamental political differences.

In the summer of 1862, after Willie died, Mary invited the medium "Lord Colchester" out to the Soldiers' Home, where, in the darkened library, the journalist Noah Brooks discovered, "he pretended to produce messages from the dead boy by means of scratches on the wainscoting and taps on the walls and furniture." Even Mary became suspicious when she came to realize that Colchester was actually threatening her with unpleasant rather than comforting revelations if she did not obtain a pass for him to travel to New York. Brooks was delighted to expose the man's scam later, with Mary's approval. He turned the tables and threatened Colchester instead with a stay in the Old Capitol Prison, and the "Lord" was not heard from again.

Mary was far from being just one of a few neurotic or gullible misfits taken in by the spiritualist movement. From two million adherents in 1850, their numbers grew to seven million by 1863, and to an estimated ten million after the war. The losses of thousands upon thousands of sons, fathers, and husbands in the war, and the happy chance perhaps to hear from them in "Summerland" rather than wait for a reunion in heaven some time in the far future, was achingly tempting for the women left behind to cope with loss in the stifling ways demanded by society in those days.

This new movement was dominated by women practitioners, who seized upon these "other powers" to compensate for their lack of economic or political power. They gave their female adherents some relief from their heavy responsibilities as the primary care-givers to the sick and the dying, and as the most visible and custom-constrained mourners for the dead. Always unorthodox, Mary refused to accept the conventional clergy's monopoly on acceptable channels to the eternal. As her biographer Jean Baker says, she "easily adopted a therapy that flattered her intuition and histrionic talent, and de-pended on magic." There was also a certain sensuality to the séances that may have appealed to her. The feasibility of this "spiritual tele-graph" was strengthened by the success of the real telegraph, and the phenomenon gave some comfort in an age dominated not only by a terrible war but also by other social and technological upheavals. In Mary Lincoln's case, it offered an explanation for some of her painful physical symptoms, such as "all the needles running through my body," which, according to the spiritualists, might very well have been calls from beyond.

Lincoln was said by some to be a practicing spiritualist himself, but any interest he showed in the popular phenomenon was prima-rily intellectual. He could only be called a spiritualist, concluded historian Richard Current, if by that is meant "any person who has a sensitivity to the unseen and incorporeal, who looks for influences from other than rational sources, who is guided by the vision and the dream." He reportedly asked the secretary of the Smithsonian Insti-tution, his friend Dr. Joseph Henry, to figure out how Lord Colches-ter might have produced his particular sound effects. Henry con-cluded that by expanding or contracting his arm muscles with a device strapped to his arms, Colchester could have caused rappings at a distance, even while holding hands with participants on his left and right.

By accompanying Mary to some séances, even going along with her holding some in the White House, perhaps opening himself up to ridicule, Lincoln was essentially demonstrating his loyalty to and concern for his wife. Mary's faithful friend, the well-born, well-connected Washington socialite, Elizabeth Blair Lee, testified to that when she said, "Mary has her husband's deepest love. This is a matter upon which one woman cannot deceive another."

First-hand observations at the Soldiers' Home of the couple's relationship to each other only confirm the opinion of those who agree with her, that the Lincoln marriage was a solid one.

CHAPTER 5

The Lincoln Marriage

LINCOLN'S FRIENDS back in the Springfield days could always tell when Mary Todd Lincoln was away from home. "We were pretty sure to be apprised of her absence [by] some slight disorder in Lincoln's apparel, and his irregularity at meal time," remembered Henry B. Rankin, once a devoted young student in Lincoln's Springfield law office. Until recently, Rankin's memories were thought to be the last remaining significant personal reminiscence of Lincoln for the many still intrigued by the Lincolns' relationship. That is, until fresh first-hand accounts of Lincoln's life at the Soldiers' Home began to surface during the National Trust for Historic Preservation's historical research on the site.

Rankin was being charitable about Lincoln's startling appearance, which was pretty much always cause for comment, sometimes astonishment, even when, as president, he could have commanded the best of everything in dress and nourishment. Sergeant Smith Stimmel, an observant young rider from Ohio in the president's last cavalry escort to and from the Soldiers' Home, saw Lincoln up close for over a year. "When [Lincoln] was well groomed, and had on his best clothes," Stimmel observed, "he presented quite a fine appearance." (The coat Lincoln wore to Ford's Theater on April 14, 1865, proved that. The quilted silk lining was stitched in elegant patterns.) "But," Stimmel went on, "he was not very careful about the style and fit of his everyday clothes, and evidently his everyday suit was not made to order, for his arms always seemed too long for his

81

Ohio cavalryman Sergeant Smith Stimmel left valuable personal reminiscences of Lincoln and his relationship with Mary Todd Lincoln.

coat sleeves, and his legs too long for his trousers. His summer coat was usually a cheap, black alpaca, which hung quite loosely upon him. He wore an old-fashioned silk hat, which showed that it had seen considerable service. It had several dents in it, and the fur or nap was usually rubbed the wrong way." Stimmel eventually figured out why that was. If and when Lincoln noticed the salutes of army officers, the usually distracted man "threw up his long arm and knocked off his tall hat, and then tumbled it back on his head, and brought his big hand down on the crown to press it firmly in place. ... But I don't want you to get the idea that President Lincoln always saluted that way," cautioned Stimmel. "That was a hurry-up salute. It was his business to get that hat off quickly, and the quickest way he could get it off was to knock it off."

Dealing with Lincoln's lack of interest in such mundane matters as food and clothing was pretty much a losing battle for Mary Todd Lincoln, even when she was at home. He just wasn't interested in either. Perhaps the most outlandish outfit that Lincoln somehow got away with in Springfield consisted of a short frock coat and jeans that ended sixteen inches above his ankles. His huge, aching feet (size fourteen) were always a problem. So Lincoln usually received visitors at the Soldiers' Home in his carpet slippers, and once, as he slipped them off, a constantly jiggling big toe protruded from a huge hole in one dark stocking. When Lincoln visited Fort Stevens, part of the capital's system of fortifications closest to the Soldiers' Home, during General Jubal Early's raid on Washington in July 1864, a young officer noticed that Lincoln's coat sleeve had a hole in it. Bullets were flying, but if one had hit the president's coat, attention would surely have been paid.

After twenty years of marriage, and by then living at the nation's most distinguished address, Mary still had not given up trying to make her husband "look like somebody." Her devoted assistant, William Stoddard, gave her credit for some success in "her efforts at securing greater care in matters of [his] dress, but the care was almost entirely her own, he merely submitting to occasional new clothes with more docility, including gloves on state occasions." He would sometimes even bend down to her so that she could smooth his coarse black hair. For Mary's devotion to her husband was total, constant to the end of her own life. He was "always . . . lover—husband—father & *all all to me*—Truly my all," she wrote in one of her many gallant letters after the assassination.

But what was Mary Todd to Lincoln? Was she the "hellcat" Lincoln's cocksure young secretary John Hay called her? Was she the insane albatross around Lincoln's neck that many even today believe she was? And how good or bad was their marriage? Was it the "domestic hell . . . the ice cave with no soul, fire, cheer, or fun in it," as Lincoln's law partner, William Herndon, presented it? Would a man as honest as Lincoln have married a woman he did not love? Mary Todd Lincoln's close friend and dressmaker, the former slave Elizabeth Keckley, thought not. "I believe that he loved the mother of his children most tenderly . . . we are indifferent to those we do not love, and certainly the President was not indifferent to his wife. She often wounded him in unguarded moments, but calm reflection never failed to bring regret."

Vehemently opposing views still persist, admittedly with evidence for both. "Lincoln himself," one friend observed, "would not make any woman happy ... he was too much allied to his intellect to get down to the plane of domestic relations." But eyewitnesses at the Soldiers' Home corroborate the position of those who assess the marriage as a devoted if difficult one, and Mary as an effective partner for most of their marriage, without whose push and polish Lincoln might never have made it to the White House, and without whose care Lincoln might not have survived as long as he did after he got there. "I shall never live to see peace," he told Harriet Beecher Stowe. "This job is killing me." Mary knew that. Getting him out to the Soldiers' Home for at least some peace and privacy was critical to keeping him alive.

Some first-hand accounts of the Lincolns' relationship from observers at the Soldiers' Home are quite precise, others are more casual, offhand, but all are touching and revealing. The comments of Sergeant Charles Derickson of the 150th Pennsylvania Regiment's Company K, the "Bucktails" who guarded the president at the Soldiers' Home from the fall of 1862 to the day he died, are the most poignant. Ida Tarbell interviewed Derickson later for her pioneering biography of Lincoln. He painted a striking picture of Mary Lincoln standing at the window of her bedroom at the Soldiers' Home in her nightgown and nightcap early in the morning, anxiously watching her husband leave for the city, always afraid he might not come back. She had received directly enough gory threats against her husband's life to be justifiably terrified. David Bates of the War Department Telegraph Office told of her once finding in her mail a picture of Lincoln with a noose drawn tightly around his neck, red spots inked to cover the front of his shirt. She finally asked her admirer Stoddard to winnow out the worst of these.

Tarbell's notes of Derickson's most intimate observation of the Lincolns' physical relationship are wonderfully suggestive even in their brevity. "Mr. Lincoln," she scribbled, as Derickson talked, "has no fear one night an orderly came up to Soldier's House with a note for Mr. L. demanding immediate reply. Mr. D was on guard— he found front door open walked upstairs. Mr. L's bedroom door ajar—knocks—who's there? Come in Sergeant. There are matches on the mantle light the gas—he & Mrs. L in bed—gets up—reads— answer goodnight [sic]." It would have been too much to ask of young

Derickson to keep this sight to himself. It might even have provided the basis for rumors at one point during the war that Mary Todd was pregnant.

Physical attraction does seem to have been an important ingredient in the Lincoln marriage, despite the fact that Lincoln, in Mary Todd's own words, was "not pretty." But she insisted that "people are perhaps not aware that his heart is as large as his arms are long ... I would rather marry a good man—a man of mind—with a hope and bright prospects ahead for position and power than to marry all the houses—gold—in the world." As for Lincoln, he told a White House guest, "My wife is as handsome as when she was a girl, and I, a poor nobody then, fell in love with her, and what is more I have never fallen out." "He was as true as steel to his wife during his whole married life," William Herndon admitted, even though he and Mary detested each other. Herndon's cruel public insistence after Lincoln's death that Ann Rutledge was the only woman Lincoln ever loved was a factor in Mary's eventual flight to Europe to remove herself from the torment of that false revelation.

Elizabeth Lee, although one of Mary's close friends, nevertheless wrote somewhat cattily to her husband, Phil, on March 1, 1862, that Mary's sister, Elizabeth Edwards, was "ten times better looking than Mary." But when Lincoln first met Mary in Springfield, she was a spirited belle who, one admirer said, could "make a bishop forget his prayers," and another, that "she was the very creature of excitement." Before multiple tragedies struck the Lincoln family in Washington, Mary made a favorable impression even on those who came to scoff. Instead of a frontier rube, they found an unusually well-educated, politically informed, charming, and fashionably dressed woman, a "Republican Queen," they called her, some sarcastically, some sincerely.

Benjamin French, the commissioner of public buildings, worked closely with Mrs. Lincoln on refurbishing both the Soldiers' Home and the White House, and he was flattered by her "very strong" invitation to visit her at the Soldiers' Home. On first acquaintance (September 8, 1861) he wrote in his journal, "Mrs. Lincoln is evidently a smart, intelligent woman, & likes to have her own way pretty much. I was delighted with her independence & her ladylike reception of

Mary Todd Lincoln's typically luxurious finery contrasted with Lincoln's total indifference to clothes and food. Willie (left) and Tad (right) were much indulged children.

me." Later, he wrote (November 24, 1861), "Mrs. Lincoln looked remarkably well & would be taken for a young lady at a short distance. . . . She seems much at her ease, & strove to be very agreeable and was so." On December 22, 1862: "I like Mrs. L. better and better the more I see of her and think she is an admirable woman. She bears herself, in every particular, like a lady." The year before, on December 22, 1861, in a hint of the abuse Mary was to face for the rest of her days, he wrote, "Say what they may about her, I will defend her." French apparently did that. But like so many others, for so many reasons, he had become disenchanted by the end. On May 24, 1865, he wrote: "I went up and bade her goodbye, and felt really very sad, although she has given me a world of trouble. I think the sudden awful death of the President somewhat unhinged her mind, for at times she exhibited all the symptoms of madness. She is a most singular woman. . . ." He added, on January 14, 1866, "That she had been awfully belied I know."

Always a fighter, sharp-tongued Mary came to regard French as an "old rascal." There were rumors that "shifty" French was not entirely innocent of involvement in the disappearance of silver and vases from the White House. Mary was falsely accused of taking everything when she finally left the capital in May 1865, but, in fact, others had plundered the White House while she lay upstairs, trying to pull herself together.

Sergeant Stimmel, of course, saw the Lincolns from a less prestigious vantage point than French. But he was cool-headed, mature, well-respected by his peers, and observant. He wrote in his memoirs that the Lincolns

> seemed to be very congenial to each other. She was an interesting little woman, full of life and activity, and took great interest in her husband's welfare. During the summer and fall she often rode out with him from their summer home, and on other occasions. When the weather was a little chilly, the President wore a man's gray shawl over his shoulders, and as they got into their carriage I have often seen her adjust the shawl about his shoulders in an affectionate manner.

These carriage rides, for Mary, were her way of luring Lincoln away from his work and into the fresh air, which she loved, and for her to grab a few increasingly precious moments alone with her husband as the war went on. Mary would not be the first politician's wife to complain that "a politician is owned by everybody, and his wife has many lonely hours," and that "power & high position do not ensure a *bed of roses*." Fanny Seward, the young daughter of Lincoln's secretary of state, made special note of seeing the couple on their regular afternoon drives. A few years after the assassination, Mary gave her daughter-in-law "a very fine carriage rug . . . I prize it very much as it so often covered my dear husband—please guard that carefully."

Lincoln must have enjoyed these rides himself. He could have said no—he had plenty of excuses to avoid her company. But sensitive as he was, he surely knew that they did her as much good as they did him. "I was such an excessively indulged wife—my darling husband was so gentle and easy," she remembered. Knowing how important she considered these outings, Lincoln telegraphed her during one of her trips that he was "tolerably well," but he confessed, "have not rode out much yet but at last got new tires on the carriage wheels, & perhaps, shall ride out soon."

The editors of Mary Lincoln's life as revealed in her extraordinary letters point out that Lincoln respected her judgment more than most Victorian husbands, and kept her informed, too, of what was happening on the battlefield when she was away. He complained about the noise made by the clanking and clattering of his first rambunctious cavalry escort (Scott's Nine Hundred of New York) because it was hard for him and Mary to hear each other talk above the noise, and he wanted to know what she had to say.

As a young suitor, he'd been transfixed by her sparkling conversation, and she carried that considerable talent to Washington. On the very day of the assassination, he made sure she didn't invite anyone to ride with them, as she sometimes did to divert him. "I prefer to ride by ourselves to day." Mary remembered how joyful he was that afternoon as they talked about their future together.

The Lincolns liked to drop in on the infantrymen and cavalrymen camped on the Soldiers' Home grounds. (Mary did not like Lincoln's telling the soldiers that their coffee was more drinkable than hers.) Sixteen-year-old drummer boy Harry M. Kieffer wrote of the Soldiers' Home years later, "Many a mark of favor and kindness did we receive from the President's family. Delicacies, such as we were strangers to then, and would be for a long time to come, found their way from Mrs. Lincoln's hand to the camp on the green hillside." John Fleming of Company K paid Mary a great compliment when he wrote, "Misses lincoln [sic] was down yesterday all through our camp. She is a clipper." In those days, it meant a very splendid specimen of humanity or horse flesh! There were other tributes to Mary. The Lincolns' youngest sons liked to visit a camp named for their mother. Someone composed a "Mary Lincoln Polka."

Mary carried her concern for her husband's health even to the battlefront, staying overnight in tents, once during a snow storm. These trips could not have been too comfortable or too safe for her, but in answer to those who asked why she did it, she said, "the change will benefit him." She had always relished excitement and adventure. She even went with him to see the fighting at Fort Stevens during that potentially disastrous raid on Washington by General Jubal Early in July 1864.

Together the Lincolns took what one Mary Lincoln biographer called revolutionary steps to welcome black school children to the White House grounds for a festival, invite black Washingtonians into White House receptions, and ask Frederick Douglass to tea at the Soldiers' Home. Together they visited the contraband camp on the route to the Soldiers' Home, set up to shelter slaves fleeing the war zones.

All this "togetherness" certainly implies the continuing compatibility of interests that attracted the couple to each other in the first place: poetry, theater, politics. What other woman would have relished Lincoln's gift of election returns from the last three Illinois legislative contests?

Sergeant Stimmel astutely recognized that "Mrs. Lincoln was very different in her makeup from her husband." The opposites most simply began with their physical appearance: he was six feet, four inches and lean; she was five feet, two inches, and pleasingly plump. Over the years her colorful descriptions of her weight problem evolved from "periodic exuberances of flesh" to "the great bloat," the result, doctors now believe, of tragically undiagnosed and untreated diabetes, whose symptoms coincide closely with the complaints Mary made so often in later years, which were so severe and bizarre that most people concluded madness must be the cause.

Sadly, perhaps because of Lincoln's teasing that they were "the long and short of it," the two were never photographed together. Personality differences were also striking: he reticent, private, enigmatic, she voluble and volatile; he self-contained, undemonstrative, she in constant need of emotional support and companionship; he cool, dignified; she hot-tempered, impatient, sharp-tongued, self-destructive. Perhaps her insistence on dressing beautifully and sensually at the very highest end of fashion, for which she was viciously criticized, was an effort to counter his decidedly low-end appearance.

In one of the most tantalizing letters Mary Todd Lincoln ever wrote, a few months after the assassination, on July 11, 1865, she revealed to another close friend, Mary Jane Welles, "This morning,

This Lincoln family picture was a figment of the artist's imagination, meant to satisfy the insatiable public demand for such idealized images of home and family.

I have been looking over & arranging a large package of *his* dear, loving letters to me, many of them written to me, in the long ago, and quite yellow with age, others, more recent & *one* written from his office, *only* the *Wednesday* before, a few lines, playfully & tenderly worded, notifying, the hour, of the day, *he* would drive with me!" [her punctuation] It is painful to think what these letters might have told us about the Lincolns' marriage, but they have disappeared. Whether Mary ultimately misplaced them in the traumatic years after Washington, whether they might have been burned in the Chicago fire, or whether Robert Todd Lincoln, their only surviving son, always publicity-detesting and intensely private, may have considered them too personal, too sentimental, and destroyed them, we do not know.

Hints of the Lincolns' mutual affection and mutual dependence are evident in the few letters and telegrams that survive from their life at the Soldiers' Home. In perhaps the most tender and companionable letter of all, on August 8, 1863, after discussing some financial investments and the weather, Lincoln went into great detail about the adventures of Tad's goat at the Soldiers' Home: "My dear wife . . . The day you left Nanny [Tad's goat] was found resting herself, and chewing her little cud, on the middle of Tad's bed. But now she's gone! The gardener kept complaining that she destroyed the flowers, till it was concluded to bring her down to the White House. This was done, and the second day she has disappeared, and has not been heard of since. That is the last we know of poor 'Nanny.'" Later, he wrote, "I really wish to see you . . . I would be glad for you to come" (Lincoln to Mary, September 20 and 21, 1863, after one of her long absences). She replied, "Am anxious to return" (Mary to Lincoln, September 22, 1863).

It's clear that Lincoln left Mary in charge of household matters, despite her inability to stay within a budget. In November 1862, Lincoln wrote asking if he should not move back to the White House, where Stoddard insisted she was "absolute mistress of all that part of the White House inside the vestibule and of all the upper floor east of the private portion of the mansion." It was getting cold at the Soldiers' Home, and the cook and housekeeper were complaining. In June 1864, he informed her that all was well, and that their belongings had been moved out to the Soldiers' Home, for what would turn out to be their last summer there.

The philandering General Daniel Sickles was a surprisingly good friend of both Lincolns. He spoke, perhaps in envy or wonder, given his own disastrous marital experiences, of what he observed in his visits to the Lincolns at the Soldiers' Home and the White House. "In their domestic relations and in their devotion to their children, I have never seen a more congenial couple. He always looked to her for comfort and consultation in his troubles. Indeed the only joy poor Lincoln knew after reaching the White House were his wife and children. She shared all his troubles and never recovered from the culminating blow when he was assassinated." "At all times," said David Bates of the War Department Telegraph Office, "Lincoln showed a most tender regard for Mrs. Lincoln, and great affection for his sons, especially Tad." Henry Rankin put their relationship most eloquently: "They were in harmony on the larger affairs in their lives."

It's interesting to speculate on what Lincoln would, or would not, have become had he married either of the two women he is supposed by some to have really loved, Ann Rutledge of New Salem, and Matilda Edwards, Mary's cousin. According to her brother, Robert Rutledge, Ann "was esteemed the brightest mind of the family, was studious, devoted to her duties of whatever character, and possessed a remarkably amiable and loveable disposition. She had light hair and blue eyes." These were qualities Lincoln must have admired. But Ann surely did not have the benefit of Mary's superior education, her cultured upbringing, nor most likely the ambition and profound belief from the start in his potential, qualities that helped him achieve the presidency. Henry Rankin believed Mary to be

> the most forceful and alert personal influence in his life . . . we should recall that but for her ambition, her husband might never have been President. . . . Lincoln needed far more than most men a refined and well-appointed home. She gave him this to the most exacting details of neatness and punctuality. More than that, she believed in him and loved him devotedly. She had faith that a great future awaited him. She stimulated his ambition to work and seek the prominence he won. . . . She was an inspiration to Lincoln.

With touching sensitivity, Rankin stayed behind as Lincoln went home to tell Mary of his election victory. "The moment was too sacred," Rankin knew.

As for Matilda Edwards, it seems she wasn't interested in Lincoln anyway, nor in any of the other smitten Springfield bachelors. She was "decidedly unworldly," rejecting the advances of Stephen A. Douglas because of his bad morals, and declining an invitation to a Springfield ball because it was not the Christian thing to do. "I hope," she wrote piously to her brother, "I shall ever have strength to resist those worldly fascinations which if indulged in bring a reproach upon the cause of religion."

Hardly the adventurous, unorthodox, and courageous woman Lincoln did marry, to whom he vowed that "Love is eternal," and who, if born in our time, with the medications now available to deal with emotional and physical pain, would quite probably have sought political office herself.

CHAPTER 6

Lincoln's Achilles' Heel

ABRAHAM LINCOLN was a marked man from the day he was elected president in November 1860. It was a wonder to his worried friends and colleagues that he survived as long as he did—well over a year longer, in fact, than another doomed president elected exactly one century later. Staying at the isolated Soldiers' Home in no way enhanced his security. It was in fact his Achilles' heel.

Both President Lincoln and his wife realized that if anyone really wanted to kill him, they would. "No vigilance could keep them out," Lincoln conceded. Mary, in chilling agreement, wrote a friend a few months after the assassination at Ford's Theatre on April 14, 1865, "I firmly believe, that if he had remained, at the W. H. on that night of darkness, when the fiends prevailed, he would have been horribly *cut to pieces*. Those fiends, had too long contemplated, this inhuman murder, to have allowed, *him*, to escape." [punctuation Mary Lincoln's]

Throughout his presidency, Lincoln seemed determined to ignore the threats that began to arrive even before the family left Springfield for the inauguration that rainy day in February 1861. Over time, Lincoln was aware of at least eighty; he kept these stuffed into a pigeonhole in his desk at the White House. His secretaries kept the rest from him. He simply refused to worry, even when his hat was shot off late one night in August 1864, as he rode out alone to the Soldiers' Home. He told the soldier who found the bullet-holed hat later that he wanted no one to know about it.

"The President was too intelligent not to know that he was in some danger," wrote his secretary John Nicolay. "but he had himself so sane a mind, and a heart so kindly even to his enemies, that it was hard for him to believe in political hatred so deadly as to lead to murder."

But others could. A fearful admirer, Walt Whitman, watching Lincoln arrive in New York on his inaugural journey later that month, remembered—perhaps too melodramatically, some say—the "sulky, unbroken silence" that greeted the president-elect as he got out of his carriage at the Astor House. "The crowd that hemmed around consisted, I should think, of thirty to forty thousand men, not a single one his personal friend, while, I have no doubt (so frenzied were the ferments of the time) many an assassin's knife and pistol lurked in hip—or breast-pocket there—ready, soon as break and riot came." Lincoln simply stretched once or twice, "looked with curiosity upon that immense sea of faces," walked up the hotel stairs, and disappeared.

By the time Lincoln reached the last stage of the inaugural journey—from Baltimore to the capital—evidence of a possible attempt on his life was so strong that Lincoln was finally convinced to change his plans, arriving in Washington at 6 A.M., six hours ahead of schedule, wearing an old overcoat and a soft hat, trusting no one would recognize him (an old friend at the station wasn't fooled for a second). Lincoln was humiliated by the scornful fuss made over what one hostile Baltimore paper called this "wretched and cowardly conduct of the President-elect," made worse by another reporter's invention that Lincoln had entered the capital in disguise, "wearing a Scotch plaid cap and a very long military cloak." This fiasco did not make Lincoln any more kindly disposed to increasingly urgent suggestions that he accept protection. "I cannot be shut up in a cage and guarded," he insisted.

Attempts to assure Lincoln's safety once he arrived in Washington were not made any easier by the precarious position of the capital itself. It was in constant danger from hostile forces inside the city as well as all around it. Mary Lincoln, "one of the best rebel haters . . . in Washington," was convinced, with justification, that

Washington was so full of Confederate spies, supporters, and sympathizers that Lincoln teased he'd be doing nothing during the war but building prisons to contain them if he paid attention to her urgings that he arrest and jail them all.

Lincoln's own letters record the continuing external threats to the city that persisted for more than three years. In September 1861, frustrated and worried about how badly the war was going, he scolded the governor of Indiana, who was as short of arms for his state and neighboring Kentucky as was everyone else at that early, unprepared stage of the war. "While I write this I am," he wrote, "if not in *range* at least in hearing of cannon-shot, from an army of enemies more than one hundred thousand strong. I do not expect them to capture this city; but I *know* they would, if I were to send the men and arms from her, to defend Louisville, of which there is not a single hostile armed soldier within forty miles, not any force known to be moving upon it from any distance." [emphasis Lincoln's] At six o'clock one morning in September 1862, Lincoln climbed the signal tower at the Soldiers' Home to see what the firing he heard nearby was all about. He decided that it was not a "general engagement."

Two years later, when Confederate General Jubal Early threatened Baltimore and Washington in his famous July 1864 raid, and Lincoln had come under fire at Fort Stevens, the President tried to calm a group of panicked Baltimore residents. "Let us be vigilant but keep cool. I hope neither Baltimore nor Washington will be taken." War-weary Washingtonians seemed by then to have become used to being surrounded by danger. The Smithsonian Institution's first African American employee, Solomon Galleon Brown, an accomplished poet, wrote on July 15, 1864 to Secretary Joseph Henry, that "many in Washington have been much frightened at the annual visit of the Rebels to their friends in Maryland." And that same summer, the editor of the *Army-Navy Journal* in New York City bitingly wrote, "The annual expedition of the Confederate forces into Maryland and Pennsylvania has been inaugurated this year at about the same time, and with rather more than the usual success." He went on to say that this predictability provided "July almanac makers with another 'about this time may be expected' passage for their wares."

The prize capture would have been the president himself. As early as April 1861, reports of a sweeping kidnapping plan (Lincoln, his family, *and* the cabinet) appeared so credible that General Winfield Scott, Lincoln's chief military adviser at the time, urged Mary Todd Lincoln and the children to pack up and go back to Springfield. One Baltimore editorial writer, of secessionist sympathies, made the unlikely claim, given Mary's loyalty to her husband and her courage, that she'd prefer to go back home rather than live in Washington under such a complete "reign of terror."

Other Confederate kidnapping plans are known to have been hatched: to seize the president alone, carry him to Richmond, and use him as a hostage for the release of thousands of Confederate prisoners—perhaps even to bring the war to a negotiated close favorable to the Confederacy. John Wilkes Booth's initial idea in early 1865 was to do just that, and at least one attempt was aborted when Lincoln did not appear as planned at Campbell Hospital. He opted for Lincoln's assassination instead, after Richmond fell and Lee surrendered, although Gideon Welles was convinced Booth had planned to shoot Lincoln at the Capitol the year before.

The Soldiers' Home became the chief focus of Confederate plans. Enemies could appreciate as well as journalist Noah Brooks that "the lonely situation of the President's summer residence would have afforded a tempting chance for a daring squad of rebel cavalry to run some risks for the chance to carry off the President." Enough friendly visitors got lost on their way out there to see Lincoln to have made it appear possible that his enemies might, too. But the president's habits were too regular, his usual route up the Seventh Street Road too vulnerable, to have put off the determined.

Realizing this, one concerned, modest Washington bachelor, Joseph C. G. Kennedy, wrote to Lincoln's secretary, John Nicolay, offering the president a temporary shelter at his inconspicuous but convenient house at 380 H Street. "It seems to me," he wrote, "that it might not be difficult for a few desperate rebels to land from a boat enter the White House and carry off the President or do him bodily harm, no more precarious [than] to attempt taking him from the Soldiers Home . . . his greatest security consists not in being where he would naturally be supposed to . . . sojourn."

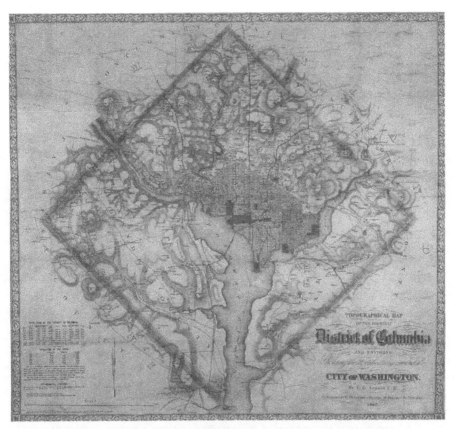

The Soldiers' Home was about three miles northeast of the White House, deep in the country not far from the Maryland border. By 1862 sixty-eight forts and batteries ringed the city.

One of the first plotters, John Walker Taylor, a young Confederate officer, even carried his plan to Confederate president Jefferson Davis at breakfast in the Richmond White House, probably in mid-1862. Taylor had cased Lincoln's routine in Washington, and reported to Davis that:

Lincoln does not leave the White House until evening, or near twilight, and then only with a driver, he takes a lonely ride two or three miles in the country to a place called the Soldiers' Home, which is his summer residence. My point is to collect several of these Kentuckians whom I see about here doing nothing, and who are brave enough for such a thing as that, and capture Lincoln, run him down the Potomac, cross him over just where I crossed, and the next day have him here.

Davis disapproved of the plan, because he knew that Lincoln was so strong he would fight to the death, and at that stage of the war, Davis was not desperate enough to risk it.

Twice more, Lincoln's sojourns at the Soldiers' Home provided an ideal opportunity. In the winter of 1863–1864, Colonel Bradley T. Johnson proposed making a sudden, quick strike at the cottage with two hundred Confederate cavalry, carrying Lincoln off as Taylor had proposed. A Confederate agent, Thomas Nelson Conrad, picked up the plan in August 1864, and plotted to capture Lincoln as he approached the entrance to the Soldiers' Home. The agent discovered, too late, that well before then President Lincoln had reluctantly accepted a cavalry escort to and from the Soldiers' Home, and a company of infantry to guard him during the family's stays at the home and the White House. Even so, Lincoln tried constantly to elude them, or dismiss them at the slightest excuse. Such protection seemed to him "like putting up the gap in only one place when the fence was down all along."

"Often," wrote drummer boy Harry M. Kieffer,

did I see him enter his carriage before the hour appointed for his morning departure for the White House, and drive away in haste, as if to escape from the irksome escort of a dozen cavalrymen, whose duty it was to guard his carriage between our camp and the city. Then when the escort rode up to the door, some ten or fifteen minutes later, and found that the carriage had already gone, wasn't there a clattering of hoofs and a rattling of scabbards as they dashed out past the gate and down the road to overtake the great and good President.

Company K, of the 150th Pennsylvania "Bucktails," had become the president's guard in early September 1862. Much as he scorned Lincoln, General McClellan had come to agree with Mary Todd Lincoln, Secretary of War Stanton, and others that Lincoln really must have some protection, whether he liked it or not, and wrote curtly to Lincoln that he had so ordered it.

The letters home of Company K's Private Willard Cutter revealed how dangerous the location of the Soldiers' Home was, with or without the prospect of a Confederate kidnapping raid:

9/10/62 (Camp Soldiers Home) We took a spy yesterday he was passed through to see the president and went on the top of the

Private Willard Cutter, of Meadville, Pennsylvania, was the most prolific letter writer we know of in Company K, and he left us a vivid picture of life in the Soldiers' Home camp and in the capital, and of the Lincoln family.

Soldiers' Home took out his spy glass and was looking at our forts and went to go out and was stopped he could not give account of himself . . . so they walked him in the city to be tried there . . . there was 17 Rebels captured half a mile from here last night.

That same month, several Midwest papers reported that "a couple of horsemen" had approached the main gate at the Soldiers' Home complex "and made some careless inquiry of the sentry as to the time Mr. Lincoln generally came out." This terrified Mary Todd Lincoln, and led to the assignment of the cavalry escort.

Private Cutter wrote his mother again on October 17, 1862:

(Camp Soldiers Home)
The news came at 7 o'clock night before last that the Rebbles [*sic*] were on the other side of the Potomac and Mrs. Lincoln had to have the guard doubled for fear the Rebbles would take the Place and all the guns were loaded for the first time in three weeks.

On August 3, 1863:

We have got an old secesh not fur from our camp he ordered one of our boys off of his farm the other night . . . he called them Yankee sons of B . . . when his apples are ripe we will give him a call some nite I guess . . . he was going to shoot two soldiers about two weeks ago for going across his farm.

Again, on July 11, 1864:

Ever since we have been here the rebs have been near the city or advancing and [it] was rather a scary place for the President to stay and several times he went to the City to stay Sunday night the sec. of war come up at 11 after Abe well Abe said he didn't think there was any danger but he went along at that time the Rebs was only 1 1/2 or 2 miles from here and once in a while we could hear the crack of a gun then we felt we wanted to see the fun as well as the rest of the folks.

The English lawyer George Borrett, arriving uninvited at the Soldiers' Home with two companions well after eight o'clock one evening in 1864, noticed that "the house is some way beyond the Federal lines and the neighborhood is infested with guerillas, to whom the President's head would be worth its weight in gold." Borrett was relieved to see that "troops [were] encamped picturesquely about the grounds" and that he and his party were actually challenged at the door by a sentry. But all they needed to be allowed to enter the house was simply to say they were there to see Mr. and Mrs. Lincoln.

What made Lincoln take the risks he did by staying at the Soldiers' Home for one-quarter of his presidency, thirteen months in all? Walt Whitman thought it might be pride. He wrote his mother on June 30, 1863: "It would be funny if [the Reb cavalry] should come some night to the President's country house where he goes to sleep every night; it is in the same direction as their saucy raid last Sunday . . . I really think it would be safer for him just now to stop at the White House, but I expect he is too proud to abandon the former custom." Sergeant Smith Stimmel wrote in his memoirs that on one morning ride back to the White House from the Soldiers' Home, Lincoln

got into a serious discussion with the lieutenant in charge of the
escort, about the "peculiar structure of a cow"—trotting off into a
field with the soldier so that he could confirm his observation on
their lopsided construction! (This was one of many practical jokes
Lincoln played on gullible companions.) "Under the great strain and
burden of his official life during those strenuous times," Stimmel
concluded, "He absolutely needed some real diversion. There was no
chance for him to go fishing or duck-hunting, or even bear-hunting.
He knew himself well enough to make use of such opportunities as
his morning and evenings afforded him and enjoy those little diver-
sions however trifling they might be as a welcome relief from the
stress and burden of official duties." And once at the Soldiers' Home,
he "could get a good night's rest, which he very much needed . . .
he was never really off duty, but it was a time when he could relax
a little."

Captain David Derickson of Company K believed "there was no
fear or timidity in Mr. Lincoln's makeup. In fact I thought him
rather careless or thoughtless as to his personal safety." Others called
his behavior irrational. But was there more to it than that? Why did
he stand on the parapet for two days at Fort Stevens as bullets from
Confederate rifles flew around him and wounded a soldier next to
him? Or land and actually stroll on a beach held by the Confederates
near Norfolk, Virginia? Or enter Richmond and walk around with
just a small party soon after the rebels withdrew, when he admitted
that "anyone could have shot me from a second-story window"? Or
insist on going to the theater and church unescorted? Or walk late at
night through the dark grounds near the Soldiers' Home, or between
the White House and the War Department where he could easily
have been mistaken for an intruder, accosted, or worse? One of
Booth's accomplices, Lewis Payne, revealed from prison that he'd
been close enough to Lincoln right there to have shot him.

In an essay titled "Lincoln's Military Fantasies," historian Gary
Prokopowicz suggests more complex motives. To be an effective
wartime leader, Lincoln believed he had to show his own personal
bravery, his own courage in some way, since he could not do so on
the battlefield. He had to demonstrate a willingness to share the risks
of what he as president was requiring so many thousands of others

to do. The hospitals and the cemetery near the Soldiers' Home were constant reminders of those costs. This was a matter of honor, made even more personal for Lincoln in that a number of friends had made the supreme sacrifice, including one so close, Edward Baker, he and Mary had named their second son for him.

We know that Lincoln believed that "there are a thousand ways of getting at a man if it is desired that he should be killed." Sadly, as Mary Lincoln told William Herndon in 1866, the Lincolns had begun toward the end of the war to think that they "had passed through 5 long—terrible—bloody years unscathed."

And of all the ways Lincoln had seemed to be courting death all those years, tragically, John Wilkes Booth needed only that one.

CHAPTER 7

Lincoln's Favorite Storytellers

LINCOLN ONCE TOLD his very staid quartermaster general, Montgomery Cunningham Meigs, that anyone who had not read *Orpheus C. Kerr's Letters* must be a heathen. A New York journalist, poet, and novelist, Robert Henry Newell, created the character, whose name itself was a comment on the bane of Lincoln's existence, the "office seeker." According to Frederick Douglass, Lincoln recommended the letters to an even less likely candidate for enjoying a laugh than Meigs—the harried General Ulysses S. Grant. "I have had a good deal of satisfaction reading that book," he told Grant, who quickly got the point of the particular Kerr story Lincoln told him—that he hoped Grant would not turn into another McClellan, demanding the skies, but delivering little. Douglass even bought a copy of *Kerr's Letters* himself, but we do not know what he thought of them.

Of the three humorists we know Lincoln read, to himself and to others at the Soldiers' Home as a way to dispel his anxiety and his melancholy, *Kerr's Letters* make the most interesting reading, because they satirize—in readable English—practically everyone and everything of concern of the day, from long-winded orators, well-meaning but clueless do-good women, and pompous diplomats to soldiers' poor marksmanship, bad army food and clothing, cowardice, and even the *Trent* crisis that could have brought on war between the Union and Great Britain.

One of Kerr's letters, concludes the *Dictionary of American Biography,* "deserves perhaps a permanent place in the history of American burlesque writing, containing parodies of the best-known authors of the day in their supposed attempts to compose a new national anthem." Here it is.

LETTER VIII.

The Rejected "National Hymns"

Washington, D.C., June 30, 1861

[Kerr writes that he is on his way to New York to look into how the competition for the best national hymn is going, with the winner's prize a generous award of five hundred dollars. He finds that the best-known poets of the day regarded the competition as just too vulgar for their attention. And others, of course, were too proud to admit that they really needed the money. Nonetheless, eleven hundred and fifty submissions were received, and Kerr happily managed to rescue from the rag man some of the best rejects.]

National Anthem

By H. W. L——, of Cambridge

Back in the years when Phlagstaff, the Dane, was Monarch
　　Over the sea-ribbed land of the fleet-footed Norsemen,
Once there went forth young Ursa to gaze at the heavens—
　　Ursa, the noblest of all the Vikings and horsemen.

Musing, he sat in his stirrups and viewed the horizon,
　　When the Aurora lapt stars in a North-polar manner,
Wildly he started—for there in the heavens before him
　　Fluttered and flew the original Star-Spangled Banner.

The committee had two objections to this: in the first place, it is not an "anthem" at all; secondly, it is a gross plagiarism from an old Scandinavian war song of the primeval age.

Next, I present a

National Anthem

By the Hon. Edward E——, of Boston

Ponderous projectiles, hurled by heavy hands
　　Fell upon our Liberty's poor infant head,
Ere she a stadium had well advanced
　　On the great path that to her greatness led;

Her temple's propylon was shattered;
　Yet, thanks to saving Grace and Washington
Her incubus was from her bosom hurled;
　And, rising like a cloud-dispelling sun,
She took the oil, with which her hair was curled,
　To grease the "Hub" round which revolves the world.

This fine production is rather heavy for an "anthem," and contains too much of Boston to be considered strictly national. To set such an "anthem" to music would require a Wagner; and even were it really accommodated to a tune, it could only be whispered by the populace.

　We now come to a

National Anthem

By John Greenleaf W——,

My native land, thy Puritanic stock
Still finds its roots in Plymouth Rock,
and all thy sons unite in one grand wish—
To keep the virtues of Preserv-éd Fish.

Preserv-éd Fish, the Deacon stern and true,
Told our New England what her sons should do,
And should they swerve from loyalty and right,
Then the whole land were lost indeed in night.

The sectional bias of this "anthem" renders it unsuitable for use in that small margin of the world situated outside of New England. Hence the above must be rejected.

　Here we have a very curious

National Anthem

By Dr. Oliver Wendell H——,

A diagnosis of our hist'ry proves
Our native land a land its native loves;
Its birth a deed obstetric without peer,
Its growth a source of wonder far and near.

To love it more behold how foreign shores
Sink into nothingness beside its stores;
Hyde Park at best—though counted ultra-grand—
The "Boston Common" of Victoria's land.

The committee must not be blamed for rejecting the above, after reading thus far; for such an "anthem" could only be sung by a college of surgeons or a Beacon-street tea-party.

Turn we now to a

National Anthem

By Ralph Waldo E——,

Source immaterial of material naught,
    Focus of light infinitesimal,
Sum of all things by sleepless Nature wrought,
    Of which abnormal man is decimal,

Refract, in prism immortal, from thy stars
    To the stars blent incipient on our flag,
The beam translucent, neutrifying death;
    And raise to immortality the rag.

This "anthem" was greatly praised by a celebrated German scholar; but the committee felt obliged to reject it on account of its too childish simplicity.

Here we have a

National Anthem

By William Cullen B——,

The sun sinks softly to his evening post,
    The sun swells grandly to his morning crown;
Yet not a star our flag of Heav'n has lost,
    And not a sunset stripe with him goes down.

So thrones may fall; and from the dust of those,
    New thrones may rise, to totter like the last;
But still our country's nobler planet glows
    While the eternal stars of Heaven are fast.

Upon finding that this did not go well to the air of "Yankee Doodle," the committee felt justified in declining it; being furthermore prejudiced against it by a suspicion that the poet has crowded an advertisement of a paper which he edits into the first line.

Next we quote from a

National Anthem

By Gen. George B. M——,

In the days that tried our fathers
  Many years ago,
Our fair land achieved her freedom,
  Blood-bought, you know.
Shall we not defend her ever
  As we'd defend
That fair maiden, kind and tender,
  Calling us friend?
Yes! Let all the echoes answer,
  From hill and vale;
Yes! Let other nations, hearing,
  Joy in the tale,
Our Columbia is a lady,
  High-born and fair;
We have sworn allegiance to her—
  Touch her who dare.

The tune of this "anthem" not being devotional enough to suit
the committee, it should be printed on an edition of linen-cambric
handkerchiefs, for ladies especially. . . .
  We next peruse a

National Anthem

By Thomas Bailey A——,

The little brown squirrel hops in the corn,
  The cricket quaintly sings;
The emerald pigeon nods his head,
  And the shad in the river springs,
The dainty sunflower hangs its head
  On the shore of the summer sea;
And better for that I were dead,
  If Maud did not love me.

I love the squirrel that hops in the corn,
  And the cricket that quaintly sings;

> And the emerald pigeon that nods his head,
>   And the shad that gayly springs.
> I love the dainty sunflower, too,
>   And Maud with her snowy breast;
> I love them all;—but I love—I love—
>   I love my country best.

This is certainly very beautiful, and sounds somewhat like Tennyson. Though it was rejected by the committee, it can never lose its value as a piece of excellent reading for children. It is calculated to fill the youthful mind with an emotion palpitating for all.

.... And this is the last of the rejected anthems I can quote from at present, my boy, though several hundred pounds yet remain untouched.

> Yours, questioningly,
> ORPHEUS C. KERR

Readers who remember the challenges of memorizing Longfellow's "Song of Hiawatha," "Evangeline," or "The Village Blacksmith" will recognize the parody of his style. And those who conquered "Snowbound," "Barefoot Boy," or "Barbara Fritchie" will recognize John Greenleaf Whittier. Another literary giant of Lincoln's time, not so well known today as he was then, is Edward Everett, who admitted to Lincoln after Gettysburg that his two-hour oration there didn't stand a chance of being remembered compared to Lincoln's two-minute address.

Other authors being parodied are listed here. Sketches are based primarily on entries in the *Dictionary of American Biography*.

Oliver Wendell Holmes, a popular and distinguished essayist of the day, novelist, poet, and teacher of anatomy, quintessential Boston Brahmin, and father of Civil War hero and Supreme Court Justice Oliver Wendell Holmes Jr.

Ralph Waldo Emerson, a thought-provoking, unorthodox writer, lecturer, and cultural leader in midnineteenth-century America. A philosopher of transcendentalism, he was critical of materialism, formal religion, and slavery. Emerson believed in the integrity of the individual as one who should try to harmonize one's life, not with conventional, outmoded religion, but with a spiritual universe governed by a mystic "Oversoul," and that all power and wisdom come from nature, "the dress God wears." People did make fun, like Kerr, of his occasionally somewhat overblown prose. Emerson met Lincoln in 1862, who "impressed me more favorably than I had hoped." After Lincoln's murder, Emerson wrote that Lincoln had turned out to be "a man without vices . . . he had a vast good nature which made him tolerant and accessible to all. . . . This good nature became a noble humanity . . . with what increasing tenderness he dealt when a whole race was thrown on his compassion."

William Cullen Bryant, well-respected poet and eloquent editor of the *New York Evening Post*, which supported the new Republican party in 1856. Bryant introduced Lincoln at Cooper Union, and he believed that war was necessary to deal with the secessionists. He was critical of Lincoln's moderation and slowness to issue an emancipation proclamation, but supported him for re-election in 1864. "Our great poet of nature."

General George Brinton McClellan, controversial Civil War general, who opposed Lincoln in 1864 as the candidate of the Democratic Party.

Thomas Bailey Aldrich, Civil War correspondent for several years, crafter of charming poems, editor, and author of the happy *The Story of a Bad Boy*, his best prose work.

George Boutwell, Lincoln's commissioner of internal revenue, once made the startling comment that "three forces—the army, the navy, and the *Nasby Letters*—caused the fall of the Confederacy." Petroleum V. Nasby was another favorite storyteller. He was the 1861 creation of the Ohio journalist and political satirist, David Ross Locke, and Lincoln was one of his most enthusiastic admirers. "For the genius to write these things I would gladly give up my office," he told the sophisticated abolitionist Senator Charles Sumner, who admired Nasby, too, and on the very last day of his life, Lincoln kept reading Nasby letters for so long he was late for dinner. It seems incredible today that anyone would like such stuff, and even then, Secretary of War Stanton was among those who found them "balderdash." "Was there ever such nonsense?" he exploded once to his assistant secretary, Charles Dana, after Lincoln had interrupted an important discussion to read Nasby to the participants. "Was there ever such inability to appreciate what is going on in an awful crisis? Here is the fate of this whole republic at stake, and here is the man around whom it all centers, on whom it all depends, turning aside from this monumental issue to read the G . . d . . . . . trash of a silly mountebank."

Few could stomach Nasby today, but critics have claimed that Petroleum V. Nasby is "an historic figure of genuine importance." Stanton and other disdainers underestimated the salutary effect of Locke's satire not only on Lincoln, but on the soldiers in the Union army and supporters of his policies in the North. For Nasby could be seen as a caricature of all they were fighting against: a Southern-sympathizing country preacher who was semiliterate, corrupt, cowardly, lazy, lying, and dissolute, "the incarnation of the most ignorant, reactionary, and sordid elements in American politics." Nasby made Lincoln laugh, made his political opponents look ridiculous, and made Locke wealthy.

It is difficult to find a Nasby "paper" today that would not offend somebody, and the outrageous spelling, a popular device in those days, would be the despair of teachers. Here is one of the most innocuous, on how Nasby deserted to the Confederate side:

> I hev deserted, and am now a sojer uv the Confederacy. Jest ez soon ez our regiment struck Suthrin sile, I made up my mind that my bondage was drawin to a close—that I wood seeze the fust oppertoonity uv escaping to my natural frends uv the sunny South. Nite before last I run the guard, wuz shot at twict (reseevin two buck-shot jest below the hind buttons uv my coat), but by eggstrrordinary luck I escaped. Had infantry bin sent after me I shood hev bin taken, for I am not a fast runner; but the commandant uv the post wiz new at biznis, and innocently sent cavalry. Between the hossis they rode, and the stopping to pick up them ez coodsent stick onto ther flyin steeds, I had no difficulty in outrunning em.
> At last I encountered the pikits uv the Looisiana Pelicans, and givin myself up ez a deserter from the hordes uv the tyrant Linkin

wuz to wuntz taken afore the kernel. I must say, in this conneck-shun, that I wuz surprised at the style uv uniform worn by the Peli-cans. It consists uf a hole in the seet uv the pants, with the tale uv the shirt a waving gracefully therfrom . . . I notist all this time the kernel was eyein my clothes wistfully. I hed jest drawd em, and they wuz bran-new. Sez the kernel:—

Mr. Nasby, I reseeve you gladly ez a recroot in the Grand Army of Freedom. Ez you divest yourself uv the clothes uv the tyrant, divest yerself uv whatever ligrin affecshuns yoo may hev for the land uv yer nativity, and ez yoo array yerself in the garb uv a Suthrin soljer, try to fill yer sole with that Suthrin feelin that ani-mates us all.

Naturally, Nasby ends up with the tattered rags of the Confederate soldiers, and as he leaves the "kernel" an adjutant pulls him aside "and askt me ef I coodent git three more to desert. Wun glance at their habilyments showd why they wuz so anxious for deserters."

I candidly confess that Linkin takes better care uv his sojers than Davis does. The clothin I hev described. Instid of regular rashens, we are allowed to eat just whatever we can steel uv the planters, and, ez mite be expected, we hev bin campt here three months, the livin is getting thin. Yet a man akin endoor almost any thing for principle.

Artemus Ward was also a favorite character of Lincoln, created by another journalist, Charles Farrar Browne. Ward was supposed to be a showman who traveled around the country with an exhibition of wax figures, "Figgers of G. Washington, John Bunyan, General Tay-lor . . . besides several miscellanyus moral wax statoots of celebrated priruts & murderers &c ekalled by few and exceld by none." Before reading the draft of the Emancipation Proclamation to his cabinet on September 22, 1862, Lincoln chose to read aloud one of Ward's shorter pieces, "High Handed Outrage at Utica." Lincoln and Browne never met, although one of his more excruciating pieces was an imaginary meeting with Lincoln in Springfield, after his election in 1860. If the reader can put himself in Lincoln's predicament, already besieged by the office seekers who were to be the bane of his existence for four years, it's possible to see why Lincoln got such enjoyment from the character, who was a sensation in England as well.

> "Good God!" Cried Old Abe, "they cum upon me from the skize—down the chimneys, and from the bowels of the yerth!" He hadn't more'n got them words out of his delikit mouth before two fat offiss-seekers from Wisconsin, in indeverin to crawl atween his legs for the purpose of applyin for the tollgateship at Milwawky, upsot the President eleck, & he would hev gone sprawlin into the fireplace if I hadn't caught him in these arms. But I hadn't more'n stood him up strate before another man cum crashing down the chimney, his head striking me viliently again the inards and prostratin my voluptoous form onto the floor. "Mr. Linkin," shouted the infatooated being, "my papers is signed by every clergyman in our town, and likewise the skoolmaster...I workt hard for the ticket; I toiled night and day! The patrit should be rewarded!"

Even a year into the war, a Massachusetts newspaper could write that "Lincoln's cheerfulness is enough itself to produce confidence in a nation." But not many months later, Admiral John A. Dahlgren, a close and valued friend and adviser, observed that "the President never tells a joke now." To Illinois congressman Isaac Arnold, Lincoln confessed after the dreadful defeat of Burnside at Fredericksburg in December 1862, "If I could not get momentary respite from the crushing burden I am constantly carrying, I should die. I feel I shall never be glad anymore." And he told his cabinet that they needed "this medicine" as well as he did. Hoary as the humorists he loved seem to us now, we should be grateful to them for helping to keep him functioning as long as they did.

CHAPTER 8

Lincoln and Freedom

EIGHTEEN-YEAR-OLD ANNA HARRISON couldn't have cared less that Washington looked like a "mudhole" when she and her family arrived in the nation's still raw young capital in the spring of 1862. They had just ended a dangerous run for it from a Virginia plantation over a hundred miles to the south. Anna's "old master and missus were dead, and we heard that our young master had been killed in the war. So we hitched up the ox cart and I led my family away to the Free State." The war was in its second bloody year.

By that summer, Anna and her family had found shelter of sorts—in one of the camps frantically being set up around Washington to look after the flood of slaves who, like Anna, were fleeing with high hopes from rebel territory across to Union army lines. "Contrabands" they were called, and at first no one knew quite what to do with them. Hundreds crowded into a deadly, disease-ridden slum called "Murder Bay," not far from the White House to the southeast. But Anna and her family had better luck. They found Camp Barker, an enclave of tents near the president's usual route up Vermont Avenue from the White House to the Soldiers' Home several miles to the north. "I used to see Mr. Lincoln almost every day riding out to the Soldiers' Home that summer. Of course, we did not know what he was doing, but he was such a great man."

What Lincoln was doing at the Soldiers' Home that summer, unbeknownst to Anna and almost everyone else, was anguishing over and shaping what would emerge on September 22, 1862, as a preliminary Emancipation Proclamation, containing what Lincoln had himself described a year before as a potential "thunderbolt"—the "bombshell" sentence—that on January 1, 1863, "all persons held as slaves within any state, or designated part of a state, the people whereof shall then be in rebellion against the United States, shall be then, thenceforward, and forever free."

Many years later, on a cold winter's day, Anna, now ninety-two years old, made her way to the Soldiers' Home to honor the man and the message that just a few months after her escape in 1862 would finally set her and the rest of the four million slaves in the country on the arduous path to freedom. She and many other freed men and women had traveled that path well, as Lincoln would come to realize. She'd married another former slave, Thomas Chase, who'd become a lawyer. Their children and grandchildren had entered the professions. All those years, Anna cherished the belief—and legend, one of many surrounding Lincoln's life, has supported her—that the Soldiers' Home was the place where the Emancipation Proclamation was written. She wanted to see the very room where Lincoln had worked on it.

At long last, we know enough about Lincoln's life at the Soldiers' Home to validate Anna's memory that she was close enough to the real story, making the Soldiers' Home one of the most moving sites in the world's still unfinished struggle for human dignity, a "legitimate cradle of liberty" in the eyes of one Lincoln scholar. After their traumatic winter at the White House, devastated by Willie's death in February, the shrinking Lincoln family had moved out at last to the Soldiers' Home in early June for the summer of 1862, their first. Lincoln's relieved private secretary, John Nicolay, wrote on June 15 to his fiancée, Therena Bates, "The President comes in every day at ten and goes out [to the Soldiers' Home] again at four. I am very glad of the change for several reasons; particularly as it gives us [Nicolay and Lincoln's other private secretary, John Hay] more time to ourselves, the crowd only coming when they know the President to be about." The next day, Lincoln's commissioner of public buildings, Benjamin French, who had made all the arrangements for Willie's funeral that winter and who worked very closely with Mary Todd Lincoln to see that her White House social events went off without a hitch, was relieved to see that Mrs.

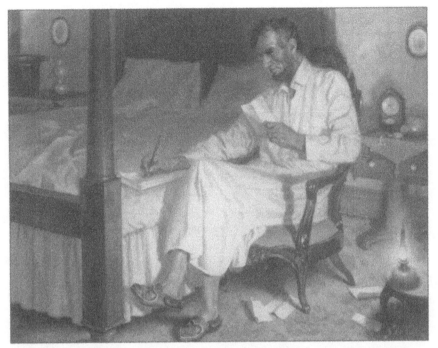

This portrait of Lincoln working on the Emancipation Proclamation at the Soldiers' Home was painted in 1959 for the 150th anniversary of his birth. Long lost, it appears for the first time here since it was found in March 2005.

Lincoln "seemed to be in excellent spirits and delighted at getting out of the city" to the Soldiers' Home. And we know, too, that at least Lincoln was still at the Soldiers' Home well beyond September. As late as November, he wrote to Mary Lincoln, away in Boston, asking plaintively if the family shouldn't move back to the White House because it was getting so cold at the Soldiers' Home that the cook and housekeeper were grumbling.

Hannibal Hamlin of Maine, Lincoln's first vice president, was the highest-ranking eyewitness at the Soldiers' Home itself to Lincoln's working on the Emancipation Proclamation there. His grandson, Charles, used the intimate notes Hamlin's son had taken during the war to recount in his two-volume biography of Hamlin a meeting of the vice president and Lincoln at the Soldiers' Home in mid-June 1862. This was a surprising month before Lincoln would reveal his intentions to issue a proclamation to Secretary of State William Seward and Secretary of the Navy Gideon Welles as the three men rode in a carriage to the funeral of Edwin Stanton's infant son, James.

On June 18, 1862, Hamlin was with Lincoln at the White House, and mentioned that he planned to leave later that day for Maine on a brief visit. Lincoln's reaction startled Hamlin at first. "I order you to sit in that chair, and afterwards ride with me to supper," Lincoln said, then laughed. "In a short time," Hamlin continued,

> the President and Vice President, escorted by a file of soldiers, rode horseback out to the Soldiers' Home. . . . After supper, President Lincoln invited Vice President Hamlin into his library, and after locking the door . . . opened a drawer in his desk and took therefrom the first draft of the military proclamation freeing four million slaves. The President and the Vice President then sat down, and Mr. Lincoln slowly read the instrument over to his associate, after which he asked for criticism and suggestions. "There is no criticism to be made," Mr. Hamlin replied. "Oh, yes, there is; at least you can make some suggestions," answered Mr. Lincoln, laughingly, and he repeated his invitation. "Finally," said Mr. Hamlin, in his account of the interview, "I did make, I believe, three suggestions, two of which Mr. Lincoln accepted."

A letter marked "strictly private" from Lincoln to Hamlin six days after the preliminary proclamation was issued in September, reinforces the plausibility of this intimate revelation. The president was responding to Hamlin's letter praising him for issuing "the great act of the age," and was worried that "troops come forward more slowly than ever. . . . The North responds to the Proclamation sufficiently *in breath* but breath alone kills no rebels." Not long after that June 18 meeting, Hamlin had spent another night at the Soldiers' Home with Lincoln, bemoaning General McClellan's failure as commander of the Army of the Potomac. For some time Hamlin had thought McClellan should be removed, and a few weeks after his second Soldiers' Home meeting with Lincoln, the president had indeed let McClellan go.

Hamlin had wanted for a long time to move faster on emancipation than Lincoln did, but recognized years later, "I was more radical than Lincoln. I was urging him, he was holding back . . . and he was the wiser." This was typical of loyal Hamlin. He'd been no happier or busier as vice president than had John Adams, who'd hated the job. "I'm the fifth wheel of the coach," Hamlin felt. His chief utility may have been his reluctant willingness to give up his powerful Senate seat to balance the 1860 Republican ticket between East and West. When a different national political balance was thought to be needed in 1864, he was dropped at the last minute from the ticket in favor of Andrew Johnson, then military governor of Tennessee. Hamlin was stunned, and went to his grave in 1891 convinced by John Nicolay and others that Lincoln was too honest and too good a friend to have maneuvered behind his back to get him off the ticket. Others, it seems, did that. Noah Brooks noted that when Lincoln was told of Johnson's nomination, he "made an exclamation that emphatically indicated his disappointment thereat." John Nicolay wrote to Hamlin's son a few years after Hamlin died, "Mr. Lincoln stated to me that your father should be renominated at Baltimore; that privately and personally he would be pleased if the convention would renominate the old ticket of 1860." How different the nation's agonizing history after the Civil War might have been had Hamlin been the man to succeed Lincoln, not the humorless, rigid, unpopular racist Johnson.

Hamlin knew from experience that "Lincoln would not as a rule say what he thought or announce plainly what he intended to do." All through the summer of 1862 Lincoln seemed to want to throw people off the emancipation scent. His famous letter to Horace Greeley in late August ("My paramount object in this struggle is to save the Union, and is not either to save or destroy slavery.") was perhaps the most intriguing, subtle example. Lincoln's meeting at the Soldiers' Home with the Reverend Elbert Porter of the Dutch Reformed Church one July evening was typically diverting. Lincoln was still debating within himself the wisest formula for emancipation, which he had come to see, at the very least, as a military necessity. Lincoln hinted at a solution that night to Reverend Porter, but revealed only his appreciation of the complexities that lay behind what some considered too much caution on his part, others far too little. As Frederick Douglass put it later: "Viewed from the genuine abolition ground, Mr. Lincoln seemed tardy, cold, dull, and indifferent; but measuring him by the sentiment of his country, a sentiment he was bound as a statesman to consult, he was swift, zealous, radical, and determined." To Reverend Porter, Lincoln argued:

> This American slavery is no small affair, and it cannot be done away with at once. It is part of our national life. It is not of yesterday.

It began in colonial times. In one way or another it has shaped nearly everything that enters into what we call government. It is as much northern as it is southern. It is not merely a local or geographical institution. It belongs to our politics, to our industries, to our commerce, and to our religion. Every portion of our territory in some form or another has contributed to the growth and increase of slavery. It has been nearly two hundred years coming up to its present proportions. It is wrong, a great evil indeed, but the South is no more responsible for the wrong done to the African race than is the North.

The relatively anonymous but beloved nurse Rebecca Pomroy also witnessed Lincoln's struggles at the Soldiers' Home as he composed the proclamation. Lincoln considered Mrs. Pomroy "one of the best women [he] ever knew" and she saw a lot of the president during those critical summer months of 1862. A widow, who had lost three sons as well, Mrs. Pomroy had come to Washington in 1861 to volunteer as a nurse to the war wounded. She'd taken care of her sick husband long enough to think she'd qualify and she certainly did, distinguishing herself over the war years as a brave, immensely humane, strong-willed protector of her battered charges against corruption and cold hearts. Mrs. Pomroy had impressed even Dorothea Dix, the Union's formidable superintendent of nurses during the war. Dix had recommended Mrs. Pomroy to the president when he asked her to suggest the ideal person to take care of Tad Lincoln as he recovered from the typhoid that killed his older brother. From then on, Mrs. Pomroy was called again and again to the White House, and to the Soldiers' Home, to care for the Lincolns, for "holding up my hands in time of trouble," as he put it. Exhausted as she usually was from her hospital work, she went. Her most critical assignment was nursing Mary Lincoln at the Soldiers' Home in July 1863. Mrs. Lincoln had apparently jumped in panic from a runaway carriage after the coachman had fallen from his seat, which may have been deliberately loosened by a saboteur. She injured her head so badly that her son Robert Todd later said he believed her health had been permanently affected. Pomroy's strong character, and the confidence both Lincolns had in her, were such that her reminiscences about the Emancipation Proclamation, though compiled in her later years by Anna Boyden, have much validity.

One day Mr. Lincoln rode up from the White House to the Soldiers' Home and engaged Mrs. Pomroy in conversation upon the subject. He said I am having a hard struggle; this Proclamation is weighing heavily upon me night and day. I shall encounter bitter opposition, but I think good will come of it, and God helping me, I will carry it through. The next day, while taking her back to the hospital, it was the sole topic of his conversation. He was more cheerful, for he had finished writing the document the night previous.

Appropriately, the most vivid account linking the Soldiers' Home to the proclamation comes from an artist. Francis B. Carpenter arrived at the White House in February 1864, to work for six months on the now famous painting of President Lincoln reading his preliminary draft of the Emancipation Proclamation to the Cabinet on September 22, 1862. Carpenter had even moved into Lincoln's office from his studio in the State Dining Room, to sketch the president as he went about his daily business. Several years after Lincoln's murder, Mary Lincoln, fiercely protective of her husband's image, wrote to a friend of her indignation that Carpenter was daring to write about Lincoln on the basis of such short acquaintance. "To think of this strange, silly adventurer, daring to write a work entitled 'The Inner Life of Abraham Lincoln.' Each scribbling writer, almost strangers to Mr. L. [*sic*] subscribe themselves, his most intimate friend!" This was a rather sharp, not atypical, shift from her 1865 letter to Carpenter that mentioned "his unerring skill," her husband's "high respect," and revealed to Carpenter intimate details of the couple's last days together, which have been treasured by historians ever since. Mary had even sent Carpenter one of Lincoln's seemingly endless supply of canes on Christmas Day, 1866.

"It had got to be midsummer, 1862," Lincoln told Carpenter one day in Lincoln's "official chamber."

Things had gone from bad to worse, until I felt that we had reached the end of our rope on the plan of operations we had been pursuing; that we had about played our last card and must change our tactics or lose the game. I now determined upon the adoption of the emancipation policy, and, without consultation with, or the knowledge of the cabinet, I prepared the original draft of the

proclamation, and, after much anxious thought, called a cabinet
meeting upon the subject . . . I said to the cabinet that I had
resolved upon this step and had not called them together to ask
their advice but to lay the subject matter of a proclamation before
them, suggestions as to which would be in order after they had
heard it read. . . . Nothing was offered that I had not already fully
anticipated and settled in my own mind, until Secretary Seward
spoke . . . "I suggest, sir, that you postpone its issue until you can
give it to the country supported by military success, instead of
issuing it, as would be the case now, [following] upon the greatest
disasters of the war!" It was an aspect I had entirely overlooked.
The result was that I put the draft of the proclamation aside, as
you do your sketch for a picture, waiting for a victory. From time
to time I added or changed a line, touching it up here and there,
waiting progress of events. . . . Finally came the week of the battle
of Antietam. I determined to wait no longer. . . . I was then staying
at the Soldiers' Home. Here I finished writing the second draft of
the preliminary proclamation, came up on Saturday, called the cabinet together to hear it and it was published the following Monday.

By January 1, 1863, when the final proclamation was issued—
and it wasn't a sure thing at all in many minds that Lincoln really
would go through with it—he had done more than "touch it up," a
painterly phrase more likely the artist's than the politician's. He'd
made significant changes from a very first draft he'd read to the cabinet on July 22, even from the preliminary proclamation Lincoln
announced publicly on September 22.

Endorsing the enlistment of black men—free or freed—into the
Union army was a critical addition to the final version. Gone was the
president's long-fought-for but in the end fruitless conviction that
gradual, voluntary emancipation, with compensation to slave owners,
was the wisest, least chaotic way to destroy the institution. And after
considerable effort to find a place for emancipated slaves to emi-
grate to (his secretary, John Hay, thought that idea was "a hideous,
barbarous humbug") Lincoln had also dropped the idea of colonization (although the concept may in fact have been another of Lincoln's shrewd ways to prepare the public for the more realistic solution, "the sugar around the pill of emancipation"). Blacks were not
interested in leaving the country they had contributed so much to

African American soldiers were vital to the Union victory.
More than 186,000 served in the Union army and navy, and
38,000 gave their lives in the Civil War.

build, including the White House, the Capitol, perhaps even Riggs's villa. By then, all but 1 percent of the blacks in the country were native-born. "Our minds are made up to live here, if we can, or die here, if we must," said Frederick Douglass.

So Lincoln had finally played that last card he described to Carpenter. It had not been easy. On record for years against slavery—"a great moral wrong ... an unqualified evil"—Lincoln had for a long time been convinced that slavery would die out on its own by the end of the century if it was confined to the states where the Constitution left it legal, holding tenaciously to the position that the Constitution did not allow its abolition where it already existed. But as

commander in chief of a nation at war, emancipation could be justified as a military necessity, a legitimate use of his war powers, if he
dared use it.

Joshua Speed, who shared a room with Lincoln in Springfield,
and was perhaps his closest friend, believed that "Lincoln saw the
necessity for [the proclamation] long before he issued it. He was
anxious to avoid it—and came to it only when he saw that the measure would subtract from [the Confederate] labor force and add to our
army quite a number of good fighting men." Slave labor was arguably the Confederacy's most valuable weapon: slaves worked in the
mines, the factories and the cotton fields, and served on the front
lines in vital support capacities. "The Negroes are part of the enemy,"
said one Northerner. "We shall be whipped as sure as fate, if we
fight with one of our hands tied behind our backs." Lincoln eventually realized that. After they had begun to fight later in 1863 for the
Union, which had been badly battered time and again for two years,
he said to those who were still reluctant or opposed, "Keep [the
power of the black soldier] and you can save the Union. Throw it
away and the Union goes with it."

Anna Harrison Chase remembered during her visit to the Soldiers' Home how ecstatic she was when she heard the news of the
proclamation. "How we laughed and cried when he set the slaves
free." But Lincoln really hadn't done that. The proclamation affected
only those slaves in precisely identified parts of rebel-held territory.
The eight hundred thousand slaves in the states that had remained
loyal to the Union were not covered by it. Lincoln had not wanted
to risk losing their political support, their resources, or their strategic
locations to the Confederacy. But he had finally given up trying to
persuade them to accept the idea of gradual, voluntary, compensated
emancipation. They wouldn't. It was time to take the chance, and
his timing was right. "It is my conviction," Lincoln wrote later, "that
had the proclamation been issued even six months earlier than it
was, public sentiment would not have sustained it."

Some of the more ardent abolitionists were disgusted with the
proclamation, forgetting that the Declaration of Independence had-
n't resulted in the colonies' immediate liberation, either. Lydia
Maria Child, a sharp-tongued, dauntless Boston author who'd been
fighting hard for years for immediate emancipation of all slaves, and

who'd volunteered to nurse John Brown after he was wounded at Harper's Ferry, wrote, "The ugly fact cannot be concealed that it was done reluctantly and stintedly, and that even the degree that was accomplished was done selfishly; was merely a war measure, to which we were forced by our own perils and necessities." But many other leading antislavery men and women—Harriet Beecher Stowe, author of *Uncle Tom's Cabin*, the so-called "slave poet" John Greenleaf Whittier, Henry Wadsworth Longfellow, an admirer of Lincoln, who was moved to tears by his poetry, and many other cultural leaders of the day—were enthusiastic. "A great day," wrote Longfellow in his diary January 1, 1863. "The President's Proclamation for Emancipation of Slaves in the rebel States goes into effect. A beautiful day, full of sunshine, ending in a tranquil moonlight night. May it be symbolical." His hope was justified. The goal of the war had now been radically enlarged, and people began to realize it whether they liked it or not. Even Lydia Child eventually admitted that she had "constantly gone on liking [Lincoln] better and better." To the opposition, it was "a bloody, barbarous, revolutionary, and unconstitutional scheme." An anti-administration Pennsylvania paper raised a widespread concern that it was "a cold-blooded invitation to insurrection and butchery."

What about the African Americans, those who were already free, and the freed to be? In his monthly paper, Frederick Douglass, the most famous of them all, gave it a mixed review, but a few months later called it "the greatest event of our nation's history." Slave George Payne poignantly rejoiced quietly, "for I am free or will be in a few minutes." The Washington correspondent of the black Philadelphia paper, the *Christian Recorder,* spoke for the voiceless, some of whose property value, to owners oblivious to human dignity, had even been sometimes pitifully assessed at as little as fifty cents, or as useful chiefly as human gambling chips. He more than made up for Lincoln's uncharacteristically but purposely flat prose: "That proclamation, over which the triumphant notes of heaven rolled along the confines of bliss, with evidences of higher ecstasies, than customarily, reverberated in overpowering rapture, across the boundaries of light and felicity, will tell upon the annals of eternity in character, of such splendor, as shall gild the name of Abraham Lincoln forever."

The eminent twenty-first-century historian Edna Greene Medford puts it in more dispassionate terms: she writes that African Americans of the time saw the proclamation as "a document with limitless possibilities" not only as establishing a goal for themselves, but as a goad to white America to live up to the idea of equality for all. "They . . . embraced it as a sort of blueprint for complete freedom . . . a watershed in their quest for human dignity and recognition as Americans." Reverend Martin Luther King Jr. agreed: "This momentous decree came as a great beacon of hope to millions of Negro slaves who had been scarred in the flames of withering injustice." And they kept their peace.

What did Lincoln himself think? In time, according to artist Carpenter, he came to see the proclamation as "the central act of my administration and the great event of the nineteenth century." But in November 1862, Lincoln admitted to his good friend, Admiral John Dahlgren, that "it would not make a single Negro free beyond our military reach." One foot soldier agreed: "That *Rebel* Back Bone Breaker of Old Abe's, is one of the harmlessest things Ever written on paper." Captain Aldace Walker of Vermont, stationed with his troops at Fort Stevens just north of the Soldiers' Home, agreed. In one of the 288 letters he wrote to his family during the war, he said, "I very much doubt the effect of the Proclamation." Lincoln said to another visitor who had roused him from bed with important news about rebel activities in Canada, "It's a paper bullet after all, and of no account except we can sustain it . . . we must make it effective by victories." The one hundred eighty-six thousand black soldiers who eventually served in the Union army and navy contributed vitally to those victories.

But there were times when it seemed that the Union could *not* sustain it. Southern independence was still a distinct possibility as late as the gloomy, battle-weary midsummer of 1864, when Lincoln had about given up on the likelihood of his reelection in the fall. Even if he did win, Lincoln knew that his powers as commander in chief, which had allowed him to issue the proclamation as a military necessity, would be gone when the war was over—no matter how it ended. From the start, in fact, there were challenges to its legality. "The courts had always been the ghost at the emancipation banquet." So Lincoln began to work hard for a constitutional amendment—the thirteenth—which would assure without question that slavery would be abolished everywhere, for good. When he was reelected in November 1864, on the strength of critical Union victories, the chances of the amendment getting through were improved. Longfellow wrote in his diary, "Lincoln elected beyond a doubt. We breathe freer. The country will be saved." Lincoln didn't have to sign congress's resolution, but he did, on February 1, 1865. "This amendment," he said, "is a King's cure for all the evils. It winds the whole thing up." We know now that he spoke too soon.

There has never been any doubt about Lincoln's hatred of slavery. A blind man can see where the President's heart was, said Frederick Douglass. In his short campaign autobiography, Lincoln noted that his family had left his boyhood home in Kentucky for Indiana "partly on account of slavery." "If slavery is not wrong, nothing is wrong," could have been his mantra. Lincoln's quieter actions as president, before and after the proclamation, such as his refusal in February 1862 to stay the hanging of an American ship captain involved in the still flourishing slave trade, and his pushing for a treaty with Great Britain that summer allowing search of ships flying the American flag that might be carrying slaves, reaffirmed that.

But Lincoln left a trail of statements about racial equality that are used even today to support the argument that he could not accept it. Countering that is the consensus among leading Lincoln scholars, built over the past half century, that Lincoln did come to the idea of racial equality slowly, that in the White House he outgrew what prejudice he had, and that he was a symbol of man's ability to do so.

In his July 10, 1858, debate with Stephen A. Douglas, Lincoln had said that "in relation to the principle that all men are created equal, let it be as nearly reached as we can." The war, and the black community Lincoln got to know in Washington, helped Lincoln reach closer to that principle himself. "I may advance slowly, but I don't walk backward," he said. Back in Springfield that wasn't easy. By 1860, there were just 311 free blacks in the whole of Sangamon County. Illinois itself, a free state in name, could nevertheless be rabidly proslavery. So Lincoln's opportunities for direct acquaintance with blacks was limited, and in his extensive, flourishing law practice he had defended slave owners as well as blacks.

But then there was William de Fleurville, better known as Billy the Barber, a lively Springfield entrepreneur and civic leader, who shaved Lincoln (fifteen dollars for one year's worth) and trimmed his coarse, unruly hair for years. De Fleurville had fled slavery in Haiti, and was one reason "Lincoln had such confidence that the [freed] Negro would become a good citizen." In fact, the editor of the *Illinois State Journal* maintained that de Fleurville was one of just two men in Springfield who understood Lincoln (the other was Lincoln's law partner, William Herndon). Billy's barbershop was a favorite Lincoln hangout, and de Fleurville's colorful promotions were made to order for Lincoln's amusement:

> I am personally friendly to all the candidates in the approaching election. No one of them has any reason to fear my opposition. I shall exert myself to secure the election of them all. To effect this object, I would say to them that nothing is so necessary as to have "a smooth face." I am adept at making smooth faces. My terms are very moderate. I shall rise in price on some after the election.

> Old bachelors, under the operation of Billy's skill can be made to look ten or twenty years younger than they really are; thus they may at the eleventh hour, secure for themselves a wife and a dozen of little ones.

The nation's capital was another story altogether. When the Lincolns arrived in early 1861, free blacks far outnumbered the slave population, 11,131 to 3,185. This was a stunning reversal from 1800, when the ratio was 3,244 slaves to 783 free blacks. Slave trading in the District, with the appalling pens, auction houses, and shuffling coffles that Lincoln could hardly avoid seeing during his term as a freshman congressman from Illinois, had been outlawed in 1850. Just the year before, in 1849, he had introduced into the House of Representatives a resolution to abolish slavery altogether in the District. But that would not happen until 1862, and by an act of Congress, not by President Lincoln.

George Riggs, builder of the Soldiers' Home cottage the Lincolns loved, took advantage of Congress's action and filed a claim of fifteen hundred dollars as compensation for the emancipation of two of his slaves, Anthony and Mary Belt. Mary, Riggs wrote, was worth one thousand dollars of that, because Anthony had asthma and was not as able to earn as much as she could. Riggs did want Anthony to get the five hundred dollars he was felt to be worth. Nine of the 966 compensated slave owners in the District were blacks themselves. One received $2,168.10 for his slaves, very likely most if not all of them family members he wanted to liberate. Three thousand slaves received their freedom at a total cost to the federal government of close to a million dollars. But that was 1862.

Even in 1861, when Vice President Hannibal Hamlin moved into the posh St. Charles Hotel, the proprietor could still assure slave-owning guests that "The proprietor of this hotel has roomy underground cells for confining slaves for safekeeping, and patrons are notified that their slaves will be well cared for. In case of escape, full value of the negro will be paid by the proprietor."

The Lincolns, however, moved into a White House and Soldiers' Home staffed by blacks who were already free. William Slade, discreet, even-tempered, ranked at the top: he was keeper of the White House keys, arranger of all White House functions, valet, confidential messenger, and friend, who sometimes spent the night talking to Lincoln when he was too worried to sleep. Slade's granddaughter Nibbie claimed that Slade collected so many of Lincoln's scattered notes for the Emancipation Proclamation, by the final draft he "already knew every word of it." Slade accompanied Lincoln to Gettysburg, and, again, knew what Lincoln was going to say because he'd listened to Lincoln rehearse his short speech. That effusive Washington correspondent of the *Christian Recorder* was pleased to call Slade "among the brightest gems in Washington." Slade led efforts within the black community to assist contrabands like Anne Harrison who poured into the city, and he helped organize black troops in the District for the Union Army. Tad Lincoln, lonesome for companionship his own age after Willie's death, played with Slade's children at the White House and at Slade's house, which was not far from the president's mansion. In fact, blacks, including White House butler Peter Brown, occupied a broad swath of the city that ran east to west just north of it. A number of black families clustered about Ford's Theatre on Tenth Street.

Mary Lincoln couldn't have run her end of the White House or the Soldiers' Home, either, without the black staff. She needed their competence and expertise to help launch her ambitious but ill-fated campaign to become an admired first lady. She worked closely with Cornelia Mitchell, the White House cook, and "was all over the kitchen." Slade's wife, Josephine, was a good friend. Mary gave her a handkerchief from a White House reception, and it's said she gave Mrs. Slade the dress she wore that night at the theater. William Slade washed Lincoln's body after the assassination, dressed it, and cut off a lock of hair.

Both Slades were light skinned, and so was Mary's dressmaker, Elizabeth Keckley, perhaps the most significant friend of Mary Todd Lincoln's White House years, and for a few disastrous years after. This phenomenon of skin color as a determinant of position in the black social structure was apparently new to the Lincolns, but it didn't take long for them to learn about its importance. The president had brought William Johnson with him from Springfield as his valet and messenger, and intended that he be the same at the White House and the Soldiers' Home. But Johnson was very dark, and in no time, the lighter-skinned White House staff made it clear he did not belong there. So Lincoln was obliged to find him a job somewhere else, admitting to Secretary of the Navy Gideon Welles that "the difference of color between him and the other servants is the cause of separation." Another free black, Solomon James Johnson, took Billy the Barber's place as the president's barber, until he went to clerk in the Treasury Department.

Elizabeth Keckley grew up a slave, but after thirty years of terrible physical and emotional abuse, she'd finally managed to buy her freedom and her son's, only to see him killed in Missouri in the war's early days. Mary Lincoln summoned her to the White House very soon after the Lincolns arrived, for she had always been intrigued by the latest fashions, always dressed fashionably, and wanted someone with Keckley's impeccable reputation and taste to outfit her properly for her campaign as first lady. The fact that Mrs. Keckley had made clothes for Varina Davis, wife of the man who was now Lincoln's nemesis, Jefferson Davis, president of the Confederacy, must have made Mary Lincoln all the more eager to engage her, which she did after just a short interview. Keckley was a striking woman, "who would have been an outstanding personality at a social gathering of Louis the Fourteenth," said one admirer. "Wherever

A former slave, dressmaker, businesswoman, and civic leader, Elizabeth Keckley became Mary Todd Lincoln's closest friend until her memoirs unintentionally ruined their relationship.

she went people would turn to admire her carriage. She was so much out of the ordinary in looks and dress, that people would . . . wonder what nationality she belonged to."

By 1861, Keckley was already a leader in the capital's black community, and had twenty women working in her atelier. Her seven-year relationship with Mary Lincoln was intense and complex. With the president, who called her Madame Elizabeth, it was mutually respectful, peacefully supportive. Through Keckley's influence with the president, and her extensive contacts in the white community, the legendary Sojourner Truth met with Lincoln in the White House. Keckley founded and led the Contraband Relief Association, which Mary was one of the first to support generously. Keckley was one of the few people Mary could bear to see after the assassination, and for six weeks she cared for Mary until the worst of the shock had worn off. Two years later Mary wrote, "Lizzie, I am frightened to death, being here alone. Come, I pray you, by *next* train." Mary had gone to New York under an alias, hatching her humiliating scheme to sell some of her White House wardrobe, and Keckley, at considerable cost to her own business, was offering patient and loyal assistance.

Their intimate friendship ended sadly a year after that, when Keckley, hoping "to place Mrs. Lincoln in a better light before the world," published her memoirs of *Life Behind the Scenes: Or Thirty Years a Slave and Four Years in the White House*. They had just the opposite effect. Mary felt betrayed, and never spoke to her again. Elizabeth Keckley "pined away," and died in Washington a poor woman in 1907. She was eighty-nine. Mary Lincoln's picture was one of the few things she'd kept in her simple room.

Frederick Douglass was surely the best known black American to visit the White House, and his invitation to "take tea" at the Soldiers' Home evidently made such an impression on him he mentioned it in his short essay for the book *Reminiscences of Abraham Lincoln by Distinguished Men of His Time*. Lincoln and Douglass met for the first time in August 1863, so it is possible that Lincoln may have read the first of Douglass's autobiographies, published in 1845. He surely knew of Douglass's *Monthly*, one of the black publications that helped to shape national opinion on issues critical to the black population. Douglass had always been a thorn in Lincoln's side and stayed one, even after Lincoln's death, insisting that blacks were "only Lincoln's stepchildren." But in those same *Reminiscences*, Douglass, like Keckley, admitted:

> In all my interviews with Mr. Lincoln, I was impressed with his entire freedom from popular prejudice against the colored race. He was the first great man that I talked with in the United States freely, who in no single instance reminded me of the difference between himself and myself, of the difference of color, and I thought that all the more remarkable because he came from a State where there were black laws. I account partially for his kindness to me because of the similarity with which I had fought my way up, we both starting at the lowest round of the ladder.

In his own time, Douglass came to see what Hannibal Hamlin and many others saw, that "Had [Lincoln] put abolition of slavery before the salvation of the Union, he would have inevitably driven from him a powerful class of the American people and rendered resistance to rebellion impossible."

Douglass thought that Mary Lincoln was perhaps freer of racial prejudice than was Lincoln. He also believed that it was a "great injustice" to accuse her of being antiabolition. Douglass was one of her few supporters after the assassination, but Mary turned down his offer to lecture on her behalf. Perhaps in appreciation of his criticism of those who ignored her when she was no longer in a position to do them favors, Mary Lincoln did send him one of Lincoln's canes, for which he thanked her, calling it "an object of sacred interest."

Jane Grey Swisshelm, who'd been quite openly contemptuous of both Lincolns, came to the same conclusion as Douglass after she'd met them. She decided that Mary was "more radically opposed to slavery" than her husband, and had "urged him to Emancipation as a matter of right long before he saw it as a matter of necessity." In her autobiography, Swisshelm concluded, "I recognized Mrs. Lincoln as a loyal, liberty-loving woman, more staunch even than her husband in opposition to the Rebellion and its cause, and as my very dear friend for life."

The activities and accomplishments of the free blacks they saw on their carriage rides in downtown Washington, on their way to the Soldiers' Home, and even north of it, must have strengthened their positive feelings toward racial equality, as did the courage of the black servicemen whose longstanding eagerness to fight for the Union was finally satisfied soon after the Emancipation Proclamation took effect. The Lincolns would have passed the elegant, "palest" Fifteenth Street Presbyterian Church, where both Elizabeth Keckley and William Slade were prominent members, and the antislavery lecturer and editor Reverend Henry Highland Garnet presided.

They also would have passed the mansion of Alfred Lee, who was becoming rich in the grain and feed business, and the fine hotel run by James Wormley ("the rich negro on I Street. How much the negroes of this city owe to him," said William Doster, the city's provost marshal), where the English novelist Anthony Trollope stayed during his North American travels. The Lincolns would have ridden by some of the 165 other black-run businesses in the city, noticed the many black workers at the Navy Yard, and realized that others in the city were working as bakers, carpenters, nurses, educators, blacksmiths, hairdressers, dressmakers, restaurateurs, and shoemakers. They would surely have been aware of the black churches located in Georgetown, on Capitol Hill, on Vinegar Hill (now Brightwood), the oldest free black community in the city, all vigorous centers of education, political activism, social cohesion, and support in a still very hostile environment. As passionate as Lincoln was about self-improvement, he must have realized what Mary's superior education had contributed to the fulfillment of their ambitions, convincing him that education would be a key ingredient of black survival in postwar America. The Lincolns must have been impressed by the over eleven hundred black children who were attending at least fifty-two schools run by blacks in the city, some of them in operation for years, and they were hopeful about the success of the first public school set up for black children in 1862.

Despite the excruciating pressures of war, Lincoln followed the tradition of presenting prizes to public school children at the Smithsonian Institution. In one of his visits to his friend and science adviser, Dr. Joseph Henry, the institution's first secretary, Lincoln might very well have met Solomon Brown, a confidant of the Smithsonian's assistant secretary, Spencer Baird. The persistent Washington correspondent of the *Christian Recorder* saw Brown as "really the colored *philosopher* of the United States," a kind of Renaissance man who was also a published poet, lecturer on geology to black audiences, organizer of black history tours, and contributor of specimens of local flora and fauna to the Smithsonian's growing collections.

Even before Lincoln came under fire from rebel troops at Fort Stevens in July 1864, he may have been aware that some of the land—eighty-eight acres commandeered by the government to build the fort—had been owned by a free black farmer, Mrs. Elizabeth Thomas, and that her own house, along with those owned by other blacks in the Vinegar Hill area north of the fort, had had to be destroyed to build the fort's breastworks. Mrs. Thomas's stone basement was then used for ammunition storage, and some claim that it was she who gave that famous yell to the president to get down before he got shot along with the man who had been standing next to him. Mrs. Thomas was understandably distraught over the destruction of her life savings, and Lincoln, it's said, promised her that she would be repaid. He died before he could fulfill that promise, and there is no record that she ever was repaid.

In his many visits to the contraband camps, Lincoln probably never met Anna Harrison, who revered him still at the Soldiers' Home all those decades later. We know that he often visited the camp off Seventh Street not far from the Soldiers' Home, and near

Solomon Brown, the first African American employee of the Smithsonian Institution, was an accomplished poet and a prominent member of the sizable free black Washington community.

what is now Howard University. There he did get to know another escaped slave, Aunt Mary Dines. Like many slaves, she had been freed by her master in his will, only to be sold after his death by his relatives. The family that bought her taught her to read and write, so in her contraband camp Mary became a valuable scribe. She was a fine soprano, too, and Lincoln stopped by, sometimes by himself, sometimes with Mary Lincoln and other notables, to listen to her and the contrabands sing hymns and slave songs. He even joined in, and with a good voice, they said. "Well, Mary," he would say before going back to the Soldiers' Home, "what can the people sing for me today? I've been thinking about you all since I left here and am not feeling so well. I just want them to sing some more good old hymns for me again. Tell Uncle Ben [a slave preacher, the oldest man in the camp] to pray a good old fashioned prayer." They did, and Lincoln wept. "He was no President when he came to camp," Aunt Mary said. "He just stood and sang and prayed just like all the rest of the people."

And that is perhaps at the root of it all, what compelled that "large-hearted man"—as Douglass put it—to move as he did, slowly but surely, toward equality for all, with the help of the free and the freed themselves. He knew that the chance to do what he had been able to do with his life, once he'd freed himself from the bondage imposed on his labor by his father ("I used to be a slave," Lincoln said in an early speech), must be the right of everyone. On it depended the success of the American experiment in democratic government, "whose leading object is, to elevate the condition of men—to lift artificial weights from all shoulders—to clear the path of laudable pursuit for all—to afford all an unfettered start, and a fair chance in the race of life."

Had he not moved as he did, perhaps that experiment in which he believed so devoutly, and for which he suffered so mightily, might very well have failed.

CHAPTER 9

Poems on Slavery

THE POET HENRY WADSWORTH LONGFELLOW was among the eminent men and women of letters of New England who gathered in Boston on January 1, 1863, to celebrate Lincoln's Emancipation Proclamation. Longfellow's slave poems were written long before Lincoln worked on the proclamation at the Soldiers' Home, but given the Lincolns' fondness for his poetry (the couple borrowed "Song of Hiawatha" three times in three years from the Library of Congress), it's not too far-fetched to think that Longfellow's sad verses about slavery might have influenced the evolution of Lincoln's thinking.

When we think of the writings of Longfellow and the other literary giants of the midnineteenth century—John Greenleaf Whittier and Herman Melville—slavery and the Civil War are certainly not the first subjects that come to mind. The gentle, pastoral, familial images of Longfellow and Whittier and the harsh tales of the sea of Melville predominate. Only Walt Whitman is more clearly associated with the Civil War, although it may be his nursing work in Civil War hospitals and his passionate interest in Lincoln that we think of first.

Yet John Greenleaf Whittier was an impassioned and active abolitionist for thirty years, and has even been called "the slave's poet." As early as 1842, Longfellow wrote his *Poems on Slavery*. He, too, was an ardent abolitionist, an admirer of Lincoln who rejoiced at his reelection and whose poetry both Lincolns loved. Melville was so elated by the fall of Richmond that he wrote seventy-two poems that were published the year after the Civil War ended as *Battle Pieces and Aspects of the Civil War.* Walt Whitman's poems on the war appeared in 1865 as *Drum Taps,* and his ode to Lincoln, "When Lilacs Last in the Dooryard Bloom'd," is regarded as the greatest lamentation in American poetry. The poems here reflect the anguish and the horror of the conflict.

The Slave's Dream

Beside the ungathered rice he lay,
　　His sickle in his hand;
His breast was bare, his matted hair
　　Was buried in the sand.
Again, in the mist and shadow of sleep,
　　He saw his native land.

Wide through the landscape of his dreams
　　The lordly Niger flowed;
Beneath the palm-trees on the plain
　　Once more a king he strode;
And heard the tinkling caravans
　　Descend the mountain road.

He saw once more his dark-eyed queen
　　Among her children stand;
They clasped his neck, they kissed his cheeks,
　　They held him by the hand!—
A tear burst from the sleeper's lids
　　And fell into the sand.

And then at furious speed he rode
　　Along the Niger's bank;
His bridle-reins were golden chains,
　　And with a martial clank
At each leap he could feel his scabbard of steel
　　Smiting his stallion's flank.

Before him, like a blood-red flag,
　　The bright flamingoes flew;
From morn till night he followed their flight,
　　O'er plains where the tamarind grew,
Till he saw the roofs of Caffre huts,
　　And the ocean rose to view.

At night he heard the lion roar,
    And the hyena scream,
And the river-horse, as he crushed the reeds
    Beside some hidden stream;
And it passed, like a glorious roll of drums,
    Through the triumph of his dream.

The forests, with their myriad tongues,
    Shouted of liberty;
And the Blast of the Desert cried aloud,
    With a voice so wild and free,
That he started in his sleep and smiled
    At their tempestuous glee.

He did not feel the drivers' whip,
    Nor the burning heat of day;
For Death had illumined the Land of Sleep,
    And his lifeless body lay
A worn-out fetter, that the soul
    Had broken and thrown away!

          Henry Wadsworth Longfellow
          Poems on Slavery
          1842

Ball's Bluff
A Reverie

(October, 1861)

ONE noonday, at my window in the town,
    I saw a sight—saddest that eyes can see—
    Young soldiers marching lustily,
        Unto the wars,
With fifes, and flags in mottoed pageantry;
        While all the porches, walks, and doors
Were rich with ladies cheering royally.

They moved like Juny morning on the wave,
    Their hearts were fresh as clover in its prime
    (It was the breezy summer time),
        Life throbbed so strong,
How should they dream that Death in a rosy clime

Would come to thin their shining throng?
Youth feels immortal, like the gods sublime.

Weeks passed; and at my window, leaving bed,
    By night I mused, of easeful sleep bereft,
    On those brave boys (Ah War! Thy theft);
        Some marching feet
Found pause at last by cliffs Potomac cleft
    Wakeful I mused, while in the street
Far footfalls died away till none were left.

> Herman Melville
> *Battle Pieces and Aspects of the War*
> 1866

"Ein Feste Burg
Ist Unser Gott"

Luther's Hymn

We wait beneath the furnace-blast
    The pangs of transformation;
Not painlessly doth God recast
    And mould anew the nation.
        Hot burns the fire
        Where wrongs expire;
        Nor spares the hand
        That from the land
Uproots the ancient evil . . .

What gives the wheat-field blades of steel?
    What points the rebel cannon?
What sets the roaring rabble's heel
    On the old star-spangled pennon?
        What breaks the oath
        Of the man o' the South?
        What whets the knife
        For the Union's life?—
Hark to the answer: Slavery! . . .

Then waste no blows on lesser foes
    In strife unworthy freemen

God lifts to-day the veil, and shows
  The features of the demon!
     O North and South
     Its victims both,
     Can ye not cry,
     "Let Slavery die!"
  And union find in freedom? . . .

In vain the bells of war shall ring
  Of triumphs and revenges,
While still is spared the evil thing
  That severs and estranges.
     But blest the ear
     That yet shall hear
     The jubilant bell
     That rings the knell
Of Slavery forever!

          John Greenleaf Whittier
          1861

Pensive on Her Dead Gazing

Pensive on her dead gazing I heard the Mother of All,
Desperate on the torn bodies, on the forms covering
    the battle-fields gazing,
(As the last gun ceased, but the scent of the powder-
    smoke linger'd,)
As she call'd to her earth with mournful voice while
    she stalk'd,
Absorb them well O my earth, she cried, I charge you
    lose not my sons, lose not an atom,
And you streams absorb them well, taking their dear
    blood,
And you local spots, and you airs that swim above
    lightly impalpable,
And all you essences of soil and growth, and you my
    rivers' depths,
And you mountain sides, and the woods where my dear
    children's blood trickling redden'd,
And you trees down in your roots to bequeath to all
    future trees,

My dead absorb or South or North—my young men's
    bodies absorb, and their precious precious blood,
Which holding in trust for me faithfully back again
    give me many a year hence,
In unseen essence and odor of surface and grass,
    centuries hence,
In blowing airs from the fields back again give me my
    darlings, my immortal heroes,
Exhale me them centuries hence, breathe me their
    breath, let not an atom be lost
O years and graves! O air and soil! O my dead, an
    aroma sweet!
Exhale them perennial sweet death, years, centuries
    hence.

                         Walt Whitman
                         from *Drum Taps*
                         1865

CHAPTER 10

Lincoln's Secretary of War

PASSERSBY MUST HAVE STOPPED in their tracks at the strange sight outside the Soldiers' Home that summer evening, and one witness—just a child then—remembered it vividly even years later. There they were—the two most powerful men in the country—intent on a task even odder than the striking physical contrast between them: President Lincoln, a skeleton in a suit someone called him, towering at six feet four inches over his short and stocky secretary of war, Edwin McMasters Stanton. A sharp eye might have noticed that Stanton's black frock coat and tall beaver hat—given his interest in a neat, even dapper appearance, and Lincoln's total lack of interest in such matters—were in much better shape than Lincoln's. Only the president's whiskers appeared more carefully tended than Stanton's long, graying, tobacco-and-cologne-scented beard.

By the summer of 1862, just months after Lincoln appointed Stanton to his cabinet, the two men—so unlike in so many other ways as well—were working surprisingly well together. A warm friendship was developing. The mess that commanded their attention that evening at the Soldiers' Home was in fact a poignant symbol of their struggles to free themselves from the web of political rivalries, bureaucratic confusion, military ineptitude—and their own inexperience—that were hampering their efforts to organize and manage a total war that had no end in sight. The object of their concentration that evening was the plight of a small flock of peacocks that had become entangled in a cluster of cedar trees near Lincoln's cottage. The birds were a gift to Stanton's children; they and Tad were frantic when the peacocks wandered off and were lost for two days in woods nearby. To keep them from straying again, some of the old soldiers housed on the grounds had tied weights to cords on the peacocks' legs, and now these were caught in the branches. So the two men went carefully back and forth, unwinding the cords and arranging the small wooden weights so they'd slide off the branches easily, letting the peacocks fly to the ground without injury.

The intricate job done, the men walked away arm in arm, their children content, and the harried men beginning to relax at their Soldiers' Home cottages from the chaos that surrounded them in wartime Washington. The formidable Stanton even forgot his cares long enough one evening to play "mumble the peg" on the grass with his children and David Bates, once he had gone through the dispatches Bates had brought out to his cottage from the War Department Telegraph Office. For both Lincoln and Stanton there was nothing more important than their children's happiness, even, in Lincoln's case, to the point of overindulgence that sometimes dismayed others. They had grieved together, too, when their two boys, the infant James Stanton and eleven-year-old Willie Lincoln, died in 1862.

Lincoln had every reason to detest Stanton, yet in January that same year, he'd given him the most powerful post in his wartime cabinet. Stanton had been one of his harshest critics in the first year of the administration. A few months after Lincoln took office, Stanton had written to a friend, "There is no token of any intelligent understanding by Lincoln . . . or the crew that govern him, of the state of the country, or the exigencies of the times. Bluster & bravado alternates [sic] with timosity & despair—recklessness and helplessness by turns rule the hour. What but disgrace and disaster can happen?" To former president Buchanan, whom Stanton had served briefly and combatively as attorney general, he was no less scornful, blaming "the imbecility of the administration [for the] catastrophe of Bull Run, an irretrievable misfortune and national disgrace." Stanton had gone so far as to describe Lincoln to General

Rogers Groups were favorite tabletop decorations in Victorian parlors. In this "Council of War," Lincoln works with his great secretary of war, Edwin Stanton, and General Ulysses S. Grant. Illustration from the Chicago Historical Society.

McClellan as "the original gorilla." The insults went back even further. Stanton had humiliated Lincoln painfully back in 1855. By that time, Stanton was on his way to becoming one of the highest paid and best-known lawyers in the country, even better than Lincoln at colorful trial tactics. Once he'd swallowed some of the same poison his client was accused of having used, to prove his client couldn't have murdered the victim, because, as Stanton demonstrated, the victim would have thrown it up. In another critical case, he'd chartered a steamer to ram it full speed into a new bridge over the Ohio River, smashing the smokestacks and superstructure, all to prove the bridge was too low for larger river boats to reach Pittsburgh, a major terminus, where he now had his law office. Later, he'd come up with the idea of a plea of temporary insanity that saved the notorious Daniel Sickles's neck in his trial for the murder of his wife's lover.

Back in 1855, Stanton had joined a team trying a high-stakes patent-infringement case brought by Cyrus McCormick against John

H. Manny, a fierce competitor in the development of a mechanical reaper. Lincoln was invited on the Manny defense when it was thought the case would be tried in Illinois, and that a lawyer known well there might help the case. When the trial was moved to Cincinnati, Ohio, Lincoln's services became extraneous. Only he didn't know that, because it seems no one cared enough to tell him. When he appeared in Cincinnati, carefully prepared for the trial but ungainly, badly dressed, and carrying a blue cotton umbrella with a ball on the end of it, Stanton and his teammates made it painfully clear, again and again, "that long-armed creature" had wasted his time coming. Nevertheless, Lincoln decided he might learn something from Stanton's performance, and so he stayed, and did. William Herndon usually got a lively account of Lincoln's experiences at court when he got back to their law office, but this time, Herndon remembered, all Lincoln said was that he "had never been as brutally treated as by that man Stanton."

But Lincoln had a longer view. He'd become aware of Stanton's sometimes secret struggles as a member of Buchanan's cabinet to keep the wavering Buchanan from caving in to Southern demands that could destroy the Union both Lincoln and Stanton loved and would die to preserve. Always the politician, Lincoln also realized the utility of having a prominent Democrat in his cabinet. And he knew from that painful experience in Cincinnati just what he was getting: "He was," wrote William Stoddard,

> with [Stanton] long enough . . . to discover in him a peculiar executive ability, tirelessness, disregard of obstacles, and a ravenous capacity for the mastery of details, rare indeed among men, while the bluntness, directness, even the harshness amounting to brutality, were gifts eminently desirable in the Secretary of War of the United States during the years which were to follow. It was a certainty that men would have no ground whereon to accuse Mr. Stanton of favoritism or of paltering with treason and his official chief would never be in effect betrayed by weak-kneed subserviency. The latter consideration was almost beyond price in those days.

So it is perhaps easier to understand why Lincoln offered Stanton the job than why Stanton accepted it. He had been making a handsome living as a lawyer, but would have to make do with eight thousand dollars a year as cabinet secretary. His wife, Ellen, as ambitious as Mary Todd Lincoln and, like her, fond of the finest things, was spending his money on lavish entertainment and luxurious surroundings as fast as it came in. He was also supporting his mother and other relatives back in Ohio. And he realized that the severe asthma he suffered from all his life could be made unbearable by the strain of managing a war that was going badly. But Stanton himself gave the best answer as to why he quickly accepted Lincoln's offer. In a letter to his old friend Reverend Heman Dyer in May 1862, after five months on the job, he wrote,

> I knew that everything I cherish and hold dear would be sacrificed by accepting office, but I thought that I might help to save the country, and for that I was willing to perish. If I wanted to be a politician or a candidate for any office, would I stand between the Treasury and the robbers who are howling around me? Would I provoke and stand up against the whole Newspaper gang in the country and of every party, who, to sell news, would imperil a battle? I was never taken for a fool, but there could be no greater madness, than for a man to encounter what I do for anything less than motives that overleap time and look forward to eternity.

Stanton realized quite soon how wrong he'd been about Lincoln. "No men were ever so deceived as we at Cincinnati," he told an associate from the Reaper trial. Robert Todd Lincoln told of Stanton's weeping for days after Lincoln's assassination.

Lincoln had chosen his "Mars" well. "Without him I should be destroyed," he wrote to friends. Stanton thought of resigning several times, once in hopes of being appointed to the Supreme Court when Chief Justice Roger Taney died. Lincoln would have liked to do that, he said, but asked, "Where can I get a man to take Secretary Stanton's place?" Even after the fall of the Confederate capital, Richmond, in early April 1865, Lincoln said to Stanton, "It is not for you to say when you will no longer be needed here." It was Stanton who took firm hold until the shock of Lincoln's assassination had worn off the country. It was he who supervised the dressing of Lincoln's body. Fanny Seward wrote warmly in her diary of Stanton's kindnesses to her father and the family after he was gravely wounded by one of Booth's assassins.

Secretary Stoddard saw firsthand what Lincoln and Stanton grew to mean to each other over the four brutal years. "Between the two men, so different, so strangely thrown together, there grew to be a bond of mutual reliance which had in it a remarkable thread of personal, human tenderness." They shared dangers together, and hugged each other when good news came. Like Lincoln, wrote Francis Lieber, a prominent political thinker of the time, "Mr. Stanton never allowed the chariot of the war to run in the mere ruts of routine. He never withheld a fair trial from the many inventions of new weapons."

The irony of their close relationship—demonstrated so clearly that evening at the Soldiers' Home—is that Lincoln emerged from the war as the country's beloved martyr but the most neutral thing to be said even today about Stanton is that he was—and still is— "un-loved": "the vilest man I ever knew or heard of" . . . "a meddlesome, murderous quack" . . . "[an] evil genius" . . . "a dangerous foe." Even Stanton's own cousin, William, said, "I thought if anybody should treat me so [in a courtroom] I would want very much to shoot him." John Hay said he'd rather tour a smallpox hospital than ask Stanton for anything. Gideon Welles found him "mercurial, arbitrary, apprehensive, violent, and fearful, rough and impulsive, yet possessed of ability and energy." Frederick Douglass gently observed, "Politeness was not one of his weaknesses." Lincoln, who had enough enemies of his own, said, "I do not see how he survives, why he is not crushed and torn to pieces."

Lincoln is partly responsible for Stanton's unfortunate reputation. Years later, Stanton's eldest son, Lewis, explained what Lincoln had admitted himself. At a dinner for Robert Todd Lincoln in New Orleans in 1898, Lewis said that Mr. Lincoln

> brought out most clearly that an understanding existed, whereby a request or demand, made by delegations, influential men, Governors, Senators or Congressmen, that for the general welfare of the country or for political or military reasons could not be granted, and yet for political reasons could not be directly refused by him, was transferred to the Secretary of War. The President was perfectly well aware that the Secretary of War basing his answer on the laws governing the situation, military discipline or other material reasons would refuse the request and the matter would so end.

. . . You can readily see that this arrangement often saved President Lincoln from making enemies, but necessarily added to the many hostile to Stanton. . . . Stanton was the man who said "No" for the Nation.

Major A. E. H. Johnson, Stanton's private secretary, put this "good cop/bad cop" arrangement more poetically: "Lincoln's heart was greater than his head, while Stanton's head was greater than his heart." Lincoln once whimsically described the difference himself. "It has been a rule of my life that if people would not turn out for me, I would turn out for them. Then you avoid collisions." Or as Stanton's biographers put it, "Lincoln ploughed around obstructions . . . it was Stanton's habit to meet them head on."

Their relationship was not without strain. Stanton sometimes despaired of Lincoln's tenderheartedness, his administrative eccentricities, and his openness. Stanton was ruthless against political opposition and dissent. His disciplined management style was the antithesis of Lincoln's; he even admitted to colleagues that when Lincoln was away, "he was much less annoyed." He always arrived at cabinet meetings at the last minute, and "his entrance was the signal to proceed to business." He hated when Lincoln took precious time away from urgent matters to recite from one of his favorite humorists. He was ahead of Lincoln in wanting to get rid of General McClellan, in using black troops in the war, and on black suffrage. At least once he called Lincoln a damned fool. When Lincoln was told of this, he said, "Did Stanton call me that? Well, I guess I had better step over and see Stanton about this. Stanton is usually right." When Stanton sent messages out to the Soldiers' Home that Lincoln must return to the White House, Lincoln went, no matter what the hour. Mary Todd Lincoln and Stanton finally reached a truce after several run-ins, but he didn't always escape her sharp tongue. Stanton swore "joyously," but surely not in her presence.

Stanton thought that diaries and memoirs were a waste of time. So his sister, Pamphila, whose husband Christopher Wolcott was not the last to die of exhaustion working for Stanton in the War Department, tried to make up for Stanton's disregard for his legacy by saving (but never publishing) many of his letters. These reveal a softer side: generous, loyal, charming, and, unlike Lincoln, an outspoken

romantic "with boundless capacity for love." (Could Lincoln ever
have written to Mary as Stanton did to his wife, Ellen: "My thoughts
dwell upon you with deep, unutterable love"?) Lincoln knew that
"the man's public character is a public mistake," he told a colleague.
"[He] is utterly misjudged."

For a time at least, at the Soldiers' Home, and at Stanton's
refuge nearby, the two men could try to forget their responsibilities
as managers of a great war, which both believed must be kept under
civilian control, and must be won at all costs, however grim, to preserve the Union. There they could share their intense love of books
and poetry, their delight in the law, and their deep attachment to
home and family. And at least they could find some consolation that
the institution where the Soldiers' Home was located, one of the
thousand things under Stanton's charge, was "in fine order . . . the
inmates, 130 in number, seemed cheerful and contented. They are
all well clothed, and fed, and every means taken for their comfort."
Stanton stayed on as secretary of war after Lincoln's assassination,
recognized by some even then as "the greatest war minister of modern times." His dramatic success in 1863 directing the reinforcement
of beleaguered General William S. Rosecrans near Chattanooga with
twenty thousand troops in a matter of days is still seen as "the greatest transportation feat in the history of warfare up to that time . . .
the longest and fastest movement of such a large body of troops
before the twentieth century."

Stanton fought desperately for months with Andrew Johnson to
keep him from conceding too much to the defeated South, making
all the horrible sacrifices of the war seem useless, but he finally
relinquished his office in 1868 and was soon appointed to the
Supreme Court, his cherished dream. But he was too worn out to
take on the job, and died just a few days after his confirmation.

John Hay had written Stanton after the war ended, and his
words could serve as an epitaph for a man who is still much misunderstood, known, if at all, as the man who said as Lincoln died,
"Now he belongs to the ages." Hay wrote,

> Not everyone knows, as I do, how close you stood to our leader,
> how he loved you and trusted you, and how vain were all the
> efforts to shake that trust and confidence, not lightly given &

never withdrawn. All this will be [known] in time, of course, to his honor and yours. . . . It is already known, as well as the readers of history a hundred years hence will know, that no honest man has cause to quarrel with you, that your hands have been clean and your heart steady every hour of this fight, and that if any human names are to have the glory of this victory, it belongs to you among the very few who stood by the side of [Lincoln] . . . and never faltered in your trust in God and the People.

CHAPTER 11

Lincoln and the
Tools of War

Private Willard Cutter was so proud of his new rifle that even before he and the hundred members of Company K arrived at the Soldiers' Home to guard President Lincoln in late summer of 1862, he boasted in his very first letter home to Meadville, Pennsylvania, on September 4, 1862, "I have the best gun of our tent." Cutter's gun was an English-made Enfield rifle, and when he wrote home again a few days later on September 16 that he "made the best shot in the squad . . . hit very near center," he probably had no idea that kind of accuracy was just what would make the Enfield one of the most widely used infantry weapons in the Civil War.

There is little doubt that the president would have noticed exactly what kind of gun Cutter was carrying when he and the other members of the President's Guard saluted "Uncle Abe with present arms as he goes by every day to the city," as Cutter described his new role proudly to his mother on September 10, 1862. It was Lincoln's direct intervention, in fact, that got Enfields into the hands of Union troops as early as they did, for Lincoln was ardently, stubbornly interested in the tools of war as well as in the military strategies to win it. One of the unanticipated internal battles Lincoln had to fight in the first two years of the war as commander in chief was to see that the Union's army and navy became equipped with the most effective weapons. And he was concerned not only with getting much-needed improvements in the more conventional materiel but also in exploring the potential utility of an astonishing list of other weapons that reads even now as if he were arming a force for the next century rather than the nineteenth: machine guns, torpedoes, incendiary shells, rockets, submarines, and aerial reconnaissance. He even set up a secret project to develop a domestic alternative to niter, a critical substance for the making of gunpowder that the British controlled, and which made Captain Wilkes's seizure of the British vessel *Trent* such an explosive diplomatic affair. Lincoln was, in effect, throughout the war his own director of military research and development.

Visitors to the Soldiers' Home during the three summers he spent there reflected his intense interest: from the distinguished physicist and Smithsonian secretary Dr. Joseph Henry to the genial, trusting, and courageous commander of the Washington Arsenal, General George Ramsay, to the inventor of a new kind of rifle shell, John Absterdam, as well slightly shady arms peddlers such as Orloff A. Zane and Archimedes Dickson. It's possible, of course, that at times Lincoln might have regretted the installation of the latest communications technology—the telegraph—at the Soldiers' Home, but it's likely he hovered as closely over it there as he did at the War Department Telegraph Office.

Someone once described Lincoln as having more of Eli Whitney in him than Henry David Thoreau. He had been fascinated by machines, and how they worked, all his life. Once he even tried—with humiliating lack of success—to give public lectures on "Discoveries and Inventions." And he is the only president to have been awarded a patent, granted in 1849 for a device to float ships off shoals. Once he designed and whittled for Tad a toy cart that Henry Ford years later reportedly described as the "original forerunner of the steering system now developed to such high efficiency in the modern motor car."

Lincoln's private secretaries in the White House passed on to him three times as many letters from inventors than any other kind of correspondence, perhaps because these young men were not devoted to already available weapons, as were the "old fogies" in the military establishment, and because some of the ideas must have given Lincoln a much-needed laugh. William Stoddard described one: a man from Tolono, Illinois, presented Lincoln with his plan for "'a cross-eyed gun.' It was a two-shooter with diverging barrels [with which] he proposed to form a regiment of cross-eyed men who could sail up the Potomac and clean out the Rebels from both sides of the river at once.... 'I know enough cross-eyed men to make the regiment, and by thunder, Mr. Lincoln, I'm cross-eyed enough to be their colonel!'" Lincoln roared at the embarrassing failure of one experiment he witnessed, but he narrowly escaped death at another, when a rocket exploded close to him during a test at the Navy Yard.

The character Orpheus C. Kerr very early in the war found Lincoln's fascination with new ideas ripe for satire. "I went to the Navy Yard yesterday," Kerr began, "and witnessed the trials of some newly-invented rifle cannon. The trial was of short duration and the jury brought in a verdict of 'innocent of any intent to kill.'" After Kerr hears of several other novelties from the inventor, such as a scheme for seizing privateers with a pair of huge clamps, which would then hoist the ships up and into the Federal hatches, "the President's gothic features lighted up beautifully at the words of the great inventor, but in a moment they assumed an expression of doubt," and Lincoln was supposed to have disconcerted the inventor by asking what would happen if the enemy fired meanwhile.

One of the first visitors to the Soldiers' Home in the summer of 1862 may have been the commandant of the Navy Yard satirist Kerr mentioned, Captain John Adolph Bernard Dahlgren. Soon after the inauguration in March 1861, Dahlgren had become one of Lincoln's valued advisers on strategy as well as weapons, because he combined rare qualities that Lincoln needed so urgently at the time to get a huge war machine built from next to nothing: great intelligence, years of experience in the research and development of ordnance, an international reputation as the inventor of powerful naval gunnery, a shared contempt for red tape, and a mutual dislike of alcohol, not to mention an appreciation of the value to his own ambitions of a close association with the chief executive.

Dahlgren admired Lincoln, there is no doubt, despite occasional irritation at Lincoln's interest in "some inflammable humbug" or other, and Lincoln's habit of dropping in at the Navy Yard unannounced at least once a week to see "Dahl," because as Lincoln said, what he was doing there was "such a relief from politicians" at the White House. After the assassination, Dahlgren wrote, "I can say from an intimate acquaintance with the President that he was a man of rare sagacity—good genial temper and desirable firmness—that he possessed qualities of the highest order as a Ruler—indeed we know of no man so well fitted to carry the country through her trial."

Dahlgren was the striking antithesis of General James Ripley, Lincoln's chief of Army Ordnance, who labeled most new inventions that came his way as "a great evil [that] can only be stopped by positively refusing to answer any requisition for a proposition to sell new and untried arms and steadily adhering to the rule of uniformity of arms for all troops of the same kind." By the summer of 1862, Dahlgren had become so close to Lincoln that he came and went at the White House as he pleased, entertaining the president on river cruises on the Potomac, and with dinner at his house. Tad Lincoln was delighted with the miniature Dahlgren made for him of his famous eleven-inch gun, just as Lincoln had been when he first saw the gun fired at the Navy Yard on May 9, 1861.

Mary Todd Lincoln eventually felt comfortable enough with Dahlgren to confide that the president sometimes couldn't sleep at night. Polished courtier that he was (at least that's what Secretary of the Navy Gideon Welles thought of him privately), Dahlgren would never have replied that lack of sleep was nothing new for him. Typically, he'd almost lost his sight years before after nights of study, and in the space of six months in 1862, he had tested over sixty new ideas for weapons and gadgets, driving himself and his crews at the Navy Yard around the clock. Lincoln was intrigued and heartened by all that activity, given the inertia of so many of his military men, and sometimes he brought Mary Todd and the boys along on his visits. Lincoln and Dahlgren, like Lincoln and Stanton, would also share the anguish of the tragic deaths of beloved sons, Willie Lincoln and Ulric Dahlgren.

It's quite probable that on July 5, 1862, riding in Mary's carriage on the way out to the Soldiers' Home, the relentless Dahlgren hoped to put in another plea for a command at sea, or at least to enlist her to be on his side in getting one. He had desperately wanted such a command for a long time, because he knew that no matter how great his achievements in weaponry, heroism in combat was the only way to glory in the United States Navy. Realizing instantly after the *Monitor*'s historic battle with the *Merrimac* in Hampton Roads on March 9, 1862, that "now comes the reign of iron," Dahlgren even dared to ask Secretary of the Navy Gideon Welles to give him command of the *Monitor*. Welles had said no, that he'd be more useful where he was (and be less inclined to fall on his face) and on that July morning, Lincoln had backed Welles in his refusal once again to give Dahlgren a naval command. It took another year of pressure for Dahlgren to get what he wanted: command of the South Atlantic Blockading Squadron, "potentially the most prestigious berth in the fleet." And Dahlgren at last became a rear admiral, which Welles also didn't hesitate to say was a rank he gave Dahlgren only because Lincoln finally decided he should have it.

By 1863 ironclads had become such an integral part of the fleet that the name had become generic. Private Cutter of the President's Guard went to see one for himself at the Navy Yard. This one was named *Sangamon*, after the river that flowed past Lincoln's village of New Salem, Illinois. Cutter wrote his mother on November 25, 1863, that "it was worth seeing all underwater but 18 inches it had two guns in the turret one 11 inch an [*sic*] 15 inch [author's note: they were Dahlgren's] I went in the turret an down below I think it has left now for [they?] was to start for Charleston."

Lincoln had played a critical part in getting the original *Monitor* built. His interest in ironclads went way back to his days in Congress. In 1848 he'd sponsored a petition by inventor Uriah Brown to get a grant to experiment with such a concept. When John Ericsson's design for the *Monitor* was presented on September 10, 1861, Lincoln was all for it, against a whole array of naval officers young and old. His secretary Stoddard wrote later, "Mr. Lincoln had a right to express strongly, as he did, his satisfaction over the fact that he had given the *Monitor* a lift at the time when, without it, she would have remained an inventor's dream."

Thirty-five monitors, at four hundred thousand dollars apiece, would be built during the Civil War for the Union Navy, and Dahlgren guns were in the turrets that made people describe the vessel

The historic battle in March 1862 between the Union's first ironclad (left), "a tin can on a shingle," and the Confederate's Virginia *(the old* Merrimac*), "a floating barn," ended in a draw but changed naval warfare forever.*

"a cheesebox on a raft." Dahlgren himself had seven in his command, one or the other often serving as his flagship.

Lincoln came quickly to appreciate that for advice and insights on scientific and technological matters, it was fortuitous that the office of Dr. Joseph Henry at the new Smithsonian Institution was a short walk from the White House. They too became friends. Henry did not bother to attend one bizarre and unsuccessful signaling experiment between the tower at the Smithsonian Castle and the tower of a building near the Lincolns' cottage, but he did go out to the Soldiers' Home two years later, on August 24, 1864. David Bates from the War Department Telegraph Office and several colleagues at the Smithsonian demonstrated nighttime signaling from one tower to the other "by means of a calcium light, which could be displayed and screened at will by the use of a button, operated by hand, in the same manner as a telegraph key is manipulated, representing the dashes and dots of the Morse alphabet." This experiment was clearly a success.

Dr. Henry interested Lincoln in the military potential of balloons, and as a result, in the summer of 1861, together "they ushered into being the first successful military air force in American history." It began on June 11, 1861, when Henry brought Thaddeus Sobieski Constantine Lowe, a twenty-eight-year-old balloonist, to the White House. Lowe had already flown from Cincinnati to South Carolina, and tried several times to cross the Atlantic. On June 18, Lowe sent Lincoln a telegraph from a balloon about a half mile away from the White House, the first electrical communication from an aircraft to the ground. Then Lincoln brought Lowe to see General Winfield Scott, his seventy-five-year-old military adviser, who wasn't interested. A month later, a frustrated Lincoln insisted on action from Scott, and so Lowe got his "air corps." By 1862, it included seven airships, and a Navy vessel on the Potomac that could be called the nation's first aircraft carrier. Soon after first Bull Run, Lowe went aloft to see where the Confederate army had gone, and he conducted aerial observations and photo reconnaissance throughout McClellan's Peninsula Campaign and later battles. But by May 1863, his pay, his budget, and his staff had been so reduced by Major General Joseph Hooker that Lowe resigned and turned to other inventions and enterprises.

But not before Private Willard Cutter wrote to his mother May 25 and June 9, 1864, that Lowe was back in town with his balloon. "[It] goes up several times most every day [and it costs] five dollars for a trip . . . they have a rope attached to it and can let it go up and come down just as you like." Given his meager soldier's salary, it's unlikely Cutter took a ride, but he did satisfy his curiosity about science and technology when he wasn't on guard duty, by visiting the Patent Office (where he got weighed and saw the patents on display), and the Smithsonian Institution (December 28, 1863). "There is a lump of copper there that weighs 14,00 lbs [*sic*] then there is one room full of pictures of Indian Chiefs of different tribes and birds I seen a lump of lava and a lump of brimstone 18 inches through or more one could not see all the things in a week." Two years later (January 30, 1865) he wrote to his brother that "there was a big fire here last Tuesday, the Smithsonian Institute [*sic*] was burnt the upper story of the Main Building was destroyed with about all the things there was in them."

Private Cutter and some of the boys in the President's Guard were directly involved in setting up for one of Lincoln's last weapons experiments, this time with Alfred Berney's "liquid fire," which was so impressively effective on May 9, 1863, it brought out the city fire department. Cutter was understandably almost at a loss for words when he tried to explain what he saw to his brother a few days later (May 13, 1863). "The man lit a piece of paper and set fire to the oil there was a stream of fire as far as the pump could [throw?] . . . it made the biggest [*sic*] smoke I ever seen." After several abortive attempts to use incendiary shells against Charleston, Lincoln turned his attention away.

We think of Lincoln as so tenderhearted and compassionate that it is hard to recognize him as the man who said, "I won't leave off until it fairly rains bombs," or who told Grant to "hold on with a bulldog grip, and chew and choke as much as possible," or who was ecstatic about the success of General Sherman's march through Georgia and Carolinas (another Union general, Philip Sheridan, had said of his similar Shenandoah campaign that "a crow flying over it would have to carry its own rations"), or who made the first recorded purchase of machine guns in history.

Perhaps in doing so, Lincoln was thinking himself of what the designer of the *Monitor*, John Ericsson, said about another machine gun that Lincoln favored. It was a weapon so effective that it was "one of the many strides which mechanical science is now making to render war so destructive, long to continue the disgrace of civilization." Robert J. Oppenheimer would echo that thought a century later at the first test of the atom bomb.

CHAPTER 12

Lincoln's Quartermaster General

THE TOOLS OF WAR were of little value to Lincoln if the men and the means were not ready to use them. To see that they were was the awesome responsibility of Lincoln's quartermaster general, Montgomery Meigs. By July 1862, Meigs had become such a trusted adviser to Lincoln, he felt he had to ride out to the Soldiers' Home and wake up the president to share his concern about what General George McClellan was doing in his bogged-down effort to capture Richmond. By then, McClellan's Peninsula Campaign on the Virginia coast was, in Meigs's vehement opinion, a disaster. "The true cause," he wrote to his father a few days later, "is the false military move which placed an army in a narrow peninsula where it was easily checked by inferior forces until the gathering hordes of a barbarous people driven by a wide sweeping conscription enforced by a merciless military despotism . . . overwhelm(ed) our gallant freemen decimated . . . by malaria & mud & storms & toil."

There's little doubt Lincoln heard the same harsh evaluation that night. But by then Lincoln was accustomed to Meigs's straight talk—and his middle-of-the-night interruptions. Meigs had rushed to the White House at three in the morning of July 22, 1861, to report to Lincoln what he'd seen of the Union defeat at the Battle of Bull Run.

George McClellan may have been called "the Young Napoleon" by his admirers, but for Meigs, the real Napoleon set the standards he used throughout the war to judge his own operations. "[I now have] the fullest powers & more money & more means of war at my command ... than any other man since Napoleon," he wrote his father halfway through the war. And as the war came to its bloody close, Meigs wrote to his cherished wife, Louisa, that Sherman's army in Savannah was ready to march north with "such troops as would have made Napoleon ready to encounter the world." No one would have argued that Meigs himself had much to do with that achievement.

And yet, during the entire war, General Meigs, a brilliant West Point graduate, hadn't led soldiers in the field for more than two days. He had finally got his chance, and a minor one at that, defending a line not far from the Soldiers' Home during Jubal Early's July 1864 raid on Washington.

The war assignment Meigs preferred, and got from Lincoln in June 1861, was unglamorous and prosaic, but so vital to the war effort and so herculean in scale that Secretary of State William Seward said at the end of the war, "Without the services of this eminent soldier the National cause must either have been lost or deeply imperiled." A century and a half later, that evaluation hadn't changed: he was "the unsung hero of Northern victory," wrote Civil War historian James McPherson, "[creator of] the military machine that Grant and Lincoln were able to use to produce victory." In the first year of the war, that meant, for starters, buying five million pairs of shoes for an army that walked most of the way, employing ten thousand women at one supply depot alone to sew uniforms, organizing wagon trains full of supplies stretching as much as forty miles on a narrow road. "Pup" tents and standard sizes for uniforms were just a few of his corps' innovations that left their mark on the armies of the future.

Lincoln had never heard of Montgomery Meigs until shortly after the inauguration in March 1861, introduced by his new secretary of state, William Seward, Meigs's close friend from his earlier service in Washington. It didn't take him long to realize what a find Meigs was. In just three weeks, in a secret operation for Lincoln and

Lincoln's quartermaster general, Montgomery Meigs, was an "unsung hero of Union victory." His architectural and engineering achievements (in the background) still mark the nation's capital. Illustration courtesy of Picture History.

Seward in April 1861, Meigs had managed, over a distance of a thousand miles, to plan, provision, and execute a mission to secure Fort Pickens off the Florida coast for the Union as the war began at Fort Sumter. It was an extraordinary, if highly controversial, feat of daring, speed, and logistical inventiveness. During a tour with Seward and Meigs of the new Washington Aqueduct the following month, Lincoln had learned of Meigs's achievements in Washington in the 1850s. He'd had charge of spending eight million dollars of public money on two enormous projects, and had accounted for every penny. Not only had Meigs designed and built the aqueduct, which was now providing the capital with an ample and urgently needed daily supply of fresh water, he had overseen the ambitious extension and rich decoration of the Capitol building, and engineered the start of construction of its new cast-iron dome. In another of the war's many ironies, Jefferson Davis, secretary of war in 1860 and, at that time at least, a great man in Meigs's opinion, said Meigs "was both constructor and architect [of the Capitol extension] in fact, though he never took the name."

Lincoln was impressed by all this. "I do not know one who combines the qualities of masculine intellect, learning and experience of the right sort, and physical power of labor and endurance so well as he." He got what he wanted: Meigs would be his quartermaster general. Meigs believed that was a better use of his brains and skills than field command. An experienced engineer, he preferred a very different battlefield. He couldn't wait to take on "the present already rotten system" of contracting for the staggering variety and volume of supplies the Union army would need for the next four years: from shoes for men, mules, and horses, to hay and harnesses, wagons and hospitals, even to ships, railroads, and bridges. Corruption had become so bad before Meigs took over on June 16, 1861, particularly in the West under John C. Fremont's command in St. Louis, that by July a special committee of the House of Representatives was already holding hearings, and what it found filled a two-thousand-page report a year later. In no time the press was reporting that "the Quartermaster General Meigs is admirably managing the thieves and plunder mongers who infest Washington." Later, one historian summed it up: "By the late summer of 1861, the United States possessed an army of half a million, rationally organized and probably as well or better supplied and equipped as any army in history."

Meigs hadn't known much about Lincoln either when they first met, but what he'd read in the press hadn't impressed him. "I hope the prints do him injustice. He certainly does not seem to come much to the level of the great mission. I fear that a weak hand will command the ship." The next day, he heard Lincoln's inaugural address and changed his mind. "It was a noble speech as delivered, delivered [*sic*] with a serious & solemn emphasis befitting the occasion. . . . No time was wasted in generalities or platitudes . . . each sentence fell like a sledge hammer driving in the nails which maintain states . . . the impression is favorable. Treason sank out of sight & loyalty sat in the sun light. The country is safe though there is yet tribulation . . . on it."

Tribulation for Meigs would come in many more forms than unscrupulous contractors. At times, he and Lincoln despaired—for money, men, military success. Lincoln even came to Meigs's office one day, crying, "What shall I do?" But Meigs's weapons were powerful: a ferocious belief in the righteousness of the Union cause, and a willingness to use harsh means to protect it: "Did I command the army which will take [Charleston] I should be sorely tempted to go through the ancient ceremonial & literally plow up its foundations & sow them with salt."

Even more effective were his stunning competence and his renowned integrity ("too damned honest," said J. B. Floyd, James Buchanan's secretary of war). Secretary of War Stanton was so confident of Meigs's ability to accomplish any task, he said he'd sign his name at the bottom of a piece of paper and Meigs could write above it "what he would." General William Tecumseh Sherman felt the same. "The handwriting of this report is that of General Meigs, and I, therefore, approve it, but I cannot read it." By the end of the war, Meigs had overseen "the spending of one and a half billion dollars, about half the direct cost of the Union war effort."

Lincoln and Meigs were temperamental opposites, but they worked together well. To Lincoln, the South was not the enemy, but to Meigs it certainly was, particularly after the murder of his soldier son, John, by Southern guerrillas. Lincoln could tolerate Meigs's short fuse, a temper so hot that Secretary of War Simon Cameron, Stanton's feckless predecessor, admitted to Meigs himself that he was afraid of it. Meigs on the other hand thought Lincoln's "considerable firmness . . . generously yields too often to his kindness." But he liked Lincoln's "fresh sense & honesty . . . which it [was] always pleasant to come into contact with . . . he honestly str[ove] to bring out a happy result the restoration of peace & union."

Meigs was not above chiding the president with interference in the performance of his job (once for suggesting a candidate for a position with the Quartermaster Corps). "I trust that the President will not permit the recommendation of any person's friends to induce him to interfere."

Meigs stayed at Lincoln's bedside until he died, and as he, General Grant, and an honor guard took the coffin to Union Station, Meigs said, "The last of our great and good President left the city. He will live in history with Washington. The one connects his name with republican liberty. The other with personal liberty & emancipation."

Meigs stayed on as quartermaster general until 1882. His farewell to the Corps was eloquent and telling.

> It moved vast bodies of soldiers over long miles; it collected a fleet of over 1,000 sail of transport vessels upon the great rivers and upon the coast; it constructed and equipped a squadron of ironclads which bore an important part in the operations in the coast . . . it supplied the army while organizing and while actively campaigning over long routes of communication by wagon, by rail, by river, and by sea, exposed to hostile attack and frequently broken up by the enemy; and having brought to the camps a great army, it, at the close of hostilities, returned to their homes a million and a quarter men.

We can still sense Meigs's imposing presence in Washington at three of his post–Civil War creations: Arlington Cemetery, which Meigs chose as a location when the graveyard at the Soldier's Home ran out of space, the Smithsonian's Arts and Industries Building, and what is now the National Building Museum. Such was Meigs's reputation still that he was mentioned specifically as the principal in congressional bills approving the construction of both structures, and Lincoln's only surviving son, Secretary of War Robert Todd Lincoln, made sure that he was.

CHAPTER 13

Lincoln as Commander in Chief: The Soldiers

ON MAY 18, 1861, a Mr. Robert Colby of New York City wrote the new president a very long letter—with a multitude of exhortations in it for improving his image as commander in chief. "For God's sake," Mr. Colby urged, "consult somebody, some military man as to what you ought to do [when you are] in military presence . . . the Commander in Chief of the armies of the United States . . . must pretend to be a soldier Even if he don't know any thing of tactics at all—You had better let some officer put you through a few dress parades in your leisure moments, if you can get any, and get some military habit on you so you shall feel natural among military men— Don't let people call you a goose on these *very, very* important relations to the Army."

If the indignant but well-meaning Mr. Colby lived through the next four years of war he would have realized how completely mistaken he was with his advice. It was precisely because of Lincoln's inability to be anything *but* himself that he became a successful commander in chief, judged by many historians to be the greatest of them all.

Lincoln had been in office just two and a half months when Colby wrote him. The war had begun on April 12, 1861, and already, while Congress was in recess, he had taken it on himself to call up well over a hundred thousand volunteers, using his constitutional powers as commander in chief. It was painfully clear to him that the tiny, totally unprepared regular army of sixteen thousand troops he'd inherited, led by the heroic, wise, but tottering General Winfield Scott, now seventy-five ("If I could only mount a horse . . . but I am past that") would not be enough, even for a war that many assumed—until the Union army's rout in its first test at Bull Run—would be over in a few months.

Lincoln knew that whatever the country faced in the months—possibly years—ahead, he would need the goodwill of the ordinary soldier. He would have agreed with writer Colby on at least one thing, that "unless the spirit and loyalty of the soldiers are kept up and encouraged in every way, the country is to suffer immeasurably before these troubles are disposed of." So in those first frantic months, Lincoln did everything he could to make himself highly visible and supportive to them. By June, he'd managed to review tens of thousands of volunteers from all over the country, as they poured into the capital and paraded down Pennsylvania Avenue past the White House. Sometimes he stood smiling and waving as long as five hours, Walt Whitman observed, while thirty thousand men marched by. He'd gone out on the Potomac River to see one regiment arrive by boat, and as late as July 1864, he was even down at the Sixth Street wharf when reinforcements landed to save the city from Jubal Early's jab at the capital's northern edge, not far from the Soldiers' Home. By the time the war ended, he'd spent a total of forty-two days in the field with the Army of the Potomac, and he'd met individually with two thousand soldiers to hear their individual problems. Some may have grumbled or even laughed at his appearance or demeanor, as Colby had pointed out, but Lincoln was long since inured to ridicule.

By the time Company K of the 150th Regiment of Pennsylvania Volunteers arrived at the Soldiers' Home on September 7, 1862, to be the President's Guard—for the next three years, it turned out—Lincoln had so solidified his reputation as the common recruit's best friend, he was already "Uncle Abe" to Private Willard Cutter of Company K, in his second letter home to his family in the small town of Meadville, Pennsylvania (pop. fifteen hundred) on September 10, 1862. ("The Soldiers' Home is the nicest place I ever seen," Cutter added.) Not long after that, Lincoln had become an even

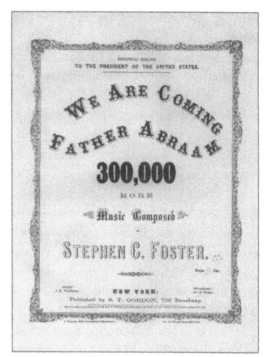

This song sold over 2 million copies, helping boost volunteer enlistments in the Union army. Civil War songs became increasingly sadder as the war dragged on.

closer relative to the troops. "Never," wrote biographer Ida Tarbell, "did a man better deserve a title than did he, the one the soldiers gave him, 'Father Abraham.'"

Lincoln's preparation for the role of commander in chief was minimal, compared to Confederate President Jefferson Davis's military credentials (West Point graduate, combat experience during the war with Mexico, impressive secretary of war under Franklin Pierce). He even mocked his own brief military service publicly. He said during his only term as congressman from Illinois in 1848:

> By the way, Mr. Speaker, did you know that I am a military hero? Yes, sir, in the days of the Black Hawk War I fought, bled, and came away . . . it's quite certain I did not break my sword, for I had none to break; but I bent a musket pretty badly on one occasion— by accident. . . . I had a good many bloody struggles with the mosquitoes, and although I never fainted from loss of blood, I can truly say I was often very hungry.

Underneath that farcical description of his eighty days as a volunteer back in 1832 was Lincoln's satisfaction that the men serving with him had chosen him as their captain over another more likely candidate. And from that brief experience, he learned how vital decent food and prompt pay were to soldiers' morale—or more accurately, how dispiriting—and more likely—the lack of both could be. For the rest of his life, he would take the side of volunteer soldiers and veterans. Four of the men of Company K spent their last years, in fact, in Soldiers Homes that had been established around the country with his encouragement.

When Congress got back in town in July 1861, Lincoln was ready with a request for four hundred thousand more men, arguing shrewdly against the likely criticism that "the people will save their government if the government will allow them. . . . So large an army as the government has now on foot, was never known before, without a soldier in it but who has taken his place there of his own free choice." (Of the two million men who ultimately served in the Union army, 94 percent would enlist as volunteers.) What was more, Lincoln told Congress, the caliber of the volunteer was such that from almost any regiment you could select "a President, a Cabinet, a Congress, and perhaps a Court, abundantly competent to administer the government itself."

The more isolated, intimate atmosphere of the Soldiers' Home made it an ideal place for Lincoln to take the measure of the citizen soldier in whom he had such faith. Company K's deportment and performance for three long years did little to shake it. In November 1862, when it appeared that the company might be reassigned to the front, or replaced by others wanting their privileged position, Lincoln wrote a short note:

> Whom it may concern: Captain Derrickson, with his company, has been, for some time keeping guard at my residence, now at the Soldiers' Retreat. He, and his Company are very agreeable to me, and while it is deemed proper for any guard to remain, none would be more satisfactory to me than Capt. D. and his Company.

(The slip of the pen in the word *retreat* perhaps reveals Lincoln's hope, ultimately dashed, for some peace for himself at the cottage, or perhaps his despair that retreat was too often the direction Union troops seemed to take in battle.)

Company K had finally arrived at the Soldiers' Home after a snafu typical of any army, especially one that had had to be built up almost from scratch. "We had orders to go to a fort about 7½ miles and was bout ½ mile of there and had orders to go back for [Stonewall] Jackson was in sight so we had to turn and go back to Washington for the night next morning we went 3 miles from the City and stoped for the day we thought but at 6 we had to march to where we are," wrote Private Cutter to his mother on September 10, 1862.

"Where we are" was a tent encampment for the hundred-odd men of Company K, located "in a small sloping field, or paddock, just outside of the neatly kept grounds of the Home, but in view of the buildings," wrote the regiment's historian later. The location had its grim aspect. "Less than one hundred yards from the Company Camp [is a cemetery] where two thousand Pennsylvanians are buried there was forty 2 one Saturday and Thirty one yesterday all die in the hospital." Private Cutter shared this sad information with his brother, who often seemed to get more bad news, and in stronger language, than did his mother.

Company K was fortunate. None of its men were buried there, and comparatively few even spent time in the hospital. Several military hospitals were located not far from the Soldiers' Home. The churches, government buildings, and private homes that had been converted to temporary hospitals at the start of the war by 1862 had been replaced by army tents or board barracks arranged all over the city in neat rows, sheltering, as Walt Whitman put it, "these thousands, and tens and twenties of thousands of American young men." Biographer Tarbell wrote, "By the end of 1862, Mr. Lincoln could scarcely drive or walk in any direction about Washington without passing a hospital. Even in going to his summer cottage at the Soldiers' Home, the President did not escape the sight of the wounded . . . as he drove home after a harrowing day at the White House, the President frequently looked from his carriage upon the very beds of wounded soldiers." If he happened upon an ambulance train on his way out to the home, he would ride along for some time, talking with the wounded. All this, of course, tore Lincoln to pieces.

Only six men died in the Company's three years of duty as the President's Guard, only one violently. Private John Fleming, a twenty-four-year-old cooper, and Private Cutter, a twenty-five-year-old carpenter, noted each death in letters home: John Glancy, twenty-five ("one of the strongest men in our Com. he was only sick about two weeks") and Andrew Hart, twenty, died of smallpox. Hart's mother applied for a pension on the grounds that her son had been her sole source of support by then. Evidently he had not been vaccinated, even though in March 1863 Fleming wrote to his family that the whole company got "Vaxinated," and he had such a bad reaction to it he was off duty for several days. Harrison Williams, age eighteen ("a nice young man and had a good many friends he was the tallest man in our Com[pany]"), and John Graham died of the typhoid fever that had killed Willie Lincoln; Solomon Allen died of spinal meningitis. Simon Nichols, age twenty-four and the father of two, reportedly died from an accidental gunshot wound to the stomach, although his troubled record in Company K makes one wonder if it were not self-inflicted. Fleming and Cutter knew most of the men who died because, like most of the volunteers in the Union army, they'd all been recruited from the same locale, Meadville and surrounding towns. Five in the company were German-born, two were Irish. (Cutter signed one of his letters home "Hans Vanderbrunn," another "Patrick O. Ryley," and sometimes he was just "a bold soger.") Coming from rural America as they did, they were more susceptible than urban soldiers to childhood diseases like measles and mumps. So a quarter of the company had to be hospitalized at one time or another. Cases of pneumonia, bronchitis, rheumatism, diarrhea, and malaria were also noted meticulously in the company records, even a few sexually transmitted diseases for those perhaps not constrained by the community values they brought with them, and possibly tempted by the hundreds of brothels in the city.

It's unlikely that the men of Company K read the May 11, 1861, issue of *Scientific American*, which contained advice "to our young soldiers." It reminded them that "in a campaign more men die from sickness than by the bullet." It instructed them how to keep warm and dry "when on guard duty during a rain storm," how to make a comfortable bed when there was not much straw to be found, and

These "spit and polished" young soldiers of Company K, "Bucktails" of the 150th Pennsylvania Volunteers, guarded Lincoln at the Soldiers' Home and the White House for three years and became part of the Lincoln family.

offered a suggestion at least half of Company K followed, to "let your beard grow so as to protect the throat and lungs."

Company K had been one of four companies organized in August 1862 by young Henry Huidekoper, just out of Harvard, and son of a prominent, politically active Meadville family. He was "saucy," Private Cutter thought, in the way he pleaded with the president in February 1863 to release the company to rejoin the rest of the regiment in the field. Huidekoper had organized four companies, including K, to be part of the already battle-seasoned 150th Pennsylvania Volunteers Regiment (called the "Bucktails" for the deer's tail that decorated their caps). He'd been made a lieutenant colonel at the outset, and was considered qualified, it seems, for having studied on his own at college a book on tactics, another on courts-martial, and practiced drilling on the lawns of the college. Years later, in a speech at Gettysburg, where he'd lost an arm in that costly historic battle, he described the kind of men who'd been mustered into service at Meadville on August 29, 1862.

> After fifteen months of strife between the north, half in earnest, and the south dead in earnest, another call for troops was made, and then it was you who responded to the country's demand—the second crop—middle-aged men with families dependent on them, young husbands sworn not to forsake their wives, young boys just old enough to pass muster and hardly strong enough to carry the sixty-pound loads imposed on them.

Company K was fairly typical of any Union army company in both age range and occupations. It was an older army than those in the next century, with a median age of twenty-four: twenty-one members were in their teens (three were just seventeen), thirty-two were between twenty and twenty-five, twenty-five were between twenty-five and thirty, five were between thirty and forty, and just two were over forty. Twenty-three were listed as farmers, fourteen as carpenters, nine as laborers, and eight as students (five were graduates of Meadville's Allegheny College). There were five coopers, four shoemakers, four wagonmasters, three lumbermen, two clerks, two teamsters, two boatmen, one miller, one printer, painter, blacksmith, carriage maker, coach trimmer, and lastly, one musician, the troubled Simon Nichols.

Years later, John Nichols, the unfortunate Simon's younger brother, told of their first encounter with Lincoln at the Soldiers' Home. It seems the company had no idea what they'd be doing once they arrived, except that they were to guard some army officer or other. They'd had nothing to eat for about twenty-four hours, and soon after daybreak, the cook, a "colored 'mammy' who was the cook" came to the door of the cottage and invited them in, ten at a time. Nichols was one of the first.

> When the soldiers were seated, they noticed that a chair had been reserved at the head of the table for someone, and pretty soon the president, Abraham Lincoln, entered and said, "Good morning, boys, I am informed that your company has been detailed to act as my bodyguard." This was the first intimation that the soldiers had as to whom they were guarding and they were a mighty proud set of men to think that almost raw recruits had been assigned to such

an important post. . . . They enjoyed that particular breakfast and none of them will ever forget it. President Lincoln ate with them and enlivened the situation by telling some of his droll stories and jokes.

It is a wonder that Lincoln maintained his awesome physical strength, considering how little he ate. He couldn't have cared less about food—perhaps an egg and a cup of coffee for breakfast, a biscuit and a glass of milk and sometimes a plate of fruit for lunch, and at dinner he'd peck at one or two courses. Noah Brooks was breakfasting with Lincoln once and realized that he didn't even notice what he was eating. He'd been given a glass of milk, and when Brooks commented on how unusual that was for a Westerner to drink at breakfast, Lincoln answered, "Well, I do prefer coffee in the morning, but they don't seem to have sent me any." When Mrs. Lincoln was at the Soldiers' Home while he remained at the White House, he would sometimes order something sent over from the Willard Hotel. Mrs. Lincoln, on the other hand, had been known in Springfield for her elegant dinners, and her White House spreads were magnificent. It was not surprising that the mother of growing boys would be concerned for how well the "boys" of Company K were eating. She arranged, among other things, that "a midnight luncheon should always be ready for the guards on duty as in turn they were relieved from their posts." She provided turkeys at Christmas and Thanksgiving and sent barrels of apples, apple butter, and other delicacies.

If Willard Cutter was at all typical, the soldiers of Company K flourished at the Soldiers' Home. "We have all we want to eat and drink," he wrote on September 21, 1862, and, "I never felt better in my life" on October 8, 1862. "[An] old woman is around most every day to sell cakes and pies, Milk, Apples, and a little of Everything," he wrote on November 9, 1862. He'd weighed 156 pounds when he left Meadville. By January 11, 1863, he had gained almost twenty pounds, and reported that another man in the company "was getting as fat as a pig." John Fleming wrote home on that date, "I weigh more now than I have for two years." Tad Lincoln liked to stop by for beans or bread and molasses.

Another regiment did Company K much better. In January 1862, the Lincolns had dinner with the New York Fifty-fifth Regiment, commanded by Regis de Trobriand, stationed north of the White House. The cooks were French, and Lincoln announced that it was the best meal he'd had in Washington. If the men of the regiment fight as well as they cook, he said, it would do well in battle. Most troops were not that lucky. General Joseph Hooker became a favorite partly for providing "soft" bread to his troops. Soldiers begged their families to send tea, butter, cheese, mince pie, rye bread. Otherwise, more often than not, it was "three hard tack and a pint of coffee for breakfast, three hard tack and a piece of Salt Horse for dinner, hard tack and coffee for supper. Poor grub that."

As Lincoln took Company K's measure, so did they take his. Company K, and Lincoln's cavalry escorts to and from the Soldiers' Home (first, Scott's Nine Hundred from New York, later, the Union Light Guard from Ohio) were in the best position to observe whether Lincoln's concern for the soldier was for show or for real. Tested and consistent over three years, it had to be real. Lincoln got to know each member of the Company by name, Ida Tarbell learned. "'He always called me Joe,' I heard a veteran of the guard say, a quaver in his voice," she wrote. "He loved his soldiers as his own children," said Harry Kieffer, drummer boy. "We always felt that the President took a personal interest in us. He never spoke absent-mindedly, but talked to the men as if he were thinking of them," said Sergeant Smith Stimmel of the Union Light Guard.

"He talked to the members of our company as if we were brothers," John Nichols remembered. Lincoln's respect for the citizen soldier seemed ingrained. "When he was absorbed in thought," he would often pass by the soldiers on guard, who would remain at present-arms well after Lincoln had passed by. When asked why they did that, the answer was that Lincoln would usually remember at some point, stop, turn around, lift his worn stovepipe hat, bow, and then continue on his way. And how could a sentinel resist an invitation from the president to sit down on the Soldiers' Home porch steps with him and Tad for a game of checkers on a "bright moonlight night"? Or an order to come in out of the rain? "Sentinel," Lincoln once asked, "Why not come under the porch out of the storm? It is contrary to orders, Mr. President. Do you know who commands the army and navy of the United States? You do, Mr. President. The President then said, "I command you to come under the porch out of the storm. He obeyed and never walked in the storm unless necessary."

Company K's captain, David Derickson, was astonished on his first ride with Lincoln into the city from the Soldiers' Home when Lincoln decided that Derickson just had to meet the army's new general in chief, Henry Halleck, and his chief aide, whom Derickson happened to know from Meadville (and Lincoln, always well informed about local politics, knew that he did).

> When the carriage stopped Lincoln requested me to remain seated, and he would bring the gentlemen down to see me, the office being on the second floor. In a short time, the President came down, followed by the other gentlemen. When he introduced them to me, General Cullum recognized and seemed pleased to see me. In General Halleck, I thought I discovered a kind of quizzical look, as much as to say, "Isn't this rather a big joke, to ask the commander-in-chief of the Army down to the street to be introduced to a country captain?"

Sergeant Charles Derickson, the captain's son, told Ida Tarbell that he once went right to the president for his permission to submit a requisition (for what, he didn't say) to "a lofty aide" on Halleck's staff. The aide asked him "who has had the audacity to go to the President with a matter of this kind?" Derickson responded that it was not audacity. "We are all friends down there & we can get what we want. A general in the office looked at the order and said, 'God, they'll be wanting pianos down there next' but signed the requisition." Henry Huidekoper remembered "Lincoln's manner was so easy, so simple, and so friendly that I had no hesitation in going into his office . . . when I dropped into his room Lincoln always had a pleasant word of greeting for me." The McCall brothers, Levi and Samuel, also went right to Lincoln for help. Their sister was married to a major in the Confederate army, who was very ill in a Union prison camp in Ohio. He'd tried unsuccessfully to be released on parole so he could get to Meadville to be taken care of. Lincoln saw to it that he was freed immediately.

It was only natural that Lincoln's great height (6'4") would be a good icebreaker as he interacted with Company K and troops elsewhere. Harrison Williams was the tallest man in Company K

(6′2½″). "One evening, the Sergeant of the Guard found the President and Williams back to back with their hats off, trying to see which was the taller." (Williams died of typhoid fever later, and Lincoln felt badly that if he'd only known, he'd have gone to the hospital to see him.) Lincoln lost at least one such contest to a six-foot-six-inch seventeen-year-old, Mahlon Staaber, in another Pennsylvania company. Then Lincoln advised him to "eat no pies or pastry in any form . . . not to use any intoxicating beverages . . . when lying down to sleep, I should always rest the head lower than the chest and should expand my lungs." The tall boy weighed only 140 pounds, and Lincoln told him he was worried that he might not survive in the service. The boy did, and became chief of police in Reading, Pennsylvania.

Armies have always sought to keep morale high. Troops on a three-day pass in Baghdad in 2004 during the Iraq war had at their disposal in one of Saddam Hussein's palaces a sauna, a pool, a hundred-seat movie theater, a weight room, and twenty-four-hour food service, including steak and lobster. Company K's devices for relaxation in camp were much simpler. One of their entertainments that amused Lincoln was called "the trained elephant" (two men, the Kepler brothers, positioned under an army blanket, performed various tricks with their legs, manipulating a trunk made from a small pliable piece of wood wrapped in another blanket). "While the Elephant was going through his exercises one evening, the President strolled into camp and was very much amused by the wonderful tricks the Elephant could perform. In a few evenings he called again and brought a friend with him, I think a Senator, and asked the Captain if he would not have the Elephant brought out again as he would like to have his friend see him perform, which of course was done, and very much enjoyed by the President & Friend." Years before, Lincoln had confessed to friends, after sneaking away to a simple country show as they traveled the judicial circuit, that he had a lot of catching up to do before he was as familiar as they were with more sophisticated forms of entertainment. Perhaps he appreciated the same lack of sophistication evidenced in the elephant game, and must have approved the forays some of the men made into the city on precious passes to visit the Smithsonian Institution, the theater, and other cultural events the capital had to offer. Throughout the war, Lincoln often used the theater as an escape himself.

The trained elephant was just plain fun for most of Company K, but one wonders if a few of the men might have seen something more in it. When Private John Fleming saw General Grant for the first time at a typically frantic White House reception in 1864, he wrote, "He looks as if he had seen the elephant," a colloquial expression meaning any "awesome but exciting experience." Despite their enormous pride in being the President's Guard, the company's enviable reputation, and their relatively comfortable living conditions, some in the company were frustrated not to be where the action was, even though they knew the rest of the 150th was taking heavy casualties at Gettysburg, at Cold Harbor, in the Wilderness, and other major battles. Cutter expressed that restlessness in his own way. He wrote to his grandmother in January 1863, "As to the fighting quality [of Company K] it is first rate for one of our company was savage enough to kill a warf rat in a bayonet charge one night while on Guard." And by the spring of 1864, he confessed that "for my part I would like to have a little fright before I go home." John Fleming felt the same. "I am getting almost tired of this kind of soldiering I would like to go to the front and try it a whill [sic]." Even Walt Whitman said he "had desire to be present at a first class battle," although he'd seen the horrific aftermath in his hospital work. Company K did see some action during Early's July 1864 raid to the north of the Soldiers' Home. No one got hurt, and they were back in camp in a few days.

Lieutenant Colonel Henry Huidekoper wanted particularly badly to get into the fight, and finally managed to, losing his right arm at Gettysburg. But when he tried to get the entire company transferred to join the rest of the 150th, Lincoln, Mrs. Lincoln, and Tad all protested vehemently. Cutter described the scene to his brother in a letter dated February 19, 1863. As the company packed up its gear to leave for the front, "Mrs. Lincoln was at the window seeing all that was going on. . . . she said she was sorry we were going to leave and wished the com. good luck. that night Mr. Lincoln cried like a child and She said if the com did not leave before Morning we should not go at all. . . . she thought it was time for her to say something and she had old Abe send one of the men down to tell the lieu if the Com wanted to stay to let him know, and the Com had a vote and they all went for to stay." Lincoln's short November 1862 note praising Company K had already settled its fate for the rest of the war. So Cutter concluded, "Com K 150 we are no more."

Henry Huidekoper was convinced it was Tad's affection for Company K that was primarily responsible for its being kept on as Lincoln's special guard. If so, that did not damage the restless men's affection for the boy. They gave him his own rank (third lieutenant) and special uniform, and fed him no matter when he showed up at the camp for something to eat. His antics amused them, his influence sometimes got them out of trouble, and his gifts were generous. From one trip with his mother, Tad brought back a huge flag for the company's fifty-foot flagpole, which was topped by a brass eagle Tad had also provided. Toward the end of their service, Company K presented Tad with an album containing photographs of each of them, posed in the same way, Cutter pointed out, so their various heights could be compared. This thoughtful gift cost the men $110, a considerable sum in those days, when sixteen dollars was a month's pay for some, and a five-dollar or six-dollar remittance home could mean the difference between hunger and food, a home and the street. Years later, Private Albert See asked Robert Todd Lincoln if he might have the album, thinking that the president's only surviving son might have more precious mementos, but Robert Todd Lincoln wrote back to say that he could not think of parting with it.

The elite Union Light Guard of Ohio, Lincoln's last cavalry escort, was even more restless with "glorious inactivity." "We longed to be in it," remembered Sergeant Smith Stimmel. When one of the men said so directly to the president, he answered, "I do not myself see the necessity of having soldiers traipsing around after me wherever I go but if [Stanton] thinks it is necessary to have soldiers here, it might as well be you as someone else. If you were sent to the front, someone would have to come from the front to take your place . . . you can serve your country as faithfully here as at the front, and I reckon it is not quite as dangerous here as it is there." Then

Lincoln told one of the stories he often used to illustrate his point. An old farmer friend of his in Illinois could never understand why the Lord put a curl in a pig's tail—but he guessed the Lord knew what he was doing when he put it there.

Oddly enough, Lincoln had paid seven hundred fifty dollars in the fall of 1864 for twenty-year-old John Summerfield Staples to serve as his so-called "representative recruit" in the army. This was a not very successful idea cooked up in June 1864 to help localities fill their quotas. People with means were willing to pay up to a thousand dollars for such a recruit. Henry Wadsworth Longfellow had done it, and so had Edward Everett, whose two-hour oration at Gettysburg had preceded Lincoln's two-minute address. Lincoln met briefly with Private Staples in October 1864, told him he was a good looking, stout, and healthy looking man, and believed he would do his duty. Staples saw no fighting and died in 1888, his tombstone reminding passersby of his having served in that unique capacity. A battle-scarred veteran, William S. Snow, had offered a similar service to Lincoln several months before, but for some reason, perhaps political, Lincoln chose Staples.

In June 1863 the *Chicago Tribune,* praising Lincoln's growing strengths as a military strategist, had urged that he take personal command of the army. Lincoln had certainly entertained that idea out of frustration with too many passive Union army commanders. But the *Tribune* went on to say that "our only apprehension would be that, just as the moment of victory, his kindness of heart would impel him to call a halt, lest the enemy should get hurt."

As it was, Lincoln's persistent leniency often infuriated his military officers. Company K experienced his kindness of heart first-hand. Private George Flemming had deserted from the Soldiers' Home on October 17, 1862. The "Morning Report" of August 3, 1863 noted cryptically that he had returned to the company, and on July 13, 1864, that he had been dishonorably discharged and sent to a barren fort in the Dry Tortugas off the Florida coast in the Gulf of Mexico. Other records tell a harsher story. Flemming claimed at his court martial that he had returned voluntarily after a sore on his leg had healed and, seeing his impoverished family, resettled with relatives in Ohio. But it was charged that he had to be brought back under arrest. He was found guilty of desertion in August 1863, and sentenced "to be shot to death with musketry." (The precision of this sentence was due to the poor marksmanship of most of the soldiers, according to the authors of a recent study of Lincoln's compassionate policy.) Even though desertions numbered in the many thousands by 1864 (some families sent civilian clothes to their soldiers to enable them to flee), Lincoln looked for any excuse to save deserters from execution on what he called "butcher days" or "hanging days." He insisted on reviewing all death sentences, and Flemming's was among the many he commuted to "imprisonment for the duration and forfeiture of all pay and allowances due."

If Willard Cutter, John Fleming, and Henry Huidekoper were any indication of Company K's political sentiments, it was full of strong Union men, contemptuous of the Copperheads around Meadville. "If we are beaten our country is gon [sic]," wrote Fleming. "I am willing to sacrifice all to put down the rebs," wrote Cutter. We can only infer from what some members of Company K did during or after the war, what the company might have thought of the war's ultimate purpose, the end of slavery. We do know that Company K presented a dress to Aunt Mary Williams, Mrs. Lincoln's "colored" cook at the Soldiers' Home. (Cutter wrote to correct his mother's impression that they'd bought it for Mrs. Lincoln herself!) His letter of May 21, 1863, to his brother mentions that "our quartermaster sergeant [Sylvester Birdsall] is Captain of a Niger [sic] Company." Cutter seemed very curious to see what the black soldiers looked like, but said nothing more. Birdsall filed for a disability pension in later years, noting in his appeal that in 1863 he'd organized the first regiment of U.S. Colored Troops, and soon after became that regiment's quartermaster. (The company's "Morning Report" of June 11, 1863 noted less grandly that he was appointed a first lieutenant of that regiment's Company C.) Birdsall served for most of the rest of the war in North Carolina and Virginia, where he became seriously ill, but he later worked on Roanoke Island for the Freedman's Bureau, set up by the government to help former slaves make the painful transition to what was hoped would be their freedom.

Private Albert See, one of the few veterans in Company K, had joined it on March 3, 1863, after surviving the disaster of Chancellorsville. After the war, he and his wife went down to teach freed slaves in Georgia. He also became a preacher, and his memoir is a chilling firsthand account of the dangers newly freed slaves and sympathetic whites faced during the sad and cruel Reconstruction period. "We left to save our lives," he wrote in his memoirs. A notice had been left at their door saying, "If you do not move, you are a dead man. Signed, KKK." See and his wife stuck it out as long as they could, "fully determined to die rather than desert." But the strain was intolerable, and they eventually moved away, making one wonder again how different conditions might have been had Lincoln lived.

In the end, of course, the constant drills, the endless polishing of brass and leather, the spotless white gloves, the long hours of guard duty, and the devotion were of no avail on April 14, 1865. Company K had been hamstrung all along by Lincoln's lack of concern for his own safety, his intense antipathy toward being guarded at all, and, to a considerable extent, the limitations placed on the company's own effectiveness. This they were painfully aware of themselves. Robert W. McBride, of the Union Light Guard from Ohio, wrote later, "A daily detail from the ranks of a company of infantry from one of Pennsylvania's famous regiments, the 'Bucktails,' was posted in front of the White House, one on each side of the portico, the beats of the sentinels beginning on each side of the entrance and running east and west about as far the East and West sides of the main building. Posted thus, they were more ornamental than useful." But that was fortunately not the case in June 1863. Cutter reported to his mother that when a "crazy man" got unruly and would not leave the White House, "one of the boys that was front of the House was called on by the doorkeeper [who] went up and fetched the lad down" and he was led off to the Guard House. And on one of their first days at the Soldiers' Home, they did apprehend a spy on the grounds.

Albert See once challenged Robert Todd Lincoln himself at the door of the White House, not recognizing him because Robert was usually away at Harvard, and they had not yet met. "I brot my gun to a charge and started for him and would have stopped him but the door keeper opened the door and I was relieved . . . if he had not come to the door as he did I would have stopped him with bayonet if necessary." In July 1864, the situation was very tense at the Soldiers' Home. See was guarding the front door of the cottage. "It was rumored that [Confederate General John Singleton] Mosby was within our lines with five hundred men in disguise to take the President. We put enough credence in the report to bring the whole guard from camp and have them fully armed all night and laying close to the president's house, where they could spring to arms in a moment and defend the President." Lincoln was chatting with someone in front of the cottage when See heard a horseman approaching at full gallop. As soon as he realized the rider had passed the picket line, See said, "President, step into the house, and shut the door." Lincoln did so. It turns out that the horseman had come to deliver an urgent message from Secretary of War Stanton to come at once into the city, because it was far too dangerous to remain at the Soldiers' Home, and Lincoln obeyed again. "I presume," See wrote, "I am the only private soldier that ever gave a command to the president, but I could not wait to request. . . . If his bodyguard at the theater had been so careful as they should have been the nation would have been saved the terrible calamity that deprived the world of one of the noblest characters of the age."

CHAPTER 14

The Generals

GENERAL GEORGE BRINTON MCCLELLAN'S message to President Lincoln on September 2, 1862, was typical of his utterly contemptuous treatment of his commander in chief, the man he called, among other things, "a well-meaning baboon." McClellan informed the president that he would "endeavor to pass by the Soldiers' Home to report to you the state of affairs unless called elsewhere." Since there is no record of his arrival there, this note was probably just one more example of what John Hay called McClellan's "unparalleled insolence" toward Lincoln, who finally had enough of the "young Napoleon" and dismissed him for good a few months later, after a year of crushing disappointments.

General Ulysses S. Grant, on the other hand, could hardly bear to spend an hour at the White House, let alone the Soldiers' Home, but for reasons Lincoln could gladly understand. Grant even cancelled a dinner invitation he'd accepted, telling Lincoln quite simply that he'd had enough of "this show business . . . a dinner to me means a million dollars a day lost to the country."

It had taken Lincoln three years to find a man who could say that. "Before Grant took command . . . we did not sleep at night here in Washington," Lincoln told a colleague later. "But I have made up my mind that whatever it is possible to have done, Grant will do, and whatever he doesn't do, I don't believe is to be done. And now we sleep at night."

Until then, Lincoln had spent untold hours dealing with a succession of generals, particularly in the Army of the Potomac, who failed him in one way or another, McClellan the most notable case. Unfortunately, at the start of the war, Lincoln's chief military adviser, Winfield Scott, a wise but tottering seventy-five-year-old hero, was no longer up to the job. By the fall of 1862, Secretary of the Navy Welles noted in his diary, "Personal jealousies and professional rivalries, the bane and curse of all armies, have entered deeply into ours." Lincoln's letters dealing with the problems that resulted are a litany of frustration and anguish.

To General McClellan, May 9, 1862: "I now think it indispensable for you to know how your struggle against [the current organization of the army] is received in quarters which we cannot entirely disregard. It is looked upon as merely an effort to pamper one or two pets, and to persecute and degrade their supposed rivals."

To General Carl Schurz, November 24, 1862: "If I must discard my own judgment and take yours, I must also take that of others; and by the time I should reject all I should be advised to reject, I should have none left, Republicans or others—not even yourself. For be assured, my dear sir, there are men who ... think you are performing your part as poorly as you think I am performing mine."

To General Henry Halleck, January 1, 1863: "If in such a difficulty as this you do not help, you fail me precisely in the point for which I sought your assistance. . . . Your military skill is useless to me, if you will not do this." (A note by Lincoln at the bottom of the letter: "Withdrawn, because considered harsh by Gen. Halleck.")

To General John A. McClernand, January 22, 1863, Lincoln wrote, "I have too many *family* controversies (so to speak) already on my hands, to voluntarily, or so long as I can avoid it, take up another. You are now doing well—well enough for the country, and well for yourself—much better than you could possibly be, if engaged in open war with General Halleck. Allow me to beg, that for your sake, for my sake, & for the country's sake, you give your whole attention to the better work."

To General Franz Sigel, February 5, 1863: "General Schurz thinks I was a little cross in my late note to you. If I was, I ask pardon. If I do get up a little temper I have no sufficient time to keep it up."

To General William Rosecrans, March 17, 1863: "Truth to speak, I do not appreciate this matter of rank on paper as you officers do. The world will not forget that you fought the battle of Stone's River, and it will never care a fig whether you rank General Grant on paper, or he so ranks you."

To General Joseph Hooker, June 16, 1863: "Quite possibly I was wrong both then and now, but in the great responsibility resting on me, I cannot be entirely silent. Now, all I ask is that you will be in such mood that we can get into our action the best cordial judgment of yourself and General Halleck, with my poor mite added, if indeed he and you shall think it entitled to any consideration at all."

To General Meade after Gettysburg, July 1863, which Lincoln decided not to send: "My dear General, I do not believe you appreciate the magnitude involved in Lee's escape. He was within your easy grasp, and to have closed upon him would, in connection with our other late successes, have ended the war. As it is, the war will be prolonged indefinitely."

And of course, the classic to McClellan, October 25, 1862: "I have just received your dispatch about sore tongues and fatigued horses. You will pardon me for asking what the horses of your army have done since the battle of Antietam that fatigue anything."

One day President Lincoln had his Soldiers' Home guard assembled to tell them that they'd become part of the Lincoln family, and that he was pleased there had been no "family jars" between them, unlike the "family controversies" he'd mentioned in his letter to General McClernand, a longtime Springfield friend.

Like McClellan, not all of Lincoln's professional generals served him well, and not all his political generals served him badly. Lawyer John A. Logan, for example, served with distinction, and was buried at the Soldiers' Home. Political generals, chosen by Lincoln for their ethnic, regional, or political qualifications, "were an essential part of the process by which a highly politicized society mobilized for war," says historian James McPherson. But in the end, concludes another, Bruce D. Simpson, "the costly mistakes of at least three political generals [Butler, Banks, and McClernand] outweighed whatever political benefit their detention may have realized."

CHAPTER 15

The Political General: Daniel Sickles

By the time general daniel sickles went out to the Soldiers' Home on October 7, 1863, his right leg was already on display at the Army Medical Museum in Washington. It wasn't just Sickles's scandalous reputation that got his leg to a museum rather than to a pile of severed limbs in the field hospital at Gettysburg. The surgeon general, after talking with President Lincoln, had issued an order that "gross" specimens such as Sickles's leg be sent to Washington for examination and evaluation as part of a huge study of the medical and surgical history of the war that would be published after it was over. How, when, and whether to amputate limbs was the great surgical controversy of the Civil War.

Like everything else about the notorious Daniel Sickles—"Devil Dan" his enemies called him—having just one leg was simply another challenge. As Mark Twain put it years later, "[Sickles] seemed to me . . . just the kind of man who would risk his salvation in order to do some 'last words' in an attractive way . . . the general values his lost leg a way above the one that is left. I am perfectly sure that if he had to part with either of them, he would part with the one that he has got." Twain was right. Sickles would visit his leg regularly in the years after the war. He lived into his nineties, as controversial after the war as he was before it, and during it.

Perhaps Lincoln's most notorious political general, and a favorite of Mary Todd Lincoln's, Daniel Sickles was undaunted by the loss of his right leg at Gettysburg. Illustration courtesy of Picture History.

His leg had been shattered by a twelve-pound cannonball, amputated, and sent to Washington with a calling card, "compliments of General D. E. S.," on the second day of the battle of Gettysburg, July 2, 1863. Just two weeks later, Sickles was chafing to get back into battle, and Secretary of War Edwin Stanton, a longtime friend, faced the first of many barrages. "It will not be long before I am ready for work again—can you give me a command?"

But by October, Sickles was still without one. He may have gone out to the Soldiers' Home to see Lincoln about that, and he was still badgering the president about it over a year later. Sickles was also aggressively counterattacking criticism of his controversial actions on that July day at Gettysburg, which some believed would have led to a court martial by General George Meade if he hadn't been so badly wounded. But years later, Henry Huidekoper remembered Sickles's action as "brave and valorous."

So a visit to the Soldiers' Home by one of Lincoln's top generals, however disreputable, but surely courageous, a quality Lincoln wasn't sure he himself possessed, was hardly out of line. Lincoln may in fact have shared John Hay's sentiment that "he has wiped out by his magnificent record all old stains and stands even in his youth sure of an honored and useful life. One leg is a cheap price to pay for so much of the praise of men and the approval of his own conscience."

Sickles's fondness and respect for the president did represent a striking metamorphosis: from Tammany Hall politician loudly sympathetic to the South and contemptuous of Lincoln, to enthusiastic supporter of his presidency and the preservation of the Union, to the highest rank in the United States Army, Major General, with twelve thousand men under his command at Gettysburg—all in just three years.

And this wasn't his first visit to the president. Sickles by 1863 had become such a friend to both Lincolns that Mary Todd's half sister, Emilie, visiting the White House, noticed that "he seems on very intimate terms here." So intimate, in fact, that Sickles, by Lincoln's side, had watched his troops pass in review before the White House, become the "Cap" among those Mary Todd Lincoln called her "beau monde friends of the Blue Room," participated—skeptically—in her séances, and accompanied the Lincolns to the theater. He also used his prodigious talents as a fixer and wheeler-dealer, and had even saved the Lincolns from great embarrassment by deflecting blame from Mary Lincoln over the leaking of a presidential speech.

What *was* surprising was that a man described over the years as "an unmitigated blackguard," "a pariah whom to know was discreditable," and "a man after show and notoriety and newspaper fame and the adulation of the mob" was given much of the time of day beyond military necessity at Lincoln's precious summer refuge at the Soldiers' Home. Captain Charles Francis Adams Jr., scion of the great and righteous Quincy dynasty, was among the appalled: "I can say from personal knowledge and experience that the headquarters of the Army of the Potomac [where Sickles was based with General Joseph Hooker] was a place to which no self-respecting man would like to go, and no decent woman would go. It was a combination of bar-room and brothel."

Mary Todd Lincoln's predilection for slightly shady but scintillating characters aside, what did Honest Abe see in Devil Dan? What common ground could a faithful family man, teetotaling, frugal, rumpled, and unpolished, have found with this cosmopolitan, hard-drinking, dapper, ostentatious, charming, blatant philanderer, who once cited his motto as: "Though I see what the better things are, even so I follow the worse." ["*Video melior protoque, deteriora sequor*"]

Worst of the worse had been Sickles's murder of his wife's lover in broad daylight and in full view of the White House a few years before the war began. Acquitted by reason of temporary insanity, the first time that defense had ever been used, Sickles appalled even his closest friends, including Edwin Stanton, the toughest member of his eight-man defense team, by returning in just a few months, if only for a time, to his ostracized but still adoring wife. "Behold. Adultery couched with Homicide," someone wrote.

Lincoln and Sickles did share some interests and experiences: Both had been restless youths, one on the frontier, the other in urban settings. Both tried one possible means of making a living after another, and settling on the law as the most practical livelihood. More important, they were both politicians to the core. When he was just sixteen, Sickles had given an impressive speech at a Brooklyn rally for Democratic presidential candidate Martin Van Buren. By the time he was twenty-seven, he was the youngest member of Tammany Hall's general council, and like Lincoln, he'd served in his state legislature and in Congress.

Some of Sickles's political methods may have come close to what we now call "dirty tricks," but Lincoln had surely seen the like. And he was well aware of Sickles's improved reputation with the powerful New York press. But what was perhaps most critical to their relationship was their shared view of how to win the war, and what to do after it. Sickles was the kind of man of action Lincoln desperately needed. Within two weeks in the disastrous spring of 1861, Sickles and a Tammany crony had raised a regiment of eight companies, and by the end of summer an entire brigade, with its meals prepared by chefs from the fanciest New York restaurant, Delmonico's (their campaign headquarters), and many of the men sheltered by a huge circus tent acquired on credit from P. T. Barnum. Sickles had astounded Lincoln soon after that with his novel suggestion, taken right to the White House, that the federal government take on his state militia as United States Volunteers. This could mean a higher rank for himself, and relief from a huge pile of unpaid debts, something Sickles seemed to always manage to have, but often escaped paying.

When all that had been settled, and Sickles at last tested, however briefly, in battle, he had arranged a parade for Lincoln of his thousands of troops, supplemented by a hundred borrowed cavalrymen, in a display so imperial in its splendor that the president, who'd arrived with just one general and one orderly, had to ask, "Sickles, I'm not going to take command of an army. What is all this for?" Sickles's strategies on the battlefield may have been controversial and highly risky, but at least he moved, and his general inclination was forward, a direction Lincoln had tried to get most of his military leaders to go without much success. In October 1863, Private Cutter wrote home: "If all our officers were like him I think we would of seen the end to this war before this." And no one could now doubt Sickles's mettle under fire. The two men also shared similar views toward reconstruction: like Lincoln, Sickles believed that conciliation and magnanimity were wiser than revenge and harshness.

Sickles never did regain command of his troops, although he recovered rapidly from his amputation. Instead, in the spring of 1864, Lincoln sent him on a mission to examine conditions in those parts of the South held by the Union Army, in particular the area now governed by Andrew Johnson, whose severe rule contradicted Lincoln's belief in a reconstruction policy of compassion and generosity. But Sickles saw too much hatred against the North to be sanguine about reconstruction prospects. Later that year, after Lincoln's reelection, which Sickles supported enthusiastically as a leading Democrat for Lincoln, he was sent by Lincoln to Latin America on another mission, more arduous both physically and diplomatically. He was, among other things, to explore with authorities in Colombia the prospects of a home there for freed slaves. For some time, Lincoln believed colonization was a potential solution to the problem and their future. That idea went nowhere, and by the time Sickles was ready to come home, still hankering for a command, although he did not yet know it, the war was over and Lincoln was already dead. Sickles would never look affectionately on that "sad, earnest, good face" again.

CHAPTER 16

The Professional General: Joseph Hooker

IF DANIEL SICKLES WAS the most notorious of Lincoln's amateur generals, then Joseph Hooker was surely one of the most colorful of his professional commanders. He was called "Fighting Joe" (oddly enough, for a man who relished going on the attack, it was a nickname he loathed). When he met with Lincoln at the Soldiers' Home on September 27, 1863, he had not lost a limb like Sickles, but he had lost command of his precious hundred-thousand-man Army of the Potomac on June 28, 1863, after leading it—or not leading it, as some insisted—to a terrible defeat at the one-house crossroads called Chancellorsville. To Hooker this was an equally devastating loss. "The President may regard me as a cripple," he said, "but if he will give me a chance, I will yet show him that I know how to fight."

It took Lincoln those three months to decide to do just that. "When trouble arises, I can always rely on Hooker's magnanimity," he told his secretary, John Hay. And this time the trouble was in Tennessee. General William Rosecrans and the Army of the Cumberland were besieged and starving down south in Chattanooga. They needed rescuing urgently. The chance Hooker hoped for was Lincoln's offer of a command of twelve thousand men, surely a comedown, but he took it, said good-bye to Lincoln at the Soldiers' Home, and in a remarkably complex transfer over twelve hundred miles by rail, spearheaded by two of Lincoln's most capable men,

191

General Joseph Hooker was a colorful, popular, and courageous professional general.
He held this grand army review for Lincoln (and possibly son Tad, at left) before leading
it to defeat at Chancellorsville.

Secretary of War Edwin Stanton, and Quartermaster General Montgomery Meigs, Hooker's two corps, seven hundred wagons, and five thousand horses, arrived in just six days at a staging area fifty miles from Chattanooga to aid in Rosecrans's relief.

All summer long, before his meeting with Lincoln that September evening at the Soldiers' Home, Hooker had seemed like "a wandering ghost," journalist Noah Brooks wrote. He had fumbled his big chance, and exposed his limitations as a commander. The battle had lasted for six days, on terrain so difficult it would sorely test even General Ulysses S. Grant the following year, and accomplished absolutely nothing but the loss of over thirty thousand men. Private Albert See, who later joined Company K, was there. "We had the worse piece of woods to push through that I ever saw . . . so thick that we could not see the enemy ten feet from us." Hooker—wounded and shaken—finally ordered a retreat from General Robert E. Lee's far smaller but more daring forces that had been crucially aided by invaluable tips from local sympathizers. Lincoln's chief military adviser at the time, General Henry ("Old Brains") Halleck, was Hooker's oldest, worst enemy, and now saw his chance to force Hooker's resignation. When he ordered another general to "pay no attention to General Hooker's orders," Hooker knew he was finished as head of the hapless Army of the Potomac, the third commander in less than a year to bungle the job.

So Hooker, who loved campaigning more than anything else in life, missed out on the action at Gettysburg, a major turning point of the war, fought just days after his removal from command of the Army of the Potomac. General George Meade now led the troops Hooker had worked fiercely that winter to shape into what he boasted was now "the finest army on the planet." Bars in Washington and New York had begun serving a drink called "Hooker's Retreat." And to add further insult to injury, Halleck had Hooker arrested for traveling without a pass when he arrived in Washington from the field, hoping to restore his reputation, battered even before Chancellorsville by years of controversy and acrimony. Hooker was anything but discreet; his often venomous tongue, his blatant ambition, his overconfidence, and his sometimes rash behavior in and out of battle were responsible for most of the damage. A somewhat pompous Charles Francis Adams of the history-burdened Quincy family, no more an admirer of Hooker than he was of Sickles, described the two of them as "the disgrace and bane of the army; they are thrice humbugs, intriguers and demagogues."

That was not entirely fair. Hooker had proved himself a superb army administrator and a courageous fighter. Years later, Henry Huidekoper, who had led Company K in its earliest days of service at the Soldiers' Home, reminded veterans gathered at Gettysburg that the army General Meade inherited from Hooker for that critical battle was "in superb form as to health, discipline, and appointments. From a condition of occasional open revolt, and a period when a dead cavalryman was never seen . . . Hooker—than whom no man was ever better at such work—had brought out order, confidence and a fervid desire to again try conclusions with our oft successful foe." That assessment still holds. In just a few months, Hooker had brought about the miraculous recovery of a demoralized, sick, and poorly fed army "on the verge of disintegration." It was his great contribution to ultimate Union victory.

Company K's Private Cutter was impressed by Hooker's appearance when the general rode up to the Soldiers' Home. "He is a fine looking old man [Hooker was only forty-nine!] . . . he rode a white horse." At West Point, Hooker had been known as "the beautiful cadet," and Noah Brooks described him during the war as

> by all odds, the handsomest soldier I ever laid my eyes upon . . . tall, shapely, well dressed, though not natty in appearance; his fair red and white complexion glowing with health, his bright blue eyes sparkling with intelligence and animation and his auburn hair tossed back upon his well-shaped head . . . he was a gay cavalier, alert and confident, overflowing with animal spirits and as cheery as a boy."

Like many of the rank and file, Cutter admired Hooker as a military leader. "Hooker is doing fighting now and is giving the rebs the devil," he wrote to his brother while the battle at Chancellorsville raged. Captain Aldace Walker was also rooting for Hooker as he followed the battle from Fort Stevens, north of the Soldiers' Home, restless as were some of the men in Company K to go into action himself. (Walker's wartime letters were later published under the revealing title *Quite Ready to be Sent Somewhere*.)

Given Hooker's famous flamboyance and eye for the image, it is tempting to think that the white horse he rode to his meeting with Lincoln at the Soldiers' Home was intended to signal that he was riding once again to the Union's rescue, and many did see him that way—before Chancellorsville. But his white horse "Colonel" was just part of the package. A German officer at the Battle of Second Bull Run in 1862 was heard to say, "Who ish dat general mit a white horse and red face? He cares nothing for bullets."

One officer who learned that he would once again be under Hooker's command in Tennessee was not pleased. General Henry Warner Slocum protested: "My opinion of Hooker both as an officer and a gentleman is too well-known to make it necessary for me to refer to it in this communication. The public service cannot be promoted by placing under his command an officer who has so little confidence in his ability as I have. Our relations are such that it would be degrading in me to accept any position under him."

This was not the first diatribe Lincoln had heard against Joseph Hooker. Lincoln himself was well aware of Hooker's faults, particularly that overconfidence, "about the worst thing I've seen here since I've been down here," he said after visiting Hooker's headquarters before the Battle of Chancellorsville. So he refused Slocum's resignation, simply promising to place him as far away from Hooker as possible once they all got to Tennessee. Dealing with these personal animosities between his commanding officers took much of Lincoln's time as commander in chief, and drained much of his energy for three long years before Ulysses S. Grant took over the entire Union army in 1864. "One of the most discouraging as well as disgusting features of the present condition of things is . . . [that] it is next to impossible to hear one General speak well of another," wrote the *New York Tribune*. "Be patient with the generals," advised the Assistant Secretary of the Army, P. H. Watson, to an exasperated colonel who couldn't find Hooker when he needed him. "Some of them [and that, of course, included Hooker] will trouble you more than they will the enemy." Secretary of State William Seward, of all people, was surprised by the infighting he saw among Lincoln's military leaders. "It never had occurred to me that any jealousy could prevent these generals from acting for their common fame and welfare of the country." Lincoln by then knew better. "'I don't see why you should have expected it. You are not old. I should have known it.' He said this gloomily and sadly."

But Lincoln had always liked Hooker despite his flaws. He'd defended placing Hooker at the head of the Army of the Potomac in January 1863 against severe opposition. Secretary of War Edwin Stanton had even threatened to resign in protest. It is true "Hooker does talk badly," Lincoln admitted, "but the trouble is, he is stronger with the country today than any other man. Even if the country were told of Hooker's talk, they wouldn't believe it."

Some of Hooker's "caustic masterpieces" were indeed incredible: General George McClellan was "a baby who knew something of drill, little of organization and nothing of [its] morale." General Robert E. Lee "is weak and little of a soldier." Grant is "simple-minded . . . with no more moral sense than a dog." General Sherman "has no more judgment than a child." As for Ambrose Burnside, whom he'd replaced as head of the Army of the Potomac after Burn-side's failure at Fredericksburg, "his moral degradation is unfathom-able . . . he must swallow his words . . . or I will hunt him to the ends of the earth." At one point Hooker had even called Lincoln and his administration "imbecile and played out."

In one of his classic remonstrances, dated January 26, 1863, which came to light only after Hooker's death in 1879 (and in 1940 sold for fifteen thousand dollars), Lincoln finally let him know what he thought of him:

> I have placed you at the head of the Army of the Potomac. Of course, I have done this upon what appear to me to be sufficient reasons. And yet I think it best for you to know that there are some things in regard to which, I am not quite satisfied with you. I believe you to be a brave and a skilful [sic] soldier, which, of course, I like. I also believe you do not mix politics with your pro-fession, in which you are right. You have confidence in yourself, which is a valuable, if not an indispensable quality. You are ambi-tious, which, within reasonable bounds, does good rather than harm. But I think that during Gen. Burnside's command of the Army, you have taken counsel of your ambitions, and thwarted him as much as you could, in which you did a great wrong to the coun-try, and to a most meritorious and honorable brother officer. I have heard, in such a way as to believe it, of your recently saying that both the Army and the Government needed a Dictator. Of course it was not *for* this, but in spite of it, that I have given you the command. Only those generals who gain successes, can set up dic-tators. What I now ask of you is military successes, and I will risk the dictatorship. The government will support you to the utmost of it's ability, which is neither more nor less than it has done and will do for all commanders. I much fear that the spirit which you have aided to infuse into the Army, of criticizing their Commander, and withholding confidence from him, will now turn upon you. I shall assist you as far as I can, to put it down. Neither you, nor Napoleon, if he were alive again, could get any good out of an army, while such a spirit prevails in it. And now, beware of rash-ness. Beware of rashness, but with energy, and sleepless vigilance, go forward, and give us victories.

Unlike Halleck, Hooker loved his scolding: "It is a beautiful let-ter, and although I think he was harder on me than I deserved, I will say that I love the man who wrote it." But Hooker had not given him victories. When news reached Lincoln of Hooker's defeat at Chancellorsville, the president was aghast. Noah Brooks was with him on the night the bad news came in. "Never, as long as I knew him, did he seem to be so broken, so dispirited, so ghost-like. Clasping his hands behind his back, he walked up and down the room, saying, 'My God! My God! What will the country say! What will the country say!' He seemed incapable of uttering any other words than these, and after a little time he hurriedly left the room."

But Hooker had shown the right stuff often enough. "Get out of the way," Hooker shouted during the Peninsula Campaign, when warned of an impenetrable swamp just ahead. "I have two regiments here that can go anywhere." His division had fought the very first, long-awaited battle of the Army of the Potomac on the peninsula, and even paranoid McClellan saw fit to give him credit for saving the day at least once during that campaign. At Second Bull Run he was commended for "hearty, cordial and untiring zeal and energy." He was wounded while fighting aggressively at Antietam, and had fought hard and well at General Ambrose Burnside's debacle at Fredericksburg.

General George Meade would be the next general to reduce Lincoln to tears, when he failed to pursue Lee's army across the Potomac after the battle, a move that quite possibly could have ended the war in July 1863. But Lincoln was resilient, and as he put it in assessing Hooker's future usefulness, "was not disposed to throw away a gun because it had misfired once." Furthermore, always sensitive to the slightest shift in political currents, Lincoln knew that Hooker still had powerful admirers on Capitol Hill, especially on the powerful Congressional Committee on the Conduct of the War. Hooker's own political views seemed to be quite amenable to shifts when his ambition was at stake. After the war was over, he confirmed that he "was never anything else but a Democrat."

Hooker also had important friends in the national press, which he had cultivated for years, providing tempting copy with his exploits, issuing press releases, cosseting influential war correspondents (whom he finally required to use bylines, because anonymity led to carelessness with information that proved of value to the Confederate army). And Lincoln was grateful for Hooker's instinct for the jugular in battle, a relief from McClellan's temporizing and timidity, and rare among his top commanders. "Oh it is terrible, terrible, this weakness, this indifference of our Potomac generals, with such armies of good and brave men."

Hooker's performance as commander of the Army of the Potomac has looked better in recent years. "He did make serious mistakes, but not enough to lose the battle. No Union general in any battle in this war was so badly served by his lieutenants," writes Stephen Sears in his definitive analysis of Chancellorsville. Nor was Hooker drunk during the fighting, Sears insists, an accusation he describes as "the longest running romance of Chancellorsville." Neither did Hooker say, as his detractors there also claimed, that "Hooker had lost confidence in Hooker." Historian Mark Neely concludes

> Hooker is the victim of an unfortunate accident of naming battles. His most famous battle and defeat should not be called "Chancellorsville." Hooker's battle should be called what the battle was called a year later when Grant fought on the same ground, the Battle of the Wilderness. Hooker's defeat would be First Wilderness, like First Bull Run, and thus the explanation of the general's failure would be built in to the battle's very name—and like Grant, Hooker might be forgiven his failure in impossible terrain.

(The term "hooker" [prostitute] was in use twenty years before the war, so the general can't be blamed for that, at least.)

Hooker was chastened by his defeat, reconciled to his limitations as a commander, and he managed to acquit himself well for the rest of the war. He left his last combat command in August 1864, with the affection of his troops intact. "No General was more careful of the comfort and welfare of his men. When other corps were hungry, we always had rations; when other corps were ragged, we had clothes," wrote one soldier. "Joe Hooker fed his men the best, and fought them the best, of any of the corps commanders."

"Fighting Joe" survived until the end in Lincoln's affection, too, the final evidence of that friendship being his place as marshal in chief at Lincoln's final burial procession in Springfield, Illinois.

CHAPTER 17

The Political General: Benjamin Butler

L INCOLN'S PRIVATE SECRETARY, young John Hay, kept a diary off and on for the first three years of the war. On November 8, 1861, he wrote: "Here is a cheeky letter just recd." (He'd crossed out a stronger sentence: "It displays a wild and absurd miracle of cheek.")

"My dear Sir," wrote Benjamin Franklin Butler to the President:

I have an ambition and I trust a laudable one to be Major General of the United States Army.

Has anybody done more to deserve it? No one will do more. May I rely upon you as you may have confidence in me, to take this matter into consideration?

I will not disgrace the position. I may fail in its duties.

Truly yours,
Benj. F. Butler

No reply has ever been found. Lincoln sometimes did not know quite what to say to Butler.

Their evening meeting at the Soldiers' Home in the late summer of 1863 was one of many encounters between the two former lawyer/politicians—in Washington and in the field, "many and pleasant," Butler recalled years later. "I guess we both wish we were back trying cases," Lincoln said wistfully. Butler had been appalled by Lincoln's lack of concern for his safety as they rode alone together

Benjamin Butler was the first to figure out how to handle slaves escaping to Union lines (call them "contrabands," he said). He also brought order and better sanitation to rebellious New Orleans. Illustration courtesy of Picture History.

that night on the "quite lonely" road out to the Soldiers' Home. Lincoln, it seems, had eluded his guard once again. "We have passed a half dozen places where a well-directed bullet might have taken you off," he told Lincoln, who replied, "Oh, assassination of public officers is not an American crime." The two men disagreed vehemently on at least one other issue. Butler believed Lincoln's clemency toward deserters was dangerous. His own proposed remedy was "vigorously shooting every man who is caught as a deserter until it is found to be a dangerous business." The two men did share a fascination with new tools of war; Butler was the first American general to use aerial reconnaissance; he had a submarine built, and was even encouraging the development of what appeared to be a steam-driven helicopter when his military career ended.

Whether or not Butler ever disgraced the positions he did hold, or failed in the duties he was given, he was throughout the war the subject of heated controversy, with Butler himself continually fanning the flames. "He could strut sitting down," Lincoln said. "A gasbag," said Mary Todd Lincoln's close friend, Elizabeth Blair Lee.

Lincoln's good friend Orville Hickman Browning found Butler "a humbug." General in Chief Henry Halleck went much further. "It seems little better than murder to give important commands to such men as Butler . . . but it seems impossible to prevent it." It was indeed. Butler was hardly the only "political general" in Lincoln's volunteer army. Halleck had condemned generals Lew Wallace, John McClernand, Franz Sigel, and Nathaniel Banks in the same breath. But Butler was one of the best known and effective political figures of the day, with as many champions as enemies. So he required the kid-glove handling that Lincoln could give so adeptly until he was no longer useful politically, certainly not militarily. But-ler loved soldiering (he had wanted badly to go to West Point) but he was not very good at warmaking. His military operations were usually bungled—or worse. Quartermaster General Montgomery Meigs, a trusted adviser to Lincoln, summed Butler up after evalu-ating his performance in the field in 1864: "He is a man of rare and great ability. But he has not experience and training to enable him to direct and control movements in battle." Even hardened General Ulysses S. Grant had to admit that "as an administration officer, General Butler has no superior." But that passive role was not what Butler had in mind when he first met Lincoln in the White House in May 1861 soon after the war began. He undoubtedly was still looking for military glory (and an eventual shot at the White House himself) when he and Lincoln arrived at the Soldiers' Home two years later.

In their first encounter, Butler had been very frank with Lincoln about his political sentiments (not that Lincoln needed to be told). "You may not be aware . . . that [I] did all I could to prevent your election," Butler told Lincoln. 'All the better,' said [Lincoln]; 'I hope your example will bring many of the same sort with you.'" The "same sort" were Democrats who supported the Union and the war, crucial to victory. Butler did what Lincoln wanted—and desper-ately needed. Rallying Democrats to Lincoln's flag was one of But-ler's critical contributions to the Union cause. Every "political gen-eral" Lincoln appointed served a similar purpose: bringing to the war effort the support of their particular constituency. By one count, Lincoln gave out 187 such plums. When Secretary of War Stanton objected to the appointment of Alexander Schimmelfennig, like Carl Schurz, a German expatriate, arguing that there were better qualified officers available, Lincoln replied: "His name will make up for any difference there may be."

In every assignment Lincoln gave Butler for four years, or in operations Butler undertook on his own extraordinary initiative, he made history—and waves. Just three days after Fort Sumter was attacked on April 12, 1861, Butler was on his way from a Massachusetts courtroom to save Washington, a brigadier general in command of two regiments of Massachusetts volunteers. The capital was in real danger. "The prize to be won was gloriously magnificent," Butler wrote in his autobiography. "The capital of the nation, with its archives, its records, and its treasures, and all its executive organization, was there . . . the capture and occupation of Washington would almost certainly have insured the Confederacy a place of recognition as a power among the nations of the earth." Lincoln knew that, too. Grateful and relieved, a harried, already exhausted president went to the station to meet the first of Butler's regiments to arrive in Washington, and it was to them Lincoln said that Washington would have been in the hands of the rebels before morning if they had not come. Butler was surprised that they had not tried. He almost surely would have, if he'd been in their shoes.

As it was, a mob of rebel sympathizers and troublemakers in Baltimore had attacked Butler's first contingent on its way through the city, killed three, and wounded many others. No more would be allowed through, he was informed by the mayor and the governor. Butler decided it was smarter to go around the city, rather than fight his way through it with the rest of his troops.

Butler was superb at that kind of maneuvering. He had already become a wealthy and prominent attorney by using his head ("opposing brawn with brain"), agreeing with his adored wife and valued counselor, the former actress Sarah Hildreth, "If you can win these battles by stratagem rather than by rivers of blood, it would surely be better." Seizing railroad tracks, locomotives and carriages, a ferryboat, even the State Seal of Maryland, and calling bluffs all along the way, Butler succeeded in opening the way north for the Union. He had come to the relief of the nation's capital with spectacular success.

Butler finally arrived in Washington himself, a national hero over-night, itching for more action, and happy to learn that "Old Fuss and Feathers" Scott planned to seize recalcitrant Baltimore, and that Butler was to lead twelve thousand men to do so. Always mindful of titles as well as rank, he had also been named commander of the new Department of Annapolis, one of the titles cooked up to keep Butler's ego satisfied and out of real trouble. After consulting on his own with some influential Baltimore citizens, and analyzing the reports of his staff spy, Butler concluded that Scott's plan was unrea-sonably cumbersome, and that a thousand men could accomplish the same thing. Butler's takeover of the city was quick, clever, and bloodless, but General Scott was livid. From then on, he was out to hobble Butler, and for starters exiled him, he thought, to Fortress Monroe, on Chesapeake Bay at the tip of the peninsula between the York and James Rivers in Virginia.

In his sanitized recollection for an 1885 book of reminiscences of Lincoln by "distinguished men of his time," Butler says not a word about how bitter this exile made him. He saw it, with some justifi-cation, as banishment to what John Hay described as "that sleepy little department" on Chesapeake Bay. Butler had in fact wept tears of rage in his hotel room when he learned about it from Scott, who was still so furious he kept Butler standing at attention while deliv-ering the sentence. The same was true of Butler's account of his visit with Lincoln at the Soldiers' Home two years later: nothing at all about his astonishment at having been removed again, this time in December 1862, from his post as military governor of Louisiana and administrator of the important city of New Orleans.

Scott should have known better than to think Butler ever was out of the way. At Fortress Monroe, Butler made one of the most daring, significant decisions of the war. It took just three fugitive slaves for him to make it. The trio had slipped away from their work on Confederate fortifications nearby. Their owner, a Confederate captain, sent his agent to Butler the next morning to get them back, citing the Fugitive Slave Law. But Butler refused to hand over the three men, claiming that the Fugitive Slave Law no longer applied because the South had seceded. Furthermore, since the slaves were registered by their owner simply as property, and were, to make matters even worse, engaged in work that aided the Confederacy's war effort, Butler announced that he was confiscating the three men as "contraband of war." He then made another critical move: he put the men to work constructing a bakery for his troops, and paid them for it. Butler never liked the term "contraband," but the public did, and the word stuck. As Butler explained in his autobiography, "Everybody thought a way had been found through the slavery question ... it paved the way for the Emancipation Proclamation eighteen months later." His military secretary, the young poet-novelist Theodore Winthrop, put it succinctly: "An epigram abolished slavery in the United States."

Once again, Butler had electrified the North and, what was soon to become a habit, enraged the South. But Butler then made the mistake of ordering a confused and ill-prepared attack on a tiny village on the peninsula, Big Bethel. Scott had hindered whatever chances of success Butler might have had by withdrawing half of his best regiments before the action, and then used Butler's trouncing to remove him from command once again, compounding Butler's humiliation by replacing him with the ancient General John Wool. Ironically, Butler thought his removal might have been because his "views on the Negro question are not acceptable to the government." He had asked Washington in vain for guidance on how to handle the hordes of fleeing men, women, and children who began turning up at the fort. So to his wife Sarah he wrote, "The Negro will be free ... it is inevitable. We may patch it as we please, but the fact will work itself out."

Butler decided to leave this second command in typically sensational style. Disobeying orders, he launched an attack on two Confederate forts at Hatteras Inlet guarding the entrance to Pamlico Sound off the North Carolina coast. This time Butler's plans did work: he captured both forts and seven hundred prisoners. Butler wanted to report his success to Lincoln as fast as he could, hoping to wipe out the ignominy of his Big Bethel defeat, and to offer President Lincoln a small victory after the devastating rout of the Union army at Bull Run. A single-track railroad was all that could get him to Washington in a hurry, but Butler was warned that if he commandeered a train going north, he could very well be hit by one coming south. Butler figured that if he used only the engine car, by itself it could back up quickly enough to avoid collision. Even Butler himself described this as "hazardous bravado," but it worked. He arrived late at night in the capital, raced with his friend, Assistant Secretary of the Navy Gustavus V. Fox, to the White House, woke Lincoln up, and in one of the more memorable descriptions of Lincoln, roared with laughter as he saw tall Lincoln dancing for joy in his nightshirt with the short assistant secretary at the one bit of good news he had heard for some time.

In his autobiography, Butler somewhat sardonically summed up these remarkable exploits of the first months of the war: "I had opened the way through Annapolis for the troops to save the capital; I had fulfilled my mission at Fort Monroe, and by taking Hatteras I had atoned for capturing Baltimore and wiped out Big Bethel, all in a campaign of four months and seventeen days, besides showing the administration and the country the best way out of the slavery question. In all this time, nobody else had done anything except to get soundly thrashed at Bull Run." Butler was now mobbed by admirers everywhere he went.

A few months later he was back in Washington, with six thousand new volunteers, after an embarrassingly contentious recruiting campaign in New England. Lincoln once again had to smooth things over, this time between Butler and the abolitionist Republican governor of Massachusetts, who resented Butler's interference with his own recruiting efforts in the state. Lincoln noted that since Butler was cross-eyed, perhaps he didn't see things as others did. (Butler was also short, balding, and heavy, quite the contrast to Joseph Hooker, "the beautiful cadet.")

In a particularly disingenuous comment, Butler wrote that he was "sick of the intrigues and cross purposes" he found in Washington. Lincoln undoubtedly was, too, and perhaps thought to get Butler out of contention's way again by assigning him even farther south this time, to barren, windswept Ship Island about one hundred and fifty miles east of New Orleans. Butler suspected as much: in his autobiography he noted rumors that someone on McClellan's staff had said, "I guess we have found a hole to bury this Yankee elephant." As it turned out, an expedition to capture New Orleans was in the works, and Butler soon dug himself out of whatever hole had been intended for him by taking part in it.

After the city's capitulation to Admiral David Farragut, Butler's rule over New Orleans lasted less than a year, and by the time he was recalled once again by Lincoln in December 1863, he'd become infamous throughout the South as "Beast" Butler, and Jefferson Davis had condemned him to death as "an outlaw and common enemy of mankind." Butler's administration was severe: he hanged a man for tearing down the Union flag, he imprisoned the mayor and other dignitaries, "traitorous" women, and insulting shopkeepers, he confiscated hoards of gold and silver, and he treated so-called foreign consuls with contempt. Worst of all, at least in the eyes of the South, he'd threatened the women of the city with arrest as prostitutes if they did not stop their insults and physical abuse of Federal troops.

The good that Butler did in administering New Orleans is usually buried in rumors of corruption, which his brother, Andrew Jackson Butler, with his shady dealings, could do little to dispel. New Orleans was filthy when Butler took over its administration; he scrubbed the place clean and all but eliminated the yearly plague of yellow fever; he found a variety of ways to assess the rich of the city for funds to provide jobs and money for the poor, white and black; he eliminated specially marked streetcars for blacks and mustered free blacks into military service. He devised a "free labor" experiment to get cotton and sugar plantations producing again and sent the first barrel of sugar produced by those free blacks to President Lincoln. The *New York Herald* reported, "He is most Quixotic in his championship of the poor and distressed." The *New York Times* said: "Of all the civil and military officers that McClellan has sent forth to deal with treason, none has manifested the wisdom, firmness and skill of General Butler. The history of his administration of New Orleans will always be regarded as one of the most extraordinary and singularly interesting chapters in the annals of our war."

This Robin Hood persona would not have come as a surprise to those who knew of Butler's dogged work as a social reformer in Massachusetts, fighting for a shorter workday for mill workers in his hometown of Lowell (from fourteen to ten hours a day), and for the secret ballot, so that they could not be punished if they were seen voting against the bosses' wishes.

Butler's experience in New Orleans turned him into an abolitionist, and for the rest of his life, an ardent champion of equal
rights for black Americans. In his farewell address to "Citizens of
New Orleans," to which most likely only Union supporters in the
city listened, Butler concluded,

> I felt no hesitation in taking the substance of the wealthy, who had
> caused the war, to feed the innocent poor, who had suffered by the
> war. And I shall now leave you with the proud consciousness that
> I carry with me the blessings of the humble and loyal, under the
> roof of the cottage and in the cabin of the slave, and so am quite
> content to incur the sneers of the salon, or the curses of the rich.
> . . . I came among you, by teachings, by habit of mind, by political
> position, by social affinity, inclined to sustain your domestic laws,
> if by possibility they might be with safety to the Union. Months of
> experience and of observation have forced the conviction that the
> existence of slavery is incompatible with the safety either of your-
> selves or of the union. As the system has gradually grown to its
> present huge dimensions, it were best if it could be gradually
> removed; but it is better, far better, that it should be taken out at
> once, than that it should longer vitiate the social, political, and
> family relations of your country. . . . Such are the views forced upon
> me by experience.

It took just one more fiasco—at Fort Fisher, Virginia, in 1864—
to end Butler's military career, but hardly his political life. He went
on to a feisty career in congress, one of the most fervent converts to
radical Republicanism, and was leader of the prosecution in the im-
peachment of Andrew Johnson. He never made it to the presidency,
which of course he would have loved, for himself and his wife, of
whom he wrote:

> I had an advantage over most of my brother commanding generals
> in the department and in the field [he might have added of Lin-
> coln as well] in having an adviser, faithful and true, clear-headed,
> conscientious and conservative, whose conclusions could always be
> trusted . . . she made my home and family as happy as we could
> be. She took her place in society when at Washington, and main-
> tained it with such grace, dignity, and loveliness of character that
> no one ever said an unkind or a disparaging word of her.

His last post was governor of Massachusetts, equally controversial there as he had been everywhere else.

Charles Dana, Secretary of War Edwin Stanton's eyes and ears during the war, and later a powerful journalist, took Butler's measure more sympathetically than most. When Butler died in 1893, Dana wrote:

> Benjamin Franklin Butler has stood out as the most original, the most American and the most picturesque character in our public life. He had courage equal to every occasion; his given word needed no brackets; his friendships and his enemies knew no variableness or shadow of turning; his opinions were never disguised nor withheld; his devotion to his country was without qualifications; his faith in the future of liberty and democracy was neither intoxicated by their victories nor disheartened by their defeats; his intellectual resources were marvelous; his mind naturally adhered to the poor and the weak; and his delight was to stand by the underdog in the fight. In these qualities he was a great and an exceptional man, and his friends valued him and loved him as truly as his foes detested him. . . . He was no pretender and no hypocrite. He lived his life, a life of energy and effort, of success and of failure and he has passed to the allotted reward while we who remain may well be grateful to heaven such a man has lived.

CHAPTER 18

Lincoln and His Cabinet

When secretary of state William Henry Seward wrote to the American consul in Paris in 1862 that he went out alone to the Soldiers' Home to see Lincoln at all hours of the day or night without fear for his safety, he was trying to reassure his worried friend that Lincoln was not in danger either when he rode out there unguarded. "Assassination is not an American practice or our habit," he insisted. Coming from Seward, this was surprising. It had been Seward and his son Frederick who'd convinced Lincoln that there really was a plot to assassinate him before he even got to Washington. It was serious enough, they felt, for him to agree to travel incognito on the final stage of his inaugural journey from Springfield. But Seward could hardly have imagined that just three years after writing the consul, on the night of Lincoln's murder, he too would be an assassin's target. One of Booth's small gang of conspirators narrowly missed killing him as well, and in his own bed.

Perhaps unwittingly, Seward was also hinting to his friend at the warm friendship that had by then developed between himself and the president. It had taken some time for Seward to admit that Lincoln "was the best of us" without his original qualifier that Lincoln "needs constant and assiduous cooperation." Seward had been mortified by his loss of the 1860 Republican nomination to Lincoln. After all, he was far better known nationally, and the list of his credentials was longer and more impressive. One day not long after his humiliation, Seward was approached by a Wisconsin congressman,

Lincoln's Cabinet members finally realized he towered over them, as he does in this statue. A nineteen-year-old sculptor, Miss Vinnie Ream, won the commission for this work in 1866, unveiled in the Capitol in 1871.

urging him, as the new secretary of state, to avoid disappointing Wisconsin voters by giving a diplomatic post to the former German revolutionary, Wisconsin favorite son and Union general-to-be, Carl Schurz. Seward was normally very amiable and self-possessed. But not this time. "Disappointment!" Seward burst out. "You speak to me of disappointment. To me, who was justly entitled to the Republican nomination for the presidency, and who had to step aside and see it given to a little Illinois lawyer. You speak to me of disappointment!"

He'd led on the first ballot, even on the second, followed closely on the first, even closer on the second, by Lincoln. Other more likely contenders, the former governor of Ohio and United States Senator Salmon P. Chase, Edward Bates of Missouri, even shady Simon Cameron of Pennsylvania, never had much of a chance. By the third ballot, the contest at the huge, hectic, newly built convention hall, the "Wigwam," in Chicago was all but over. Lincoln had won. As custom dictated, neither Lincoln nor Seward was at the convention. Seward was at his family home in Auburn, New York, waiting quietly with his wife and daughter for the news that he was the nominee. Instead, his cherished daughter, Fanny, wrote in her diary:

> May, Friday, 18, 1860. Father told Mother and I—in three words, Abraham Lincoln nominated. His friends feel much distress—he alone has a smile—he takes it with philosophical & unselfish coolness.

> May, Saturday, 19, 1860. All father's friends disheartened, he alone cheerful—People act as if a great calamaty [sic] had befallen the nation and "strong men weep like children."

Lincoln went home quietly, but he could not sleep. "I then felt as I never had before, the responsibility that was upon me." He might have worried even more had he realized that Seward, once included in the new administration's cabinet, would assume that he, not Lincoln, would really be running everything. In fact, in August 1861, Seward wrote to Frances, his wife, "I look back and see that there has not been a day since last January that I could safely, for the Government, have been absent." Soon after that, Chicago journalist and Lincoln adviser, Joseph Medill, complained that Seward was "Lincoln's evil genius . . . he has been President *de facto* and has kept a sponge saturated with chloroform to Uncle Abe's nose."

Seward's wife was almost certainly not disappointed that her husband had lost the nomination; she did not relish the political life that Mary Todd Lincoln had found so exhilarating. Lincoln's first reaction on learning that he'd won the election on November 6, 1860, was to say, "I'd better go home. There's a little lady at home who would like to hear this news." As he approached their house at Eighth and Jackson, Lincoln shouted, "Mary, Mary, *we* are elected." Mary could hardly wait to get to Washington. Frances had always preferred to stay in her father's home in Auburn, no matter where her husband's political career took him. But that distaste for politics did not preclude her having convictions as strong as Mary's. She too was an admirer of the vehemently antislavery Senator Charles Sumner. Frances was also more radical on the subject of emancipation than her husband. Seward was not alone in fearing that emancipation might bring on a slave uprising in the South against "the Lords of the Lash," as Sumner called them, which in turn might cause cotton-devouring England and France to get involved as "Lords of the Loom" to protect their supplies, and that slaves might end up starving if emancipation came too soon. Seward never changed his private view that the Emancipation Proclamation was "a puff of wind over an accomplished fact . . . the emancipation proclamation was uttered in the first gun fired at Sumter." In two of the letters that the couple exchanged almost daily when they were apart, Frances argued that the slaves might want to take the chance of starving rather than be left "exposed to such horrible cruelty as is sometimes their fate." Later she wrote that Lincoln [and by inference, her adored "Henry"] "gives the impression that the mere keeping together [of] a number of states is more important than human freedom."

Lincoln's first challenge was to select the seven men who would, or at least should, serve as his official advisers—his cabinet. He began putting together a list of possible candidates on election night, but he was still balancing and juggling almost until Inauguration Day, March 4, 1861, cobbling a group together, just as the Republican Party itself had been cobbled together four years before, out of a new mix of regional, social, and economic interests held together principally by mutual opposition to the expansion of slavery into new territory. "The making of a cabinet . . . was by no means as easy as he had supposed," the admittedly inexperienced Lincoln told Thurlow Weed, alter ego of the disappointed Seward, and one of the wiliest, most controversial political operatives of his time, who had wept frustrated tears when Seward lost. Lincoln's negotiations with Seward were almost as intricate as those with Salmon Chase. Lincoln asked Chase "to accept the appointment of Secretary of the Treasury, without, however, [my] being exactly prepared to offer it to you." Chase's response was equally arcane. "I did not wish to and was not prepared to say that I would accept the place if offered."

What seems astonishing today about Lincoln's final list of cabinet appointees is that it included all four men whose ambitions for the presidency he had thwarted: Seward for State, Chase for Treasury, Bates as attorney general, and Cameron for the War Department.

This was hardly a recipe for harmony—or loyalty. (Orpheus C. Kerr has his own satirical take on the list: "Old Abe . . . selected his Cabinet officers because they all had large mouths and could laugh easily.") Lincoln did try to release their own tension by getting them to laugh from time to time, with limited success. As for Chase, Lincoln maintained that it required a surgical operation to get a joke through his head. A year and a half later, one observer likened the cabinet to "a collection of powerful chemicals, each positive, sharp, individual—but [which] thrown together, neutralize each other & the result is an insipid mess." This was not quite fair. To begin with, it was a calculated mix on Lincoln's part, a coalition of the interests and opinions Lincoln needed to understand and pull together in order to face a disintegrating Union and bitter antagonists intent on separation, even war, if it came to that.

William Henry Seward was arguably the best placed of Lincoln's final choices. He had traveled abroad, and developed a world view in which an expanded America had a powerful place. His house across from the White House was a congenial gathering place for a succession of foreign diplomats, dignitaries, and cultural leaders, even Lincoln himself. Seward later liked to bring his foreign counterparts out to the Soldiers' Home of an evening. Acquiring Canada had been in his sights for years, but the purchase of Alaska in 1867 would be his last effort to unite all of North America under one government. As Charles Dana, assistant secretary of war, put it in his Civil War recollections, Seward had what is very rare in a lawyer, a politician, or a statesman—imagination. Too often the politician got in the way of the statesman Seward tried so hard to be—far too often, Lincoln's secretary of the Navy Gideon Welles and many others believed.

Mary Todd Lincoln had warned her husband about Seward in particular when she saw his cabinet list, but then, she had little use for any of his appointees. Seward was "a dirty abolition sneak," she believed, a hypocrite who would take credit when things went right, and leave Lincoln, "a saint," with the blame if they didn't. Very early in the game, Mary had hissed at Seward, "It is said that you are the power behind the throne. I'll show you that Mr. Lincoln is president yet." Lincoln had already done that. "I can't allow Seward to take the first trick," he told John Hay, after he had maneuvered Seward out of resigning in objection to the inclusion of Chase, his bitter rival, in the cabinet lineup. Lincoln had also taken a second trick. Less than a month into the administration, Seward submitted "Some Thoughts for the President's Consideration." It was so spectacular in its boldness and vanity (a "mortal insult," Carl Schurz called it), Lincoln would have had every reason to get rid of his secretary of state on its receipt. "We are at the end of a month's administration, and yet without a policy, either domestic or foreign," Seward charged. After outlining his stunning recommendations, including the prospect of a war against France or Spain (to bring the seceding states back into the Union to face a common enemy, he reasoned), Seward concluded, "Either the President must do it himself, and he all the while active in it, or devolve it on some member of his Cabinet . . . I neither seek to evade nor assume responsibility." Lincoln answered privately, tactfully, logically. "Only the hand of iron in the glove of velvet" could have responded the way he did, believed his secretaries, Nicolay and Hay, when they revealed this extraordinary exchange only years later in their history of Lincoln's presidency. Lincoln rebutted Seward's points one by one, and ended unequivocally, "If this must be done, I must do it."

Only two of Lincoln's original cabinet appointments survived the incredible strains of the next four years, and then went on, remarkably, for another four years in their same capacities in the Andrew Johnson administration. Seward was one, Gideon Welles the other. The two men had just a few other things in common. They were the only members of the cabinet we know to have visited Lincoln at the Soldiers' Home. (Edwin Stanton sometimes occupied another cottage on the Soldiers' Home grounds.) They were also the first cabinet members Lincoln chose to reveal his plans to issue an Emancipation Proclamation. He invited both to accompany him to Gettysburg for the cemetery dedication. Both became Lincoln's good friends. Devastating family tragedies surely must have helped bind all three men together. Seward had already lost an infant daughter when the war began. (Frances would die just nine weeks after the assassination attempt on her husband's life; Fanny would die of tuberculosis in 1866.) Just three of the Welleses' nine children survived to adulthood. (Mary Lincoln's good friend Elizabeth Blair Lee, not surprisingly, thought Mary Jane Welles was "one of the saddest persons I ever saw.") Welles's four-year-old son, Hubert, died during the war, in 1863. And it was in a carriage carrying Lincoln, Seward, and Welles to the funeral for Secretary of War Stanton's infant son that Lincoln spoke to the two men of his emancipation plans.

Gideon Welles was the only member of Lincoln's inner circle to leave a comprehensive account of Lincoln's administration in a voluminous diary. (Seward intended to keep a diary, but managed to report on only one day.) On December 3, 1862, Welles wrote what Lincoln surely felt about Willie, "A light, bright cherub face, which threw its sunshine on our household, when this book was last opened, has disappeared forever. My dear Hubert, who was a treasure garnered in my heart, is laid beside his five brothers and sisters in Spring Grove." Given this sad history, it's not surprising that Welles became somewhat impatient in June 1863 with Mary Todd Lincoln's continued insistence, over a year after Willie's death, that the Marine Band's weekly performance outside the White House remain canceled. (She'd stopped Company K's band as well.) "The public will not sympathize in sorrows which are obtrusive or assigned as a reason for depriving them of enjoyments. It is a mistake to persist in it." Lincoln, caught as he often was in the crossfire between Mary's wishes and others' needs, told Welles to do what he thought best, so Welles went ahead and started the concerts again—in Lafayette Square nearby—"the people greatly pleased."

Mary Lincoln and Mary Jane Welles became very close during the war, so close that Mrs. Welles, sick as she was, answered the plea to go to the house across from Ford's Theater to try to console Mary as Lincoln lay dying. During the war the two women had made many visits together to military hospitals, unannounced and ignored by the press, which did not help bolster Mary's reputation. Thanks to their friendship, Mary's letters to Mrs. Welles, during the White House years and after, give us some of the most intimate insights into the Lincoln marriage. In a revealing comment in her December 6, 1865, letter, Mary showed her spunk, the "elasticity of spirit" others admired in Lincoln, confessing that she was tempted to try the cigarettes Welles's son had sent Robert Todd Lincoln as a souvenir of his trip to Havana! Mrs. Welles accompanied her husband at least once to the Soldiers' Home on July 26, 1864, but Welles's diary for that day indicated it was not for pleasure.

If Seward went out to the Soldiers' Home with anybody, it was likely to be one of his foreign counterparts. He proved invaluable to Lincoln on matters of protocol and diplomatic appointments; his diplomatic dispatches could be adroit masterpieces. Seward undoubtedly composed the numerous letters Lincoln was required to write to his "Great and Good Friends" around the world, such as to thank the King of Siam for a proposed gift of elephants, which, alas, had to be refused: "Our political jurisdiction . . . does not reach a latitude so low as to favor the multiplication of the elephant, and steam on land, as well as on water, has been our best and most efficient agent of transportation in internal commerce." Seward even proposed a conclusion for Lincoln's first inaugural address, and must have begun to suspect Lincoln's genius when he read what Lincoln had done with his suggestions:

> "I close," Seward proposed. "I am loth to close," wrote Lincoln.
>
> "We are not, we must not be, aliens or enemies, but fellow-countrymen and brethren," Seward suggested. "We are not enemies, but friends. We must not be enemies," wrote Lincoln.
>
> "Although passion has strained our bonds of affection too hardly, they must, I am sure they will not, be broken." [Seward] "Though passion may have strained, it must not break our bonds of affection." [Lincoln]

And finally, in the most telling improvement of all:

> "The mystic chords which, proceeding from so many battle-fields and so many patriot graves, pass through all the hearts and all the hearths in this broad continent of ours, will yet harmonize in their ancient music when breathed upon by the guardian angels of the nation." [Seward]
>
> "The mystic chords of memory, stretching from every battle-field and patriot grave, to every living heart and hearthstone, all over this broad land, will yet swell the chorus of the Union, when again touched, as surely they will be, by the better angels of our nature." [Lincoln]

Mary Todd Lincoln and Frances Miller Seward had little chance to develop any such friendship, partly because Mrs. Seward chose to stay in Auburn most of the time, and when she was in Washington, Mary's detestation of Seward spilled over to Frances with a vengeance. On September 9, 1861, Fanny Seward recorded in her diary,

> After dinner according to our previous plans, we went to call on Mrs. Lincoln . . . we were shown . . . into the blue and gold room—and all seated—quite a party to be sure—Edward drew a chair for Mrs. L. & one or two extra ones & went to tell her. . . . Well there we sat—Father, Mother, Major De Courcy, Mr. Nicolay—Fred, Anna [Fred's wife], Jenny & I—after a lapse of some time the usher came and said Mrs. Lincoln begged to be excused, she was *very* much engaged—(men. The only time on record that she ever refused to see company in the evening—she generally sits in state. . . .) So we filed out. . . . The truth of Mrs. L.'s engagement was probably that she did not want to see Mother—else why not give general directions to the door keeper to let no one in? It was certainly very rude to have us all seated first.

Sweet Fanny tried to put the best light on Mrs. Lincoln's snub by concluding her diary entry with a mention of Mary's humane intercession to save a man from a death sentence for sleeping at his post.

The few things the two department secretaries had in common were not sufficient for them to have deliberately arranged to appear together at the Soldiers' Home, although Seward, much to Welles's disgust, annoyed him and other cabinet members by taking every opportunity to nose around in their affairs while keeping them out of his own. It did not help that Welles had fought against Seward's nomination (not for Lincoln, although Welles admired him, but for Chase) and he remained, in his diary at least, Seward's most persistent and harshest critic. At the outset, Seward had certainly acted as if Welles and the navy were his subordinates, arranging arrogantly, recklessly—in the belief that he could steer the country away from war—a secret expedition to protect Fort Pickens in Florida. He bamboozled the harried Lincoln into permitting him to take one of Welles's best ships (the *Powhatan*) to do so. This turned out to be a serious blow to Lincoln's plans to resupply Fort Sumter. More than one motive has been suggested to explain Seward's behavior; Welles thought it was Seward's excessive vanity: Seward, he wrote, "prided himself in his skill and management, and had a craving desire that the world should consider him the great and controlling mind of his party, of the Administration, and the country." Welles did admit that "Seward has genius and talent. No one knows that better than himself." He was essentially a "dove," Welles a "hawk." When Seward remarked after the *Powhatan* incident that from then on "he'd better tend to his own business, and confine his labors to his own department," Welles wrote in his diary, "I cordially assented."

The two men had come to the Republican Party from different political and professional directions. Welles was an influential Connecticut newspaperman with a national reputation, a former Democrat who helped organize the Republican Party in 1856, and happily for Lincoln, had no higher ambition than a cabinet post. One wag attributed his appointment to the Navy Department to Lincoln's having perhaps thought that "any New Englander must be amphibious." Welles had served in the Navy Department for four years under President Polk, as chief of the Bureau of Provisions and Clothing. So he knew at the outset at least as much, if not more, than Lincoln's other appointees did—except Seward—about their respective departments. One post seemed as good as the other, as Lincoln put together pieces of that particular political jigsaw puzzle.

Seward was an experienced politician who'd served effectively as a humanitarian, courageous governor of New York from 1839 through 1842, and as a United States Senator from 1849 to 1861. His references to an "irrepressible conflict" and a "higher law" than the Constitution gave him a strong antislavery reputation. Seward, like Lincoln, had eventually thrown in the fading Whig Party towel, which was melding into a new Republican Party. Welles and Seward were on opposite sides of critical wartime issues and policy, from the advisability of resupplying Fort Sumter to the seizure of supposedly neutral vessels and their mails. Welles favored attack, challenge, retribution, and openness. Seward preferred conciliation, negotiation, and compromise, which others often saw as opportunism, deviousness, and recklessness. He worked desperately, if not dangerously, to avoid civil war.

Their physical appearances and temperaments were as different as their backgrounds. Henry Adams loved Seward. His classic autobiography, *The Education of Henry Adams,* contains an insightful description of the secretary of state:

> a slouching slender figure; a head like a wise macaw; a beaked nose; shaggy eyebrows; unorderly hair and clothes; hoarse voice; offhand manner; free talk; and perpetual cigar...at table, among friends, Mr. Seward threw off restraint, or seemed to throw it off, in reality, while in the world he threw it off, like a politician, for effect. [He] was never petty or personal; his talk was large; he generalized; he never seemed to pose for statesmanship; he did not require an attitude of prayer.

Adams omitted to mention that Seward liked to swear. He and Lincoln were out riding in a carriage one day when the coachman began to curse at some obstacle in the way. Lincoln asked the man if he were an Episcopalian. The driver replied that if he went to church at all, it was to the Methodist. "Oh," said Lincoln, "I thought you must be an Episcopalian, too, for you swear like Mr. Seward and he's a church warden."

As for Gideon Welles, Henry Adams did not bother to describe him. (His father, Charles Francis Adams, Lincoln's minister to the Court of St. James's during the war, believed it was Seward who ran the country for four years, not Lincoln. This infuriated Welles, who indignantly countered Adams's argument in later years.) Many did write Welles off as an old fogey—Grandmother Welles and Rip van Winkle being a few of the epithets—and Welles resented it. He chastised himself for being too reticent, instead—fortunately for us—pouring out his pungent observations with his pen. Journalist Noah Brooks's description was gently charming:

> Father Welles, as the populace term our venerable Secretary of the Navy, is not so old as he is painted, although his white beard and snowy hair—wig, I mean—give him an apostolic mien which, in these degenerate days, is novel and unusual. He is a kind-hearted, affable and accessible man. Unlike his compeer of the Treasury, he does not hedge his dignity about him as a king, but is very simple and unaffected in his manners. He is tall, shapely, precise, sensitive to ridicule, and accommodating to the members of the press...

that he is slightly fossiliferous is undeniable, but it is a slander that he pleaded, when asked to personate the grandmother of a dying sailor, that he was busy examining a model of Noah's ark.... Welles ... has all of the industry of Stanton with all of the pride of Chase, which is saying a great deal. He will not lose his place in a hurry.

And he did not. Lincoln became so fond of his secretary of the navy that he called him "Neptune." Welles deserved Lincoln's regard. "Few officials have ever had to begin a life and death struggle with the problems that beset Gideon Welles ... his ships were scattered all over the globe, many of his best officers had gone South, and more than thirty-five hundred miles of coastline had to be blockaded." He presided over the "development and deployment of the greatest national armada of the [nineteenth] century." Lincoln came to count on Welles's honesty, frankness, and good sense; he had the courage of his convictions. The two shared a strong interest in new technologies, and a willingness to take big chances, as Welles did with his enthusiasm for the Monitor class of ship. Fortunately for Welles, the politicians who so persistently besieged Lincoln with petitions for high military rank appreciated, modestly for once, that a naval command might be beyond their capabilities. So Welles was freer to chose his own officers, and he usually chose well. Admiral David Farragut, a Tennessean who remained loyal to the Union, was his prize. Welles's navy was relatively welcoming to free and fleeing blacks. By the end of the war, blacks would make up 20 percent of the navy's enlisted force, twice the percentage for the army. In 1863, Lincoln paid a lyrical tribute to Welles and his navy: "Nor must Uncle Sam's web feet be forgotten. At all the watery margins they have been present. Not only on the deep sea, the broad bay, and the rapid river, but also up the narrow, muddy bayou, and wherever the ground was a little damp, they have been, and made their tracks." When Vicksburg fell, Lincoln threw his arm around Welles, saying, "he is always giving us good news."

It is easier to imagine Lincoln and Seward at the Soldiers' Home than Welles and Lincoln there. Seward's son Frederick drew a vivid picture of Lincoln and Seward together:

As they sat together by the fireside, or in the carriage, the conversations between them ... always drifted back to the same channel—the progress of the great national struggle. Both loved humor, and however trite the theme, Lincoln always found some quaint illustration from his western life, and Seward some case in point in his long public career, that gave it new light.

They must have compared notes on their shared love of history (and even of cats). As to the nature Seward loved, Lincoln obviously had a different take on it. "I know all about trees," Lincoln told some women he met walking on the Soldiers' Home grounds, "in light of being a backwoodsman. I'll show you the difference between spruce, pine, and cedar." Lincoln would comment on how well or poorly trees had been chopped down by soldiers to make camp. He preferred trees without leaves, so he could see "their anatomy." Seward, on the other hand, tended to rhapsodize: "I wish you could be in the grounds here this bright morning," he wrote to Frances. "The chestnuts are in full bloom, and there is a humming of bees . . . their foliage like the music of a distant waterfall . . . I watch the development of vegetation with a lover's interest."

Seward's optimism was an important counter to Lincoln's tendency to melancholy. One day, Lincoln said to Seward, "I think I will telegraph to Sherman that I will not break up McClellan's command and that I haven't much hope of his expedition anyway." "No," said Seward. "You won't say discouraging things to a man going off with his life in his hand. Send them some hopeful and cheering dispatch."

Industrious Welles was all business. His penchant for maxims, which were scattered through his diary, would not necessarily make for the kind of conversation Lincoln had with Seward either:

Those who know least, clamor most.

Capitalists will not as a general rule loan or invest for patriotism, but for good returns.

All men crave power.

Let the rebel perish away from the parents whom he had abandoned.

Welles never let up on his criticism of Seward, at least in his diary, although Seward soon realized that Welles was not to be pushed around. But Welles's respect for Lincoln and the president's "intuitive sagacity" grew. He'd begun to form a good impression when he visited Lincoln in Springfield with the distinguished delegation sent to inform Lincoln officially of his nomination, hoping, too, that Lincoln might notice his cabinet potential. By September 7, 1862, he wrote:

> From what I have seen and heard in the last few days, the more highly do I appreciate the President's judgment and sagacity.

Later, he wrote:

> Lincoln's military convictions and conclusions are infinitely superior to [General] Henry Halleck's. (July 7, 1863)
>
> Lincoln's own letters and writings are generally unpretending and abound in good sense. (August 11, 1863)
>
> The President has well-maintained his position and under trying circumstances acquitted himself in a manner that will be better appreciated in the future than now. (December 31, 1863)
>
> The President's estimation of character is usually very correct, and he frequently divests himself of partiality with a readiness that has surprised me. (January 8, 1864)

To Lincoln, Seward was "a man without gall." It was he who advised Lincoln to wait for a military victory before announcing the preliminary Emancipation Proclamation. Under Lincoln's watchful eye, he grew as a statesman, and he is now regarded as one of the great secretaries of state in American history. With his geopolitical perspective, he saw the value of a transcontinental railroad, of global telegraphic communications, the acquisition of island bases in the Caribbean and the Pacific, even the creation of a canal through the Isthmus of Panama. He had steadied America's delicate relations with the major European powers, keeping them from recognizing the Confederacy as an independent nation. As for Seward's view of Lincoln, after the election of 1864, he had come to believe that "Lincoln will take his place with Washington, and Franklin and Jefferson, and Adams and Jackson, among the benefactors of the country and the human race." Toward the end of his own life, Seward rued its length. "I have always felt that Providence dealt hardly with me in not letting me die with Mr. Lincoln. My work was done, and I think I deserved some of the reward of dying there." Mary Todd Lincoln would have preferred that herself.

EPILOGUE

IT WAS THE FIRST transatlantic passage to America for the famous actress Sarah Bernhardt. But it would be the last for the little woman she observed "dressed in black, with a sad, resigned face." As the two women walked on deck, the ship suddenly rolled violently. The woman in black would have fallen headfirst down the stairs she was about to descend if the actress had not grabbed her skirt and held her back. "You might have been killed, Madam, down that horrible staircase," said Sarah. "Yes," said the woman, "but it was not God's will." When Bernhardt introduced herself, the woman revealed who she was, with some resentment. "I am the widow of President Lincoln." Bernhardt realized that she "must have done this unhappy woman the only service that I ought not to have done her. I had saved her from death."

Death finally did come for Mary Todd Lincoln two years after her final return from Europe to the United States that fall of 1880. She had survived seventeen anguished years in increasingly poor health since the assassination of her adored husband—"my all, truly my all," she said time and again. Those seventeen years were filled, as only the complex, volatile, controversial Mary Todd Lincoln could have filled them—with drama, contention, and ever more tragedy, compounded by her blaming herself for the president's death. "My own life, has been so chequered," she wrote at the end of 1865 to Elizabeth Blair Lee, "naturally so gay & hopeful—my prominent desires, all granted me—my noble husband, who was my 'light & life' and my highest—ambition gratified—and that was, the great weakness of my life. My husband became distinguished above all. And yet, owing to that fact, I firmly believe he lost his life & I am bowed to the earth with Sorrow."

Robert Todd Lincoln, Mary's eldest son, had written to his fiancée, Mary Harlan, before their 1868 wedding, "My mother is on one subject not mentally responsible. It is very hard to deal with someone who is sane on all subjects but one." That, of course, was

money. After the assassination, Mary had become even more con-
sumed with worry about her substantial debt and her future income.
No amount of money could have assuaged her grief over the loss of
her husband; no domestic arrangement could possibly have compared
to the distinction of living in the White House, or the pleasures of
her "dearly loved" Soldiers' Home. But her worries were justified
in the early years of her widowhood. All she had was what was left
of Lincoln's twenty-five-thousand-dollar 1865 salary. His substantial
estate would not be settled for three years, until 1868. Her long-
fought-for pension of three thousand dollars a year was not approved
by Congress for five years, in 1870. So in the meantime, Mary's standard of living nosedived. Her attempt to raise money through the
sale of her elegant White House wardrobe was a public relations and
financial disaster. Few were inclined to philanthropy in her cause,
although she did somehow raise ten thousand dollars to help pay off
her personal debts—to the penny. Senator Charles Sumner and Frederick Douglass were among the few who seemed to care at all about
her well-being. The generous gifts of money and houses bestowed
on other Civil War heroes made her comparative poverty even more
bitter.

Twice in those seventeen years, Mary Lincoln fled to Europe,
"putting the waters between me and unkindness," she explained.
On the first voyage, Tad Lincoln, "her bright little comforter," was
her loyal companion. But when she began her second exile in September 1876, she was all alone, in poor health, and shattered once
again by loss. Tad had died in July 1871, and what was left of her
reputation had been ruined by the insanity trial engineered in May
1875 by her only surviving son, straitlaced Robert. Such a trial and a
judgment of insanity was the only legal way under Illinois law he
could gain control of her finances, which he was convinced were in
jeopardy because of her increasingly eccentric spending habits, and
the possibility of losing her financial assets to charlatans or the ill
will of her political enemies. So Robert's motives were probably
benign, but his methods were cruel. At least there was a trial, not
just his word, which might have sufficed for commitment in all but
three states at that time. But it was a travesty: Robert had gathered
his evidence carefully, but Mary was given no time to prepare a

defense (she was told of her trial that same morning). The doctors who testified to her insanity had never examined her, and the jury deliberated just ten minutes. Mary was appalled, and never forgave her son.

Mary's courage and intelligence were put immediately into high gear to figure out how to escape the pleasant private asylum outside Chicago where she was sent after the trial. In a few months of clever, shrewd maneuvering, she was free and back in her sister's house in Springfield, where her only happiness had begun years before with her marriage to Abraham Lincoln in that very house. A year later, in June 1876, she commenced the petition to have a jury declare her "restored to reason and capable to manage and control her estate," which was now considerable. She was quite comfortably off, and soon bound again for Europe. "I cannot stay in Springfield," she told her sister, Elizabeth Edwards. "My former friends will never cease to regard me as a lunatic. If I should say the moon is made of green cheese, they would heartily and smilingly agree with me. I would be much less unhappy in the midst of strangers."

Mary did her best in Europe during the next four years. She read widely, traveled, indulged her obsession with shopping, kept informed about American politics, and tried spa after spa to heal her aching body, her intense pain made even worse from a fall that severely injured her back. But finally she had to go home. She was too sick to stay away any longer.

Records of her final medical examination in New York City by four prominent physicians, just six months before her death on July 15, 1882, were reevaluated not long ago by two physicians, one a medical historian. They came to a stunning conclusion: that Mary Todd Lincoln was a long-time victim of severe, untreated diabetes, resulting in a condition known as locomotor ataxia, a chronic spinal cord disease. Its known symptoms are so vividly bizarre, at the time they lent credence to the accusation of insanity when Mary described "being all hacked to pieces by knives . . . I'm on fire, burning up," or insisted on remaining in a dark room with only a candle for light, or that someone was pulling wires out of her eyes. There is also greater understanding today of the psychological needs that lie behind excessive spending. Post-traumatic stress syndrome may also have contributed to her odd behavior as the tenth anniversary of her husband's assassination neared, just a few weeks before the insanity trial.

In recent years, historians also have begun to offer more sympathetic assessments of Mary Todd Lincoln. During most of her lifetime, they were few. Some of her Springfield neighbors spoke well of her: James Gourley told the detested William Herndon, "I don't think that Mrs. Lincoln was as bad a woman as she is represented. She was a good friend of mine . . . a good woman." Noyes Miner, in his *Vindication of Mrs. Abraham Lincoln*, testified that she was "a devoted wife, a loving mother, a kind neighbor, and a sincere and devoted friend. Blessings on her memory." The Reverend J. A. Reed offered a compassionate epitaph at her funeral. He compared the Lincolns to "two lofty pine trees with branches and roots intertwined. Though only one was struck by lightning, they had virtually both been killed at the same time. With the one that lingered, it was slow death from the same cause."

As for Lincoln, his ranking by historians as our greatest president has held for decades. His compassion, his brilliance, his eloquence, and his martyrdom have brought him immortality. In perhaps the grandest tribute of all, Leo Tolstoy believed that Lincoln was "what Beethoven was in music, Dante in poetry, Raphael in painting, and Christ in the philosophy of life. He aspired to be divine, and he was." But does Lincoln have anything to tell us today? Does he matter? "He himself presided over the social revolution that destroyed the simple equalitarian order of the 1840s," wrote historian Richard Hofstadter. "Booth's bullet confined his life to the happier age that Lincoln understood, which unwittingly he helped to destroy, the age that gave sanction to the honest compromises of his thought."

Lincoln kept the Union from disintegrating into two, perhaps even more parts, but how united would he find us as a people a century and a half later? His own words suggest that Lincoln would caution against believing that God picks sides. "Are we on God's side?" was to him the far more important question. To those who still try to puzzle out what religious faith might attract Lincoln today, his credo would still be simple: "When any church will inscribe over its altar,

Lincoln's likeness was carved for the top of a Tlingit totem pole a few years after his assassination. It is the only known totem of a white man. Illustration from the Alaska State Museum, Juneau.

as its sole qualification for membership . . . " he insisted, "the Saviour's condensed statement of both Law and Gospel, 'Thou shalt love the Lord thy God with all thy heart, and with all thy soul, and with all thy mind, and thy neighbor as thyself,' that church will I join with all my heart and all my soul."

Lincoln would urge caution before embarking on war. "One war at a time," he told his secretary of state, William Henry Seward, when he squelched Seward's proposal to start a conflict against a European power as a way to attract the secessionists back into the Union, believing they would choose to form a united front with the North to face an external enemy.

He would appreciate that Americans are still struggling to go forward, as he did, in "the race of life," still believing in the American Dream his own life epitomizes. And he would encourage belief in the critical role of government in that struggle, as he told Congress in his Fourth of July, 1861, message, words well worth repeating: "[Its] leading object is, to elevate the condition of men—to lift artificial weights from all shoulders—to clear the paths of laudable pursuits for all—to afford all, an unfettered start, and a fair chance, in the race of life."

Above all, he would remind us that our American experiment in self-government is "the last, best hope of earth," and that it is far too precious to us and to the world to be given away through cynicism, intolerance, greed, even apathy.

ACKNOWLEDGMENTS

To see the President Lincoln and Soldiers' Home Monument come closer and closer to fruition over these past few years has been a thrill, made all the more intense for my having been asked to write a book about Abraham Lincoln's life there. I am indebted to Richard Moe, the president of the National Trust for Historic Preservation, for his faith in my ability to bring this handsome and haunting undiscovered treasure to life through words. Sophia Lynn, the Monument's meticulous project manager, has been unfailingly and warmly cooperative, and her assistants, Erin Carlson and Angela Brown, quick to respond to my requests. Watching the application of the expertise and integrity of David Overholt and Bill Dupont to the preservation of the site has been a particular pleasure. The support of Jim Vaughan and Max van Bagooly has been much appreciated, and I am deeply grateful to Matthew Pinsker and his researchers for the superb material they provided, which formed the solid base for my own endeavors, as well as his own writing.

My brilliant agent, Paul Mahon, came through once again with warm support, expert advice, and unbelievable generosity. Hana Lane, my editor at Wiley, was unfailingly amiable and expert. Editorial researcher Jane Caplan, and image researcher Ann Monroe Jacobs, were once again a pleasure to work with. Scott Schulke, my computer guru, responded with good-natured and expert assistance with viruses and other mysterious technological problems, no matter what time of day or night.

I was constantly awed by, and thankful for, the capacity of the Library of Congress to come up quickly with even the most esoteric material. It is truly a magnificent place, and the research staff is superb. I thank Evelyn Timberlake, Bruce Martin, and all their colleagues for their efficient help.

My field trip to Meadville, Pennsylvania, in search of Company K was a delight. Mike and Penni Dallas are dedicated Civil War re-enactors, and they were more than willing to share their knowledge, their research files (and their overflowing supply of period uniforms, dresses, and paraphernalia) with me. They and their fellow reenactors deserve much credit for bringing our history to life for young and old (and often woefully ignorant) Americans. LeRoy E. Fladseth was generous with stories of his grandfather, Sergeant Smith Stimmel, as were Sergeant Joseph Conroy about Company F, 150th Pennsylvania "Bucktails" and Mark Roche about Company H. Longtime friend Colonel Gordon Francis (ret.) provided expert hands-on information about comparative nineteenth- and twentieth-century military practice. Everyone at the Armed Forces Retirement Home, both residents and administrators, was ready and willing to add to my store of information about past and present life there.

Dr. Mary Beth Corrigan, archivist of the Rare Book Library at the Riggs Bank, was a stimulating authority on George Riggs and nineteenth-century Washington, as was Kathleen W. Dorman at the Smithsonian Institution Archives on first Secretary Dr. Joseph Henry, first African American employee Solomon G. Brown, and on the Smithsonian Institution's fate during the Civil War. Jane Westenfeld, reference librarian of Special Collections/Ida M. Tarbell Collection, the Pelletier Library, Allegheny College, Meadville, Pennsylvania, was ingenious in turning up valuable, wide-ranging material during my week of research in Company K's hometown. Nancy Hadley, archivist of the American Institute of Architects, arranged for my visit to the evocative AIA Rare Book Room. Paul Sledzik, curator of the Anatomical Collection at the Armed Forces Institute of Pathology, in Washington, D.C., provided valuable information on the whereabouts of General Daniel Sickles's leg and Civil War medical practice, Ron Harvey of the National Park Service explained Civil War forts, and Carolyn Lackey at the Military History Institute, Carlisle, Pennsylvania, detailed the lives of individual soldiers in Company K. The staff at the Martin Luther King Washingtoniana collection were always ready to help, as were Michael Musick at the National Archives and Bob Willard, a longtime Lincolniana collector. Thomas Schwartz, Illinois state historian, and Kim Bauer, curator of the Lincoln collection at the Abraham Lincoln Presidential Library and Museum in Springfield, Illinois, are sitting on a gold mine, which they are always ready to mine for the literary prospector.

I am particularly grateful for the advice of distinguished American historians: Dr. William Lee Miller, whose own writings on the period set a standard difficult to emulate; Dr. Cullom Davis, editor of *Law Practice of Abraham Lincoln*, Dr. Edna Greene Medford of Howard University, Dr. Jean Baker of Goucher College, Dr. Fath Ruffin of the Smithsonian Institution, Dr. John Vlach of George Washington University, Dr. James W. Loewen, Dr. Harold Hyman, John M. Taylor, biographer of William Henry Seward, and Dr. Scott Cairns, whose new dissertation on Lord Lyons, British minister to the United States during the Civil War, was very engaging. (I am indebted to Greg Bayne and fellow Civil War buffs in the United Kingdom for help in tracking him down.)

In every part of the country, I found resources to enrich the portraits of Lincoln and the other characters in this book: in Baton Rouge, Louisiana, courtesy of Judy Bolton, at the Special Collections in the Hill Memorial Library of Louisiana State University; in San Marino, California, through Dr. John Rhodehamel, Norris Foundation Curator of American Historical Manuscripts at the Huntington Library; in Gambier, Ohio, through Carol Marshall, at the Greenslade Collection, Kenyon College; in Washington, D.C., through Jo Ellen el Bashir at the Moorland-Spingarn Center of Howard University; and in St. Louis, through Dr. Anne Woodhouse, Schoenberg Curator at the Missouri Historical Society.

Thomas P. Lowry of the Index Project (*Don't Shoot That Boy!*), Nettie Washington Douglass, Edward Steers Jr. (*Blood on the Moon*), Jon Powell, Thomas Lalley, and Anne and David Richardson all provided useful insights or material on Lincoln and the other dramatis personae in his life.

I appreciate very much the information shared by many local churches and institutions in an exploration of the Civil War atmosphere in Washington: Anacostia Museum of the Smithsonian Institution (Dr. Gail Lowe, historian); Asbury United Methodist Church (Lonise Fisher Robinson, historian); the Carman Collection of Lincolniana (Joan Sansbury, librarian/curator); Church of the Epiphany (Tripp Jones, archivist); District of Columbia Public Schools (Judy Capurso, archivist); Dumbarton United Methodist (Jane Donovan); Emory United Methodist Church (Pastor Joseph Wayne Daniels Jr.);

Government of the District of Columbia Historic Preservation Office (Nancy Kassner, archaeologist at the D.C. Government's Historic Preservation Office); the Historical Society of Washington, D.C. (Gail Rodgers McCormick); Israel Metropolitan C. M. E. Church (Cynthia Mason, historian); and Mrs. Edward P. Felton.

A nationwide search to find a fascinating painting by Jes Schlaikjer of Lincoln working on the Emancipation Proclamation at the Soldiers' Home, exhibited during the Lincoln Sesquicentennial, has finally succeeded. We thank the following for their efforts to track it down: Richard Doener, Officer of the Curator, United States Senate; Michael Fowler, University of South Carolina, Aiken; Robert Harmon, Pennsylvania Academy of Design; Harold Holzer, Vice President, Metropolitan Museum of Art; Bob Willard, Historical Society of Washington; Mark Mitchell and Paula Pineta, National Academy of Design; Marc Pachter, Director, and Warren Perry, National Portrait Gallery; Judy Throm, Archives of American Art, Smithsonian Institution; Cindy van Horn, the Lincoln Museum, Fort Wayne, Indiana; and Judge Frank J. Williams, founder of the Lincoln Forum and Chief Justice of the Supreme Court of Rhode Island.

And last, but hardly least, to my father, Judge Frank E. Smith, on whose desk sat a bust of Abraham Lincoln, and whose collection of Lincolniana first whetted my interest many years ago. That seems now to have come full circle.

NOTES

Prologue

1   *sweetest, wisest soul*   Walt Whitman, *Civil War Poetry and Prose* (New York: Dover Publications, 1995), 33.

1   *mighty Westerner*   Walter Lowenfels, ed., *Walt Whitman's Civil War* (New York: Da Capo Press, 1960), 261.

1   *There were thirty-one*   In Richard Hofstadter, *The American Political Tradition* (New York: Vintage Books, 1954), 135.

2   *It was a very*   In Justin G. Turner and Linda Levitt Turner, *Mary Todd Lincoln: Her Life and Letters* (New York: International Publishing Corporation, 1972), 94.

2   *an even "greater resort"*   Ibid., 128.

3   *sitting upon the steps*   *Springfield Republican*, May 24, 1862. David Rankin Barbee papers, Lavinger Library Special Collections, Georgetown University, Washington, D.C., box 2, folder 91.

PART ONE
Lincoln's Long Journey to the Soldiers' Home

Chapter 1. Beginnings

7   *It was a shed*   William O. Stoddard, *Abraham Lincoln: The True Story of a Great Life* (New York: Fords, Howard & Hulbert, 1884), 15.

7   *The sides and roof*   In Alfred Kazin, *A Writer's America, Landscape in Literature* (New York: Alfred A. Knopf, 1988), 88.

8   *The purpose of*   In Don Fehrenbacher, *Lincoln in Text and Context: Collected Essays* (Stanford, Calif.: Stanford University Press, 1987), 137.

8   *1820 census information*   In William Lee Miller, *Lincoln's Virtues: An Ethical Biography* (New York: Alfred A. Knopf. 2002), 47.

10   *how he lay*   Noah Brooks, *Statesmen: Men of Achievement* (Charles Scribner's Sons, 1893), 182.

10   *it isn't the best*   In Ruth Painter Randall, *Mary Lincoln: Biography of a Marriage* (Boston: Little Brown, 1953), 137.

11   *It is like*   Katherine B. Menz, *The Lincoln Home: Lincoln Home National Historic Site, Springfield, Illinois* (Harpers Ferry Center: National Park Service, U.S. Department of Interior, 1983), 35–37.

Chapter 2. The Riggs Villa

13   *the lines of which*   Andrew Jackson Downing, *Treatise on the Theory and Practice of Landscape Gardening*, 4th ed. (1849), 414.

14   *I think it wrong*   John Beverly Riggs, *The Riggs Family of Maryland* (Baltimore, Md., 1939).

14 *I am engaged* Roland T. Carr, *32 President's Square: Part One of a Two-Part Narrative of the Riggs Bank and Its Founders* (Washington, D.C.: Acropolis Books, 1980), 99.

15 *I am living* Ibid., 110.

15 *this last winter* Ibid., 124.

16 *Let the soldier* Riggs Archives, Riggs Bank (Washington, D.C., February 14, 1840).

18 *When not on duty* Smith Stimmel, *Personal Reminiscences of Abraham Lincoln* (Kearney, Neb.: Morris Publishing, 1997), 21.

18 *for fear I* Private Willard Cutter letter to his mother, January 1, 1863. Typescript courtesy of Mike Dallas, Captain of Company C. reenactors, 150th Pennsylvania Volunteers, Meadville, Pa. The original letters are in the Special Collections, Pelletier Library, Allegheny College, Meadville, Pa.

Chapter 3. Washington and the White House

19 *"Eighteen Sixty-One"* Whitman, *Civil War Poetry*, 3.

20 *with a task* In David Herbert Donald, *Lincoln* (New York: Simon & Schuster, 1995), 273.

20 *the union now . . . revolution* In James M. McPherson, *Battle Cry of Freedom* (New York: Oxford University Press, 1988), 235–237.

21 *essence of anarchy* In Donald, *Lincoln*, 264.

21 *is not an absurdity* In McPherson, *Battle Cry*, 248.

21 *The tug has to* Ibid., 253.

21 *the South* Ibid., 259.

21 *was entirely ignorant* In Donald, *Lincoln*, 285.

22 *keeled over* Ibid., 289.

23 *Few know* Gideon Welles, *Diary of Gideon Welles, Secretary of the Navy with Lincoln and Johnson*, 2 vols. (Boston: Houghton Mifflin, 1911), 1:549.

23 *No one believed* *Century Magazine* 2 (1888):614–615.

23 *Any private secretary* Henry Adams, *The Education of Henry Adams* (New York: Modern Library, 1931), 107.

24 *Lincoln would have* McPherson, *Battle Cry*, 271–272.

25 *without some kind* In Joseph J. Ellis, *Founding Brothers: The Revolutionary Generation* (New York: Alfred A. Knopf, 2001), 50.

26 *abhorrent to common sense* Ibid., 74.

26 *the very dirtiest* Sarah Booth Conroy, "Firsts for Two First Ladies," *Washington Post* (November 13, 2000).

26 *stand upon* In Betty C. Monkman, "Furniture and Interiors," in *Our Changing White House*, ed. Wendell Garrett (Boston: Northeastern University Press, 1995), 109.

26 *Washington has* James Fenimore Cooper, Freedom Plaza, Washington, DC, inscription.

26 *Magnificent Intentions* Charles Dickens, *American Notes* (New York: St. Martin's Press, 1985), 11.

27 *Ten years* Adams, *Education*, 99.

27 *If you had not* Don E. Fehrenbacher and Virginia Fehrenbacher, *Recollected Words of Abraham Lincoln* (Stanford, Calif.: Stanford University Press, 1996), 269.

27 *All the roads* In David W. Miller, *Second Only to Grant: Quartermaster General Montgomery C. Meigs* (Shippensburg, Pa.: White Mane Books, 2000), 111.

28 *It's not Shurs* In Hans L. Trefousse, *Carl Schurz: A Biography* (New York: Fordham University Press, 1998), 132.

28 *an empty treasury* Carl Schurz, *Abraham Lincoln* (Boston: Houghton Mifflin, 1899), 43ff.

28 *He instinctively understood* In Trefousse, *Carl Schurz*, 146.

28 *the true representative* Ralph Waldo Emerson, *National* magazine (February 1909).

29 *The halls, corridors* Elizabeth Todd Grimsley, "Six Months in the White House," *Journal of the Illinois State Historical Society* (October–January, 1926–1927):48.

29 *Italian married Lady* *Lincoln Papers* (February 27, 1861), Library of Congress.

29 *promiscuous receptions* Fehrenbacher and Fehrenbacher, *Recollected Words*, 194.

30 *They don't want* Ibid., 498.

30 *The rebellion* In Schurz, *Lincoln*, 74.

30 *had initiated* Mark Neely Jr., *The Lincoln Encyclopedia* (New York: Da Capo Press, 1982), 234. I was led to this source by William Lee Miller's *Lincoln's Virtues*.

30 *The house* Charles Farrar Browne, *The Complete Works of Artemus Ward* (New York: Lenox Hill, 1970), 102.

31 *When I get* In Michael Burlingame, ed., *Lincoln Observed: Civil War Dispatches of Noah Brooks* (Baltimore: The Johns Hopkins University Press, 1998), 212.

31 *There were moments* Allen Thorndike Rice, ed., *Reminiscences of Abraham Lincoln by Distinguished Men of His Time* (New York: Harper & Bros., 1909), 230.

31 *seven-eighths* In Burlingame, *Lincoln Observed*, 211–212.

32 *of these I must... I think now* In William C. Harris, *Lincoln's Last Months* (Cambridge, Mass.: Belknap Press of Harvard University Press, 2004), 71.

32 *mere gleanings* Donald B. Cole, ed., *Benjamin Brown French: Witness to the Young Republic—a Yankee's Journal 1828–1870* (Hanover, N.H.: University Press of New England, 1989), 374.

32 *learned he must* Welles, *Diary*, 1:37.

32 *were to undertake* Ibid., 2:232.

33 *I have seen* Harris, *Last Months*, 67.

33 *watch and wait* Welles, *Diary*, 1:274.

33 *It is an infirmity* Ibid., 2:131.

33 *Lincoln was* Ibid., 1:240.

33 *Lincoln makes* Ibid., 2:264.

34 *when he relies* Ibid., 1:52.

34 *[he is] a much* *Galaxy* magazine (February 1873).

34 *a singular man* Welles, *Diary*, 1:520.

34 *extremely unmethodical* In James Mellon, ed., *The Face of Lincoln* (New York: Bonanza Books, 1979), 142.

34 *Mr. Lincoln was* Rice, *Reminiscences*, 401.

34 *He was an unconscious* William O. Stoddard, *Lincoln's Third Secretary: The Memoirs of William O. Stoddard* (New York: Exposition Press, 1955), 99.

34 *This poor President!* Michael Burlingame, ed., *Inside Lincoln's White House: The Complete Civil War Diary of John Hay* (Carbondale: Southern Illinois University Press, 1999), 288n122.

35 *Hell has no terror* In Richard J. Carwardine, *Lincoln: Profiles in Power* (Edinburgh: Pearson Longman, 2003), 183.

35   *If there was*   In Allen C. Guelzo, *Abraham Lincoln, Redeemer President* (Grand Rapids, Mich: William B. Erdmans, 1999), 357.

35   *If to be the head*   In John B. Larner, ed., *Records of the Columbia Historical Society* (Washington City: 1925), 27:90.

35   *The tycoon is*   In Tyler Dennett, *John Hay: From Poetry to Politics* (New York: Dodd Mead, 1933), 48.

36   *The White House*   Turner and Turner, *Mary Todd Lincoln*, 187.

36   *in the new republic*   Richard L. Bushman, *The Refinement of America: Persons, Houses, Cities* (New York: Alfred A. Knopf, 1992), 442.

36   *this damned old house*   In French, *Journal*, 382.

36   *I have but a*   In "The Musical Mr. Lincoln," *Abraham Lincoln Quarterly* (December 1949): 435–36.

37   *the stamp of*   *Columbia Historical Society*, 36.

37   *I wish you could*   Cutter, letter of November 17, 1862.

37   *it would stink*   French, *Journal*, 382.

38   *palace as splendid*   In William Seale, *The President's House: A History*, 2 vols. (Washington, DC: The White House Historical Association with the National Graphic Society, 1986), 1:222ff.

38   *at my leaving*   In William G. *Allman*, "Furnishing the Executive Mansion," in Garrett, *Our Changing White House*, 137.

39   *every Saturday*   French, *Journal*, 385.

40   *I went in*   John Fleming, *A Palace Guard's View of Lincoln: The Civil War Letters of John H. Fleming* (Santa Barbara: University of California Library, 1971), 27. Courtesy of the Lincoln Museum, Fort Wayne, Indiana.

41   *no private gentleman*   *Report of the Commissioner of Public Buildings* (National Archives), 5:1, 680.

41   *He patted me*   Elise K. Kirk, *Music at the White House: A History of the American Spirit* (Urbana: University of Illinois Press, 1986), 78ff.

42   *witness the performance*   French, *Journal*, November 24, 1861.

42   *magnificent new*   Margaret Leech, *Reveille in Washington* (Alexandria, Va.: Time Reading Program Special Edition, 1980), 342.

42   *a sink of corruption*   Burlingame, *Inside Lincoln*, 77, 312n140.

42   *filthy*   Ibid., 219.

43   *among the ladies*   Jean Baker, *Mary Todd Lincoln: A Biography* (New York: W. W. Norton, 1987), 186.

43   *They all seemed*   Tom Ledoux, ed., *Quite Ready to Be Sent Somewhere: The Civil War Letters of Aldace Freeman Walker* (Victoria, British Columbia: Trafford Publishing, 2002), 34.

44   *distributing food*   French, *Journal*, 413–444.

44   *red hot*   Louisa May Alcott, *Hospital Sketches* (New York: Garland Publishing, 1984), 38ff.

45   *plain almost*   George Washington Adams, *Doctors in Blue: The Medical History of the Union Army* (Dayton, Ohio: Morningside Press, 1985), 176ff.

46   *It is the mudyest*   Cutter, letter of January 25, 1863.

46   *The mud here*   Ledoux, *Walker*, 105.

47   *one cloud of dust*   French, *Journal*, 431.

47   *a huge mess*   Lowenfels, *Walt Whitman's Civil War*, 65.

47   *swarming*   David Macrae, *The Americans at Home* (New York: E. P. Dutton, 1952), 109.

48   *reflection of*   William Quentin Maxwell, *Lincoln's Fifth Wheel: The Political History of the U.S. Sanitary Commission* (New York: Longmans, Green and Co., 1956), 14.

48   *Oh, how I wish*   French, *Journal*, 457.

48   *My first impressions*   Whitman, *Civil War Poetry*, 63.

48   *He has a face*   Ibid., 63–64.

49   *Life was anything*   Lt. Col. Thomas C. Chamberlin, *History of the One Hundred and Fiftieth Regiment, Pennsylvania Volunteers, Second Regiment, Bucktail Brigade* (Philadelphia: McManus. 1905), 54.

49   *Pennsylvania Avenue*   In *Columbia Historical Society*, 55–56.

49   *All the sorrows*   In Seale, *The President's House*, 1:xix.

49   *I am glad*   In Francis Bicknell Carpenter, *The Inner Life of Abraham Lincoln: Six Months at the White House* (New York: Hurd and Houghton, 1879), 293.

PART TWO
Lincoln at the Soldiers' Home

Chapter 4. Embattled Retreat

53   *a soap factory*   Benjamin Brown French in *Records of the Office of Public Buildings and Public Parks of the National Capital* (May 21, 1862), 125, National Archives Microfilm publication M 371, reel 7.

53   *The Washington Canal*   Ibid., March 11, 1862, 105.

53   *The ghosts*   David Donald, in *We Are Lincoln Men: Abraham Lincoln and His Friends* (New York: Simon & Schuster, 2003), 216.

54   *[It] lies on a*   Geier Brown Renfrew Architects, *Anderson Cottage Historical Structure Report*, February 20, 1985, in *National Intelligencer* (June 28, 1842), NTHP/SH files, 8.

54   *When we are in*   Turner and Turner, *Mary Todd Lincoln* (May 29, 1862), 128.

55   *There was fifty*   Cutter, letter of September 16, 1862.

55   *There is 1800*   Ibid., letter of September 1, 1863.

55   *an almost morbid*   Burlingame, *Lincoln Observed*, 204.

56   *When we are within*   Turner and Turner, *Mary Todd Lincoln*, 133.

56   *There is more*   Cutter, letter of November 7, 1863.

56   *nice and warm*   Ibid., letter of November 9, 1862.

57   *holding a candle*   Isaac Markens, *Why Lincoln Spared Three Lives* (Fort Wayne, Ind.: Lincoln Museum, 1911), 3.

57   *He seemed to dislike*   Harold Holzer, ed. *Lincoln as I Knew Him* (Chapel Hill, N.C.: Algonquin Books, 1999), 97.

58   *beat a retreat*   Markens, *Why Lincoln*, 4.

58   *It was very*   In Rufus Rockwell Wilson, *Lincoln Among His Friends: A Sheaf of Intimate Memories* (Caldwell, Idaho: Caxton Printers, 1942), 332ff.

59   *I laugh*   In Mellon, *Face of Lincoln*, 146.

59   *Halt! Who goes*   Harry M. Keiffer, *Recollections of a Drummer Boy* (Mifflinburg, Pa.: Bucktail Books, 2000), 46–47.

59   *surrounded by*   Jay Cooke, "Interview with Abraham Lincoln," *American History Illustrated* (November 1972).

60   *Oliver Twist II*   In William C. Davis, *Lincoln's Men* (New York: The Free Press, 1999), 62.

60 *Although you had*   Charles Gwynn letter to Lincoln (March 29, 1864), Lincoln Papers, LOC.

60 *public life in*   George Borrett, "An Englishman in Washington," *The Magazine of History* 149 (1929):11ff.

61 *It was late*   John R. French, "Reminiscences of Famous Americans," *North American Review* 141 (September 1885):237ff.

63 *Madam, I owe you*   In Markens, *Why Lincoln*, 5.

63 *I go there*   In John M. Taylor, *William Henry Seward: Lincoln's Right Hand* (New York: HarperCollins, 1991), 240.

64 *ludicrous conclusion*   Orville Hickman Browning, *The Diary of Orville Hickman Browning* (June 30, 1862) (Springfield: Illinois State Historical Library) 1:(1850–1864):555.

64 *Alexander T. Stewart*   All in Baker, *Mary Todd Lincoln*, 185, 194, 258–260.

65 *I have no time*   In Lord Newton, *Lord Lyons: A Record of British Diplomacy* (New York: Longmans, Green and Co., 1913), 87–88.

66 *Go thou*   In Carpenter, *Inner Life*, 243.

66 *I am afraid*   In Newton, *Lord Lyons*, 24.

66 *our golden*   "New Glimpses" paper, NTHP/SH project notes.

66 *I fear he is*   Donald, *Lincoln*, 528.

66 *I am a little*   Davis, *Lincoln's Men*, 64.

68 *Poor Mr. Lincoln*   Elizabeth Keckley, *Behind the Scenes or Thirty Years a Slave and Four Years in the White House* (New York: Oxford University Press, 1988), 157.

68 *Says Gov*   Roy Basler et al, ed., *Collected Works of Abraham Lincoln* (New Brunswick, N.J.: Rutgers University Press, 1953–1990), CW 7: August 19, 1864, 506–508.

68 *In the loss*   Turner and Turner, *Mary Todd Lincoln*, July 26, 1862, 130–31.

68 *her affliction*   *The Independent* (August 10, 1862). LOC: Adams Building, fifth floor.

69 *How dearly I loved*   Turner and Turner, *Mary Todd Lincoln*, August 25, 1865, 267ff.

69 *washing floors*   Invoices from John Alexander, upholsterer, Washington, D.C., May 21, 1864. Records of the First Auditor, Audit 151.223, National Archives, College Park, Md.

69 *papering is*   In Mark E. Neely, Jr. and R. Gerald McMurty, *The Insanity File: The Case of Mary Todd Lincoln* (Carbondale: Southern Illinois University Press, 1986), 156.

70 *we always have*   Turner and Turner, *Mary Todd Lincoln*, September 31 [*sic*], 1862, 133.

70 *It is such a*   Ibid., July 20, 1864, 177.

71 *entertained us*   Basler, *Collected Works* 6: August 19, 1864.

71 *The strong will*   Anna L. Boyden, *War Reminiscences or Echoes from Hospital and White House* (Boston: D. Lothrop and Co., 1887), 84.

71 *For two hours*   Rice, *Reminiscences*, 156–57.

71 *A little party*   Herbert Mitgang, ed., *Washington in Lincoln's Time by Noah Brooks* (New York: Rinehart & Co., 1958), 40–41.

72 *the end of*   Burlingame, *Inside Lincoln*, August 23, 1863, 76.

72 *ever unworthy*   Gabor Borrit, ed., *Lincoln's Generals* (New York: Oxford University Press, 1994), 13.

72 *I could as well*   Howard University typescript, n.d.

72 *If it is done*   Papers of Samuel P. Heintzelman, MSS Division, LOC.

73 *Play! Play!* In Walter Hebert, *Fighting Joe Hooker* (New York: The Bobbs-Merrill Co., 1944), 86.

73 *rust[ing]* Abraham Lincoln Papers, LOC, n.d.

73 *The relations* Abraham Lincoln to General Henry Halleck, CW supplement 1, March 3, 1864, 228.

74 *his wife* "New Glimpses," NTHP/SH files, 1.

74 *were the best* Virginia Laas, *Wartime Washington: The Civil War Letters of Elizabeth Blair Lee* (Urbana: University of Illinois Press, 1991), 144 (May 12,1862).

75 *no family* Mitgang, *Washington*, 245.

75 *Boby came across* Turner and Turner, *Mary Todd Lincoln*, 37.

75 *See, Madam* Keckley, *Behind the Scenes*, 181.

76 *I generally* In Carpenter, *Inner Life*, 272.

76 *It is my pleasure* Donald, *Lincoln*, 109.

76 *he comprehended* Mitgang, *Washington*, 249.

76 *will be what* Ibid., 250.

77 *pleurisy, probably* Ruth Painter Randall, *Lincoln's Sons* (Boston: Little Brown, 1956), 209.

78 *made wonderful* In Baker, *Mary Todd Lincoln*, 220.

78 *working for* Browning, *Diary*, January 1, 1863, 1:608–609.

78 *he pretended* Mitgang, *Washington*, 66–67.

79 *any person* Richard Current, *The Lincoln Nobody Knows* (New York: Hill and Wang, 1958), 68.

80 *Mary has* Baker, *Mary Todd Lincoln*, 228.

Chapter 5. The Lincoln Marriage

81 *We were pretty* Henry B. Rankin, *Intimate Character Sketches of Abraham Lincoln* (Philadelphia: J. B. Lippincott, 1924), 164.

81 *When [Lincoln]* Stimmel, *Reminiscences*, 21.

81 *he was not* Ibid., 9.

83 *look like* Baker, *Mary Todd Lincoln*, 133.

83 *her efforts* Stoddard, *True Story*, 403.

83 *always . . . lover* Turner and Turner, *Mary Todd Lincoln*, 534.

83 *I believe* Keckley, *Behind the Scenes*, 146–147.

83 *Lincoln himself* In Michael Burlingame, *The Inner World of Abraham Lincoln* (Urbana: University of Illinois Press, 1994), 319.

84 *I shall never* In Randall, *Mary Lincoln: Biography*, 333.

84 *has no fear* David Derickson, *A Word for Mrs. Lincoln*, notes in the Ida M. Tarbell Lincoln Collection, Special Collections, Pelletier Library, Allegheny College, Meadville, Penn.

85 *people are perhaps* Douglas L. Wilson and Rodney O. Davis, eds., *Herndon's Informants: Letters, Interviews, and Statements about Abraham Lincoln* (Urbana: University of Illinois Press, 1998), 444.

85 *My wife* Turner and Turner, *Mary Lincoln*, 114.

85 *He was as true* In Miller, *Lincoln's Virtues*, 79.

85 *ten times* Laas, *Wartime*, 104.

85 *make a bishop* Turner and Turner, *Mary Todd Lincoln*, 11.

85 *the very creature* Ruth Painter Randall, *The Courtship of Mr. Lincoln* (Boston: Little Brown).

87 *seemed to be* Stimmel, *Reminiscences*, 18.

87 *a politician* In Burlingame, *Inner World*, 319.

87   *power and high position*   Turner and Turner, *Mary Todd Lincoln*, 583.

87   *a very fine*   In Neely and McMurty, *Insanity File*, 160.

87   *I was such*   Ibid., 182.

88   *tolerably*   In Randall, *Mary Lincoln: Biography*, 290.

88   *I prefer*   Turner and Turner, *Mary Todd Lincoln*, 284.

88   *Many a mark*   Harry Kieffer, 48.

88   *Misses*   Fleming, *Guard's View*, 25.

88   *the change*   In Baker, *Mary Todd Lincoln*, 227.

89   *Mrs. Lincoln*   Stimmel, *Reminiscences*, 18.

89   *periodic*   In Baker, *Mary Todd Lincoln*, 83.

89   *This morning*   Turner and Turner, *Mary Todd Lincoln*, 257.

91   *The day you*   Basler, *Collected Works*, 6:371–372.

91   *I really wish*   Ibid., 474.

91   *In their domestic relations*   Katherine Helm, *The true Story of Mary, Wife of Lincoln, Continuing the Recollections of Mary Lincoln's Sister, Emilie* (New York: Harper's, 1928), 195.

91   *At all times*   David Homer Bates, *Life in the Telegraph Office: Recollections of the US Military Telegraph Corps during the Civil War* (Lincoln: University of Nebraska Press, 1995), 208.

91   *They were in*   Rankin, *Intimate Character*, 162.

92   *was esteemed*   In Douglas L. Wilson, *Lincoln Before Washington: New Perspectives on the Illinois Years* (Urbana: University of Illinois Press, 1997), 85.

92   *the most forceful*   Rankin, *Intimate Character*, 162.

92   *decidedly unworldly*   In Wilson, *Before Washington*, 115.

92   *I hope*   In Randall, *Courtship*, 70–71.

Chapter 6. Lincoln's Achilles' Heel

93   *No vigilance*   In Donald, *Lincoln*, 548.

93   *I firmly believe*   Turner and Turner, *Mary Todd Lincoln*, 285.

94   *The President*   John Nicolay, *A Short Life of Abraham Lincoln* (New York: The Century Co., 1919), 53.

94   *sulky, unbroken*   Lowenfels, ed., *Walt Whitman's Civil War*, 270.

94   *wretched*   Edward Steers Jr., *Blood on the Moon* (Lexington: University Press of Kentucky, 2001), 21.

94   *I cannot be shut*   Fehrenbacher and Fehrenbacher, *Recollected Words*, 440.

94   *one of the best*   Derickson, "A Word."

95   *While I write*   In Robert V. Bruce, *Lincoln and the Tools of War* (Indianapolis: The Bobbs-Merrill Co., 1956), 57.

95   *general engagement*   Cutter, letter of September 16, 1862.

95   *Let us be*   Benjamin Franklin Cooling, *Jubal Early's Raid on Washington, 1864* (Baltimore, Md.: Nautical and Aviation Publishing Co. of America, 1989), 88.

95   *many in Washington*   Kathleen W. Dorman, *Interruptions and Embarrassments: The Smithsonian during the Civil War. Papers of Joseph Henry.* Smithsonian lecture series, September 25, 1966.

95   *The annual expedition*   Cooling, *Jubal Early*, 207.

96   *reign of terror*   David Rankin Barbee Papers, Box 2, file 60.

96   *the lonely situation*   P. J. Staudenraus, ed., *Mr. Lincoln's Washington: Selections from the Writings of Noah Brooks, Civil War Correspondent* (South Brunswick, N.Y.: Thomas Youseloff, n.d.), 354.

96   *It seems to me*   Lincoln Papers, LOC, June 30, 1863.

97   *Lincoln does not*   Cooling, *Jubal Early,* 25.

98   *like putting up*   Fehrenbacher and Fenhrenbacher, *Recollected Words,* 171.

98   *Often did I see*   Kieffer, 48.

98   *(Camp Soldiers Home)*   Cutter, letters of September 12, 1862, October 17, 1862, August 3, 1863, July 11, 1864, typed letters courtesy of Mike Dallas, Meadville, Pa.

99   *a couple of*   NTHP/SH files, *Cincinnati Gazette,* September 18, 1862.

100   *the house is some*   Borrett, "An Englishman," 11.

100   *It would be funny*   Whitman, *Civil War Poetry,* 67.

101   *peculiar structure*   Stimmel, *Experiences,* 8, 14.

101   *there was no fear*   Derickson, "A Word."

101   *anyone could*   Fehrenbacher and Fehrenbacher, *Recollected Words,* 192.

101   *Lincoln's Military Fantasies*   Gary Prokopowicz in John Y. Simon and Harold Holzer, eds., *Rediscovering Lincoln* (New York: Fordham University Press, 2002), 77ff.

102   *there are a thousand*   Fehrenbacher and Fehrenbacher, *Recollected Words,* 48.

102   *had passed through*   Wilson and Davis, *Herndon's Informants,* 358.

Chapter 7. Lincoln's Favorite Storytellers

104   *Letter VIII: The Rejected National Hymns*   Robert Henry Newell, *The Orpheus C. Kerr Papers* (New York: AMS Press, 1971). (Original publisher: Blakeman and Mason, 1862, vol. 1.)

109   *three forces*   Cyril Clemens, *Petroleum V. Nasby* (Webster Grove, Miss: International Mark Twain Society, 1936), xiii.

109   *For the genius*   Donald, *Lincoln,* 543.

110   *Was there ever*   Benjamin P. Thomas and Harold M. Hyman, *Stanton: The Life and Times of Lincoln's Secretary of War* (New York: Alfred A. Knopf, 1962), 330.

110   *an historic figure*   Clemens, *Petroleum,* xiv.

110   *the incarnation*   Ibid., 145.

110   *I hev deserted*   Ibid., 39ff.

112   *Good God!*   Artemus Ward, "Interview with President Lincoln," in *The Complete Works of Artemus Ward,* 102.

112   *Lincoln's cheerfulness*   Barbee Papers, *Springfield Republican* (May 24, 1862): box 2, folder 91.

112   *the President never*   Dahlgren, February 6, 1863.

112   *If I could not*   Fehrenbacher and Fehrenbacher, *Recollected Words,* 18.

112   *I feel I shall*   Ibid., 19.

Chapter 8. Lincoln and Freedom

113   *old master*   *Washington Post,* December 27?, 1947.

113   *I used to see*   Ibid.

114   *thunderbolt*   Fehrenbacher and Fehrenbacher, *Recollected Words,* 295.

114   *legitimate cradle*   Harold Holzer, NTHP/SH files.

114   *The President comes*   John Nicolay Papers, LOC, June 13, 1862.

115   *seemed to be*   French, *Journal,* June 16, 1862, 399–400.

116   *I order you*   In Charles Eugene Hamlin, *Life and Times of Hannibal Hamlin,* 1899 (Port Washington, N.Y.: Kennikut Press, 1971), 2:428ff.

116   *troops come forward*   Basler, *Collected Works,* 5:444.

116   *I was more*   In Patricia L. Faust, ed., *Historical Times Illustrated Encyclopedia of the Civil War* (New York: Harper & Row, 1986), 334.

117 *made an exclamation* Mitgang, *Lincoln in Washington's Time*, 148.

117 *Mr. Lincoln stated* Hamlin, *Life*, 2:471.

117 *Lincoln would* Ibid., 427.

117 *Viewed from* Dr. Lucas Morel, "Frederick Douglass's Emancipation of Abraham Lincoln," paper presented at the Sixth Annual Symposium of the Abraham Lincoln Institute, March 22, 2003, 11.

117 *This American slavery* Fehrenbacher and Fehrenbacher, *Recollected Words*, 368.

118 *one of the best* Ibid., 362.

118 *holding up* Boyden, *War Reminiscences*, 56.

119 *One day* Ibid., 121–2.

119 *To think* Turner and Turner, *Mary Todd Lincoln*, 464.

119 *his unerring* Ibid., 279.

119 *It had got* Fehrenbacher and Fehrenbacher, *Recollected Words*, 79–80.

120 *a hideous* Burlingame, *Inside Lincoln* (July 1, 1864), 217.

120 *the sugar* Carwardine, *Lincoln*, 211.

121 *Our minds* In Allen Guelzo, *Lincoln's Emancipation Proclamation: The End of Slavery in America* (New York: Simon & Schuster, 2004), 141.

122 *Lincoln saw* Wilson and Davis, *Herndon's Informants*, 196–7.

122 *Negroes are* George M. Frederickson, *The Inner Civil War: Northern Intellectuals and the Crisis of the Union* (New York: Harper Torch Books, 1965), 114.

122 *Keep [the power]* Benjamin Quarles, *Lincoln and the Negro* (New York: Da Capo Press, 1990), 180.

122 *It is my* In LaWanda Cox, *Lincoln and Black Freedom: A Study in Presidential Leadership* (Columbia: University of South Carolina Press, 1981), x.

123 *The ugly fact* Frederickson, *Inner Civil War*, 119.

123 *A great day* "Lincoln Liked Longfellow," *Lincoln Herald* (Summer 1952), 21.

123 *constantly* *Dictionary of American Biography*.

123 *a bloody* Guelzo, *Lincoln's Emancipation Proclamation*, 187, 189.

123 *greatest event* In Fehrenbacher, *Lincoln in Text*, 109.

123 *for I am free* Elizabeth Clarke-Lewis in *First Freed: Washington, D.C. in the Emancipation Era* (Washington, D.C.: Howard University Press, 2002), 80.

123 *That proclamation* *Christian Recorder*, Philadelphia, Pa., November 22, 1862.

124 *a document* Dr. Edna Greene Medford, "African-Americans and Lincoln's Proclamation of Emancipation," in John Simon, Harold Holzer, and William Pederson, eds., *The Lincoln Forum: Abraham Lincoln, Gettysburg and the Civil War* (Mason City, Iowa: Savas Publishing Co., 1999), 48.

124 *They . . . embraced it* Dr. Edna Greene Medford, "African-Americans and the Cult of Lincolnolatry," Springfield, Ill.: Papers from the Tenth Annual Lincoln Colloquium (October 21, 1995):58.

124 *This momentous* In NTHP/SH Special Resources Study draft (August 2002), 34.

124 *the central act* In Guelzo, *Lincoln's Emancipation Proclamation*, 186.

124 *it would not* Fehrenbacher and Fehrenbacher, *Recollected Words*, 129.

124 *That Rebel* Davis, *Lincoln's Men*, 98.

124 *I very much doubt* Ledoux, *Walker*, 40.

124 *It's a paper bullet* Fehrenbacher and Fehrenbacher, *Recollected Words*, 387.

124 *The courts* Guelzo, *Lincoln's Emancipation Proclamation*, 190.

125 *Lincoln elected* "Lincoln Liked Longfellow," 21.

125 *This amendment* In James G. Randall, *Lincoln and the Presidency: Last Full Measure* (Urbana: University of Illinois, 2000), 314.

125 *A blind man* In Prokopowicz, *Rediscovering Lincoln*, 203.

125 *If slavery* For an excellent summary of Lincoln's remarks, see William Lee Miller, *Lincoln's Virtues*, 285.

125 *in relation to* In Cox, *Black Freedom*, 5.

126 *Lincoln had such* John E. Washington, *They Knew Lincoln* (New York: E. P. Dutton, 1942), 183.

126 *I am personally* Ibid., 194.

127 *The proprietor* Sandra Fitzpatrick and Maria R. Gordon, *The Guide to Black Washington: Places and Events of Historic and Cultural Significance in the Nation's Capital*, rev. illus. (New York: Hippocrene Books, 2001), 40.

127 *already knew* Washington, *They Knew*, 111.

127 *among the brightest* *Christian Recorder*, November 29, 1862.

128 *was all over the kitchen* Washington, *They Knew*, 119.

128 *the difference* Lincoln to Welles, Basler, *Collected Works*, March 16, 1861.

128 *who would have been* Washington, *They Knew*, 217–18.

129 *Lizzie, I am* Keckley, *Behind the Scenes*, 277.

130 *to place Mrs. Lincoln* Ibid., xiv.

130 *In all my interviews* Rice, *Reminiscences*, 323.

130 *Had [Lincoln] put* Morel, 11.

131 *more radically* Turner and Turner, *Mary Todd Lincoln*, 145. Swisshelm letter to *Chicago Tribune*, July 20, 1882.

131 *I recognized* Jane Grey Swisshelm, *Half a Century*, 2nd ed. (Chicago: Jansen, McClurg and Company, 1880), 237.

131 *the rich negro* William Doster, *Lincoln and Episodes of the Civil War* (New York: G. P. Putnam's Sons, 1915), 245.

132 *the colored philosopher* *Christian Recorder*, December 27, 1862.

133 *Well, Mary* Washington, *They Knew*, 86.

134 *He was no President* Ibid., 86.

134 *large-hearted man* Frederick Douglass, undated typescript (8), MSS Department, Moorland-Spingarn Research Center, Howard University, Washington, D.C.

134 *I used to be* In Guelzo, *Abraham Lincoln*, 121.

134 *whose leading object* Basler, *Collected Works*, 4:438–439.

Chapter 9. Poems on Slavery

136 *The Slave's Dream* *Henry Wadsworth Longfellow: Poems and Other Writings* (New York: The Library of America, 2000), 24.

137 *Ball's Bluff* Herman Melville, *Battle-Pieces and Aspects of the War: Civil War Poems* (Amherst: Prometheus Books, 2001), 28.

138 *Ein Feste Burg* Robert Penn Warren, *John Greenleaf Whittier's Poetry: An Appraisal and a Selection* (Minneapolis: University of Minnesota Press, 1971), 154.

139 *Pensive on Her Dead* Whitman, *Civil War Poetry*, 38.

Chapter 10. Lincoln's Secretary of War

142 *There is no token* In Thomas and Hyman, *Stanton*, 120.

142 *the imbecility* In Miller, *Lincoln's Virtues*, 421.

143 *the original gorilla* Ibid., 422.

144 *that long-armed* Ibid., 417.

144 *had never been* Stoddard, *True Story*, 316.

144 *He was, wrote* Ibid., 316–317.

145 *I knew that* Edwin M. Stanton letter, *Journal of the Military Service Institution of the U.S.* (1886), 7:255.

145 *No men were ever* In Miller, *Lincoln's Virtues*, 426.

145 *Without him* Richard Kenin and Justin Wintle, eds., *Dictionary of Biographical Quotations* (New York: Alfred A. Knopf, 1978), 699.

145 *Where can I get* In Thomas and Hyman, *Stanton*, 337.

145 *It is not for you* Ibid., 354.

146 *Between the two* Stoddard, *True Story*, 318.

146 *Mr. Stanton never* Francis Lieber, "Edwin M. Stanton," MSS. n.d. Huntington Library, San Marino, Calif.

146 *un-loved* Thomas and Hyman, *Stanton*, 38.

146 *the vilest* In Joseph T. Glatthaar, *Partners in Command: The Relationship Between Leaders in the Civil War* (New York: Free Press, 1994), 69.

146 *a meddlesome* In Thomas and Hyman, *Stanton*, 253.

146 *[an]evil genius* Ibid., 531.

146 *a dangerous foe* Ibid., 192.

146 *I thought* Ibid., 55.

146 *mercurial, arbitrary* Welles, *Diary*, May 19, 1863.

146 *Politeness was not* In Miller, *Lincoln's Virtues*, 415.

146 *I do not see* Kenin and Wintle, *Biographical*, 699.

146 *brought out most* MSS and Archival Collections of the Department of Archives, Edwin M. Stanton MSS 1648: "Louis Hutchinson Stanton on Stanton's relationship to Lincoln" (typescript), Louisiana State University, Baton Rouge.

147 *Lincoln's heart* Bates, *Telegraph Office*, 389.

147 *It has been a rule* Ibid., 204.

147 *Lincoln ploughed* Thomas and Hyman, *Stanton*, 366.

147 *he was much less* In Harris, *Last Months*, 207.

147 *Did Stanton call* In Thomas and Hyman, *Stanton*, 390.

147 *joyously* Stoddard, *True Story*, 207.

148 *boundless capacity* Pamphila Stanton Wolcott, *Edwin M. Stanton: A Biographical Sketch by His Sister, Pamphila Stanton Wolcott* (typescript, 120), Fondren Library, Rice University, Houston, TX.

148 *My thoughts* Stanton to Ellen Stanton, March 11, 1858.

148 *the man's public* Fehrenbacher and Fehrenbacher, *Recollected Words*, 23.

148 *in fine order* NTHP/SH files, Soldiers' Home Board Minutes, 1862.

148 *the greatest war* Francis Lieber letter (LI434) Huntington Library, San Marino, Calif.

148 *the greatest transportation* Thomas and Hyman, *Stanton*, 370.

148 *the longest and fastest* McPherson, *Battle Cry*, 675.

148 *Now he belongs* In Donald, *Lincoln*, 599.

148 *Not everyone knows* In Thomas and Hyman, *Stanton*, 382.

Chapter 11. Lincoln and the Tools of War

150 *I have the best* Cutter, letter of September 4, 1862.

151 *original forerunner* Harry E. Gunn in *American Motorist* (February 1933). Lincoln Scrapbook, vol. 4, Washingtoniana Collection, Martin Luther King Library.

152   *I know enough*   In Stoddard, *Third Secretary*, 109.
152   *I went to*   Kerr, *First Series*, 84–88.
153   *such a relief*   In Bruce, *Tools*, 21.
153   *I can say*   In Robert J. Schneller Jr., *A Quest for Glory: A Biography of Rear Admiral John A. Dahlgren* (Annapolis, Md.: Naval Institute Press, 1996), 319.
153   *a great evil*   In Bruce, *Tools*, 69.
154   *now comes*   In Schneller, *Quest*, 200.
154   *potentially*   Ibid., 231.
154   *it was worth*   Cutter, letter of November 25, 1863.
154   *Mr. Lincoln had*   Stoddard, *True Story*, 298–299.
155   *by means of a*   Bates, *Telegraph Office*, 264–265.
156   *they ushered into*   Bruce, *Tools*, 85ff.
156   *[It] goes up*   Cutter letters/Dallas typescript, originals in Pelletier Library, Allegheny College, Meadville, Pa.
157   *I wont leave off*   In Bruce, *Tools*, 161.
157   *hold on with*   In Glatthaar, *Partners*, 218.
157   *a crow flying*   Henry Huidekoper, *Oration at the Union of the Survivors of the 150th Regiment*, Pennsylvania Volunteers at Gettysburg (August 13, 1894), 5.
157   *one of the many*   In Bruce, *Tools*, 209.

Chapter 12. Lincoln's Quartermaster General

158   *The true cause*   In Miller, *Second Only to Grant*, 144.
159   *[I now have]*   In Thomas and Hyman, *Stanton*, 289.
159   *such troops*   In Russell Weigley, *Quartermaster General of the Union Army: A Biography of M. C. Meigs* (New York: Columbia University Press, 1959), 314.
159   *Without the services*   In Miller, *Second Only*, 263.
159   *the unsung hero*   McPherson, *Battle Cry*, 325.
160   *was both constructor*   In Miller, *Second Only*, 40.
161   *I do not know*   In Harry C. Ways, *The Washington Aqueduct 1852–1992* (n.p., n.d.), 62.
161   *the present already*   In Weigley, *Meigs*, 161.
161   *the Quartermaster*   In Miller, *Second Only*, 130.
161   *By the late summer*   In Weigley, *Meigs*, 216.
161   *I hope the prints*   Ibid., 131.
161   *It was a noble*   Ibid., 132.
162   *Did I command*   Ibid., 285.
162   *too damned honest*   Ibid., 80.
162   *what he would*   In Miller, *Second Only*, 213.
162   *The handwriting*   In Ways, *Washington Aqueduct*, 15.
162   *the spending*   McPherson, *Battle Cry*, 235.
162   *considerable*   In Miller, *Second Only*, 175.
162   *fresh sense*   Ibid., 235.
162   *I trust*   In Weigley, *Meigs*, 227.
162   *The last of*   Ibid., 322.
163   *It moved*   Meigs's Annual Report to the Secretary of War, 1882.

Chapter 13. Lincoln as Commander in Chief: The Soldiers

164   *For God's sake*   In Harold Holzer, ed., *Dear Mr. Lincoln: Letters to the President* (Reading, Mass.: Addison-Wesley Publishing Co., 1995), 148.
165   *unless the spirit*   Ibid., 148.

165 *The Soldiers' Home* Cutter, Dallas typescript, originals in Special Collections, Pelletier Library, Allegheny College, Meadville, Pa.

166 *Never did a man* Ida Tarbell, *The Life of Lincoln*, vol. 2 (New York: Macmillan, 1917), 169. Housed in Ida M. Tarbell Lincoln Collection, Special Collections, Pelletier Library, Allegheny College, Meadville, Pa.

166 *By the way* Lincoln, *Autobiographical Narrative*, 23.

167 *the people will save* Basler, *Collected Works*, 4:437.

167 *a President* Ibid., July 4, 1861.

167 *Whom it may concern* NTHP/SH files (November 1, 1862).

168 *We had orders* Cutter, letter of September 10, 1862.

168 *in a small sloping* Chamberlin, *History*, 38.

168 *Less than one hundred* Cutter, letter of September 16, 1862.

168 *these thousands* In Daniel Mark Epstein, *Lincoln and Whitman: Parallel Lives in Civil War Washington* (New York: Ballantine Books, 2004), 127.

168 *By the end* Ida Tarbell, *Life*, 158.

169 *one of the strongest* Cutter, letter of March 28, 1863.

169 *a nice young man* Ibid., January 12, 1864.

171 *After fifteen months* Huidekoper, *Oration*, 2.

171 *When the soldiers* John Nichols, *Omaha Daily Bee*, November 25, 1894. American Military Institute files, Carlisle, Pa.

172 *Well, I do prefer* In Mitgang, *Washington in Lincoln's Time*, 246.

172 *a midnight luncheon* Chamberlin, *History*, 41.

173 *three hard tack* In Davis, *Lincoln's Men*, 209.

173 *He always called* In Tarbell, *Life*, 155.

173 *He loved* Kieffer, 48.

173 *We always felt* Stimmel, *Reminiscences*, 8.

173 *He talked* Nichols, *Omaha Daily Bee*.

173 *When he was absorbed* Robert W. McBride, "Lincoln's Body Guard: The Union Light Guard of Ohio with Some Personal Recollections of Abraham Lincoln" (Indianapolis: Indiana Historical Society, 1911), 25.

173 *Why not come under* In Albert Nelson See, *Memoirs* (typescript), NTHP/SH project files, 23–24.

174 *When the carriage* Major David V. Derickson, "Abraham Lincoln's Body Guard: Reminiscences," 2. At the Ida M. Tarbell Lincoln Collection, Special Collections, Pelletier Library, Allegheny College, Meadville, Pa.

174 *who has had* Charles Derickson interview, 9. Ida M. Tarbell Lincoln Collection, Special Collections, Pelletier Library, Allegheny College, Meadville, Pa.

174 *Lincoln's manner* H. H. Huidekoper, *Personal Notes and Reminiscences of Lincoln* (Philadelphia: Bicking Print, 1896), 9.

175 *One evening* "Life at the Soldiers Home," NTHP/SH project files.

175 *to eat no pies* Fehrenbacher and Fehrenbacher, *Recollected Words*, 401.

175 *While the Elephant* Tarbell, *Life of Lincoln*, 156–57.

176 *He looks as if* Fleming, *Guard's View*, 35.

176 *As to the fighting* Cutter, letter of January 1863. Original in Special Collections, Pelletier Library, Allegheny College. Meadville, Pa.

176 *for my part* Cutter, letter of March 31,1864, typescript.

176 *I am getting* Fleming, *Guard's View*, July 17, 1864, 35.

176 *had desire to* In Epstein, *Lincoln and Whitman*, 213.

177 *We longed to be* Stimmel, *Reminiscences*, 11–12.

178 *our only* Herbert Mitgang, ed., *Lincoln As They Saw Him*, 344.

178 *"Morning Report"* Regimental Books, National Archives.

179 *If we are beaten* Fleming, *Guard's View*, March 25, 1863, 26.

179 *I am willing* Cutter, letter of August 15, 1864, typescript.

180 *We left* See, *Memoirs*, 30–33.

180 *A daily detail* McBride, "Lincoln's Bodyguard," 20.

180 *crazy man* Cutter, letter of June 14, 1863.

180 *I brot my* See, *Memoirs*, 25.

181 *President* Ibid., 25–26.

Chapter 14. The Generals

182 *the original* Carwardine, *Lincoln*, 183.

182 *endeavor to* Lincoln Papers, LOC, September 2, 1862.

182 *unparalled* Burlingame, *Inside Lincoln*, November 13, 1861, 32.

182 *this show business* In Boritt, *Lincoln's Generals*, 175.

182 *Before Grant* Fehrenbacher and Fehrenbacher, *Recollected Words*, 148.

183 *Personal jealousies* Welles, *Diary*, 2:104.

183 *I now think* Basler, *Collected Works*, 5:208–209.

183 *If I must* Ibid., 5:509–10.

183 *If in such* Basler, *Collected Works*, 6:31.

183 *I have too* Ibid., 70–71.

183 *General Schurz* Ibid., 93.

184 *Truth to* Ibid., 138–39.

184 *Quite possibly* Ibid., 320–323.

184 *My dear General* Ibid., 327–328.

184 *I have just* Ibid., 5:474.

184 *were an essential* McPherson, *Battle Cry*, 329.

184 *the costly mistakes* Bruce D. Simpson, "Lincoln's Political Generals," *Journal of the Abraham Lincoln Association* 21 (Winter 2000): 76.

Chapter 15. The Political General: Daniel Sickles

The principal references in this chapter are from Thomas Keneally, *American Scoundrel: The Life of the Notorious Civil War General Dan Sickles* (New York: Doubleday, 2002).

185 *gross specimens* Information from Paul Sledzik, curator, Anatomical Collections, Armed Forces Institute of Pathology, National Museum of Health and Medicine, Washington, D.C.

185 *surgical controversy* Adams, *Doctors in Blue*, passim.

187 *he has wiped out* Burlingame, *Inside Lincoln*, October 20, 1863, 95.

189 *If all our officers* Cutter, letter of October 8, 1863, typescript.

Chapter 16. The Professional General: Joseph Hooker

191 *The President may* In Hebert, *Fighting Joe Hooker*, 248.

191 *When trouble arises* Burlingame, *Inside Lincoln*, September 27, 1863, 87.

192 *a wandering ghost* Ibid., 52.

192 *We had the worse* See, *Memoirs*, 12.

193 *pay no attention* Hebert, *Fighting Joe Hooker*, 245.

193 *the finest army* Burlingame, *Inside Lincoln*, September 9, 1863, 79.

193 *the disgrace* In Hebert, *Fighting Joe Hooker*, 227.

193 *in superb form* Huidekoper, *Oration*, 5.

193 *on the verge* James M. McPherson, *For Cause and Comrades: Why Men Fought in the Civil War* (New York: Oxford University Press, 1997), 156–157.

194 *He is a fine* Cutter, letter of September 17, 1863, typescript.

194 *by all odds* In Stephen W. Sears, *Chancellorsville* (Boston/New York: Houghton Mifflin, 1996), 58.

194 *Hooker is doing* Cutter, letter of May 6, 1863, typescript.

194 *Who ish dat* In Hebert, *Fighting Joe Hooker,* 129.

194 *My opinion* Ibid., 251.

195 *about the worst* Ibid., 183.

195 *One of the most* Ibid., 128.

195 *Be patient* Ibid., 119.

195 *It never had* Burlingame, *Inside Lincoln,* mid-September 1862?, 40.

195 *Hooker does talk* In Hebert, *Fighting Joe Hooker,* 106.

195 *a baby* [and following quotes] In Hebert, *Fighting Joe Hooker,* 249, 294, 291, 329.

196 *I have placed* Basler, *Collected Works,* 6:78, January 26, 1863.

196 *It is a beautiful* In Hebert, *Fighting Joe Hooker,* 170.

197 *Never, as long* Burlingame, *Lincoln Observed,* 242n72.

197 *Get out of* In Hebert, *Fighting Joe Hooker,* 97.

197 *was not disposed* Ibid., 229.

197 *was never* Ibid., 295.

198 *Oh it is terrible* Welles, *Diary,* 1:439–440.

198 *He did make* Sears, *Chancellorsville,* 437.

198 *Hooker is the* Neely, "Lincoln and the Cult of Manliness: Hooker, Lincoln, and Defeat," in Boritt, *Lincoln's Generals,* 75.

198 *No General* In Hebert, *Fighting Joe Hooker,* 287.

Chapter 17. The Political General: Benjamin Butler

199 *Here is a cheeky* Burlingame, *Inside Lincoln,* November 8, 1861, 31.

199 *I guess we* Rice, *Reminiscences,* 247.

200 *We have passed* Ibid., 252.

200 *vigorously* Ibid., 252.

200 *He could strut* In Mellon, *Face of Lincoln,* 110.

200 *A gasbag* Laas, *Wartime Washington,* 8.

201 *a humbug* Browning, *Diary,* 2:65.

201 *It seems* James M. McPherson, *Abraham Lincoln and the Second American Revolution* (New York: Oxford University Press, 1991), 70.

201 *He is a man* Richard S. West, *Lincoln's Scapegoat General: A Life of Benjamin F. Butler 1819–1893* (Boston: Houghton Mifflin, 1965), 240.

201 *as an administration* Boritt, *Lincoln's Generals,* 184.

201 *You may not be* Rice, *Reminiscences,* 248.

202 *The prize* Benjamin F. Butler, *Autobiographical and Personal Reminiscences of Major General Benjamin Butler. Butler's Book: A Review of His Legal, Political and Military Career* (Boston: A.M. Thayer, 1892), 220.

202 *If you can win* West, *Lincoln's Scapegoat,* 244.

203 *that sleepy little* Burlingame, *Inside Lincoln,* January 2–4, 1864, 140.

204 *Everybody thought* Butler, *Autobiographical,* 259.

204 *views on the* In West, *Lincoln's Scapegoat,* 106.

204 *The Negro* Ibid., 106.

205 *I had opened* Butler, *Autobiographical,* 288.

205 *sick of the* Ibid., 334.

205 *I guess we* Ibid., 336.

206 *He is most* West, *Lincoln's Scapegoat*, 156.

206 *Of all the* Ibid., 175.

207 *Citizens* Ibid., 203.

207 *I had an* Butler, *Autobiographical*, 82–83.

208 *Butler has* West, *Lincoln's Scapegoat*, 421.

Chapter 18. Lincoln and His Cabinet

209 *Assassination* In Taylor, *William Henry Seward*, 240.

209 *was the best* In Donald, *Lincoln*, 301.

210 *Disappointment!* Donald, *Lincoln Men*, 147.

211 *May, Friday* Patricia C. Johnson, "Sensitivity and Civil War: The Selected Diaries and Papers 1858–1866 of Frances Adeline (Fanny) Seward" (Ph.D. thesis, University of Rochester, 1964), 256.

211 *I then felt* In Donald, *Lincoln*, 256.

211 *I look back* In Donald, *Lincoln Men*, 156.

211 *Lincoln's evil* Ibid., 166.

211 *I'd better go* In Baker, *Mary Todd Lincoln*, 161–162.

212 *a puff of wind* In Guelzo, *Emancipation*, 222.

212 *exposed to such* In Taylor, *William Henry Seward*, 190.

212 *The making* In Donald, *Lincoln*, 265.

212 *to accept* Ibid., 264.

213 *Old Abe* Kerr Papers, 12:88.

213 *a collection* In Thomas and Hyman, *Stanton*, 383.

213 *a dirty* In Donald, *Lincoln Men*, 255.

213 *It is said* Turner and Turner, *Mary Todd Lincoln*, 135.

213 *I can't allow* In Donald, *Lincoln Men*, 149.

214 *We are at* In Taylor, *William Henry Seward*, 150ff.

214 *Only the hand* Nicolay and Hay, *Century* Magazine 35 (February 1888): 615–16.

215 *one of the saddest* Laas, *Wartime Washington*, 214n4.

215 *A light, bright* Welles, *Diary*, 1:182.

215 *The public* Ibid., 1:325.

216 *Our political* Basler, *Collected Works*, 5:125.

216 *I close* Gary Wills, *Lincoln at Gettysburg: The Words That Remade America* (New York: Simon & Schuster, 1992), 158.

217 *After dinner* Johnson, *Fanny Seward Diary*, 360.

218 *prided himself* Welles, *Diary*, 1:39.

218 *Seward has* Ibid., 1:198.

218 *he'd better* Ibid., 1:24, n.d.

218 *any New Englander* Ibid., intro., xxi.

219 *a slouching* Adams, *Doctors in Blue*, 104.

219 *Oh, said Lincoln* In Donald, *Lincoln Men*, 171.

219 *Father Welles* In Burlingame, *Lincoln Observed*, 48.

220 *Few officials* Jack Coggins, *Arms and Equipment of the Civil War* (New York: Barnes and Noble Books, 1990), 126.

220 *development* Craig L. Symonds, "Men, Machines and Old Abe: Lincoln and the Civil War Navy," in Prokopowicz, *Rediscovering Lincoln*, 49.

220 *Nor must* Basler, *Collected Works*, 6:409–410.

220 *As they sat* In Taylor, *William Henry Seward*, 227.

221 *I know all* In Harris, *Last Months*, 55.
221 *I wish you could* In Frederic Bancroft, *The Life of William Henry Seward* (New York, London: Harper & Bros., 1900). 2:186–87.
221 *I think I will* Burlingame, *Inside Lincoln*, October 17, 1861, 27.
222 *From what I have* Welles, *Diary*, 1:passim.
222 *Lincoln will* In Harris, *Last Months*, 41–42.
222 *I have always* *American National Biography*, 68.

Epilogue
223 *dressed in black* Turner and Turner, *Mary Todd Lincoln*, 704.
223 *My own life* Ibid., 302.
223 *My mother* Baker, *Mary Todd Lincoln*, 277.
224 *her bright little* Turner and Turner, *Mary Todd Lincoln*, 527.
225 *restored to* In Neely and McMurtry, *The Insanity File*, 104.
225 *I cannot stay* In Baker, *Mary Todd Lincoln*, 350.
225 *being all hacked* Norbert Hirschhorn and Robert G. Feldman, "Mary Lincoln's Final Illness: A Medical and Historical Reappraisal," *Journal of the History of Medicine* 54 (October 1999): 521–22.
226 *I don't think* In Charles Strozier, *Lincoln's Quest for Union: Public and Private Meanings* (Urbana: University of Illinois Press, 1987), 78.
226 *a devoted wife* Noyes Miner, "Mrs. Abraham Lincoln: A Vindication" (photocopy), Illinois State Historical Library, 6.
226 *two lofty pine* Turner and Turner, *Mary Todd Lincoln*, xix.
226 *what Beethoven* In Burlingame, *Inner World*, 13.
226 *He himself* Hofstadter, 105.
226 *When any church* In Mario M. Cuomo, *Why Lincoln Matters Today More Than Ever* (Orlando: Harcourt, 2004), 132.
228 *[Its] leading object* Ibid., 132.
228 *last, best hope* Ibid., 23.

ADDITIONAL SOURCES

African-American Heritage Trail, Washington, D.C.: Cultural Tourism, Washington, 2003.

Civil War to Civil Rights: Washington Downtown Heritage Trail. Charlottesville, Va.: Howell Press, 2001.

Eaton, John. *Grant, Lincoln and the Freedman*. New York: Longmans, Green and Co., 1907.

Fleischner, Jennifer. *Mrs. Lincoln and Mrs. Keckly* [sic]: *The Remarkable Story of the Friendship between a First Lady and a Former Slave*. New York: Broadway Books, 2003.

Goldsmith, Barbara. *Spiritualism: Other Powers, the Age of Suffrage and the Scandalous Victoria Woodhull*. New York: Knopf, 1998.

Goode, Col. Paul R. *The U.S. Soldiers' Home: A History of Its First Hundred Years*. n.p., n.d.

Green, Constance McLaughlin. *Secret City: A History of Race Relations in the Nation's Capital*. Princeton, N.J.: Princeton University Press, 1967.

Horton, James Oliver. "The Genesis of Washington's African American Community," in *Urban Odyssey: A Multicultural History of Washington, D.C.* Washington, D.C.: Smithsonian Institution Press, 1996.

Johnston, Allan. *Surviving Freedom: The Black Community of Washington, D.C. 1860–1880*. New York: Garland Publications, 1993.

Leibiger, Stuart. *Founding Friendship: George Washington, James Madison, and the Creation of the American Republic*. Charlottesville: University Press of Virginia, 1999.

McPherson, James M. *Drawn with the Sword: Reflections on the American Civil War*. New York: Oxford University Press, 1996.

Miller, Iris. *Washington in Maps: 1606–2000*. New York: Rizzoli International Publications, 2002.

Mitchell, Reid. *The Vacant Chair: The Northern Soldier Leaves Home*. New York: Oxford University Press, 1993.

Paludan, Phillip Shaw. *The Presidency of Abraham Lincoln*. Lawrence: University of Kansas Press, 1994.

Peterson, Merrill D. *Lincoln in American Memory*. New York: Oxford University Press, 1994.

Spilsbury, Gail. *Rock Creek Park*. Baltimore: The Johns Hopkins University Press, 2003.

INDEX

Page numbers in *italics* indicate photographs or artwork.

Printed in the USA
CPSIA information can be obtained
at www.ICGtesting.com
JSHW081544061223
53390JS00003B/122